Spanish Scientists in the New World

Spanish Scientists in the New World

THE EIGHTEENTH-CENTURY EXPEDITIONS

Iris H. W. Engstrand

University of Washington Press   *Seattle & London*

Library of Congress Cataloging in Publication Data
Engstrand, Iris Wilson.
    Spanish scientists in the New World.

    Bibliography: p.
    Includes index.
    1.   Mexico—Discovery and exploration—Spanish.
2.   Pacific coast (North America)—Discovery and
exploration—Spanish.   3.   Scientific expeditions—
Spain—History.   I.   Title.
Q115.E56   508.72   80-50863
ISBN 0-295-95764-6

To Donald C. Cutter, teacher and friend

Contents

Illustrations

following page 66

Plaza, Mexico City
Antonio Pineda's passport
Mexican Indians
Mexican muleteer
View of port of Acapulco
Cockfight in Acapulco
Plan of Botanical Garden, Mexico
Volcana of Tuxtla
Pineda dying, Philippines

following page 98

Plan of Friendly Cove, Nootka Sound
Inscribed tablet, Strait of Juan de Fuca
Nootka fields and settlement
Indian festival, Nootka Sound
Maquinna, Nootka chief
Woman of Nootka Sound
Figure of Nootka woman
Tetaku
One of Tetaku's wives
Salamanca Channel
Vernacci Channel

MAPS

Preface

O NE DOES not readily associate the history of New Spain with Europe's great age of cultural enlightenment; yet Spain's scientific achievement in the Americas during the late eighteenth century resulted directly from the advancement of knowledge in European centers of learning. The hope of the Spaniards, however, unlike certain of the French *philosophes,* was that the discovery and application of useful knowledge would improve life in a practical way. Naturalists, whose profession was uniquely suited to this role, engaged in the pursuit of truth by carefully observing, analyzing, and recording nature in all its aspects. They believed that their studies would yield beneficial products and unlock secrets to improve human existence. No less than natural philosophers, natural scientists felt that truth had to be sought and understood, but in simple arrangements rather than in abstract concepts. Observable nature, for them, held the key to man's future success.

This study examines two major Spanish enterprises during the final years of the eighteenth century with the common objectives of scientific exploration, collection, and accurate reporting. The first, the Royal Scientific Expedition to New Spain (1785–1800), organized under the direction of Martín de Sessé, established a Royal Botanical Garden in Mexico City and provided scientists for work in Mexico, California, the Pacific Northwest, Puerto Rico, Cuba, and Central America. The second, the expansive expedition of Alejandro Malaspina (1789–94), visited South America, Mexico, Alaska, the Pacific Northwest, California, the Philippines, Australia, and certain Pacific Islands. Several additional scientific efforts, such as the voyage of Jacinto Caamaño to the north of Nootka Sound and the explorations by Dionísio Alcalá Galiano and Cayetano Valdés of the Strait of Juan de Fuca in 1792, grew out of the above endeavors.

The scientists of these great Spanish undertakings represented several nationalities and brought together diverse knowledge in an exchange of their experiences. As naturalists, or natural historians, they were truly generalists and their laboratory encompassed all that nature presented. No flower, snake, spider, or tiny ant hill was likely to escape their watchful eyes. Their lives became intertwined not only because they served Spain in New World areas during the same years, but because they utilized each other's work. There was much to see, record, and classify. They also became involved with observers from England, France, the United States, and elsewhere since the scientific community excluded virtually no one because of national origin. They kept in mind Spain's concern for commercial products, but their scientific curiosity and absolute commitment to nature sent them into tangled jungles and underground caverns and to the rims of smoking volcanoes.

Although this study is essentially about the scientists and their work, special attention is given to the illustrators who accompanied them. Since the advent of photographic reproduction, the forms of visual communication have drastically changed. Professional artists, whose pen-and-ink sketches and detailed colored drawings were the only means by which journals, diaries, and other reports could be illustrated, probably reached the zenith of their influence during the late eighteenth and early nineteenth centuries. Because the scientific nature of the enlightenment emphasized the natural rather than the supernatural world, artist-illustrators were concerned with exactness and precision as an art form.

In contrast to some sixteenth-century explorers, observers in the enlightenment era did not return from travels with drawings of mermaids, flowers with human faces, or other results of rumor or vivid imaginations. The new science sought accuracy based on actual observation, and botanical and zoological plates were often accompanied by pressed plants and stuffed animals. Drawings of flora and fauna, illustrations of the dress, housing, weapons, customs, and facial characteristics of Indians, and scenes of harbors and buildings were meant to represent exactly what was there, regardless of how the artist might have wanted to express his own feelings. Sometimes, however, Indian faces do resemble their European counterparts in the less skillfully executed paintings.

Finally, Spanish cartographers, whose contributions are represented by two maps accompanying this work, deserve recognition for their skill. Able to make accurate determinations of latitude and longitude for the first time, these map makers worked constantly during the naval and scientific expeditions along the Pacific Coast. They corrected previous errors and drew many excellent charts from longboats off rocky coastlines or along unknown beaches. They personified Spain's great interest in map making, which was heightened after the conclusion of peace with England in 1783. The Ministry of Marine moved forward with plans for a series of explorations by land and sea beginning with the west coast of Africa and extending into the Caribbean and coastal areas of South America.

Following publication in 1787 of the *Atlas marítimo de España,* the Spanish government decided to improve the hydrographic maps of the west coast of the Americas and islands of the Pacific Basin. This decision, and the government's commitment to a final search for the Northwest Passage, provided major impetus for Malaspina's extensive expedition, planned initially to go around the world. Territorial considerations led to further exploration and mapping of the Northwest coastal regions. Many of these maps were catalogued by Henry Raup Wagner in his pioneer work *Cartography of the Northwest Coast of America to the Year 1800,* published in 1937. Originals are located primarily in the archives of the Ministerio de Asuntos Exteriores and the Museo Naval, Ministerio de Marina, in Madrid, and in the Archivo General de Indias in Sevilla.

Extensive research in a number of archival depositories was rewarded by voluminous documentary information regarding the personnel and accomplishments of the Royal Scientific Expedition to New Spain and the Malaspina Expedition. My principal sources were found in the Madrid archives of the Museo Naval, Museo Nacional de Ciencias Naturales, and the Real Jardín Botánico. I located additional documents in the Archivo General de la Nación in Mexico, D.F. Other valuable manuscripts and drawings were examined in the archives of the Ministerio de Asuntos Exteriores in Madrid; the Archivo General de Indias in Sevilla; the Conservatoire Botanique in Geneva; the British Museum, Kew Gardens, and Linnean Society in London; Yale University Library in New Haven, and the Bancroft Library of the University of California, Berkeley. For an explanation of the archive abbreviations used in the footnotes, see "Manuscript Collections" in the bibliography.

For generous assistance that made thorough investigation possible, I gratefully acknowledge the grant for research awarded by the Del Amo Foundation of Los Angeles and Madrid and the additional stipends given to me by the American Philosophical Society and the National Endowment for the Humanities. The University of San Diego not only assisted in financing the research, but also funded the publication of the color plates, for which I am especially appreciative. I also owe particular thanks to staff members of the various research institutions in which I worked. Although I cannot name all who assisted me, I would like to mention the late Admiral Julio Guillén, former director, Captain Roberto Barreiro-Meiro, associate director, Ana María Vigón, and Jaime Fernández Jiménez of the Museo Naval; María de los Angeles Calatayud, archivist, and Eugenio Ortiz de Vega, director, Museo Nacional de Ciencias Naturales; Irene Carrascosa, former archivist, and Santiago Castroviejo, research scientist, Real Jardín Botánico; Juan Manuel Zapatero, former director of the Servicio Histórico Militar; Julian Donahue and Ralph Schreiber of the Los Angeles County Natural History Museum; Amadeo Rea and Reid Moran of the San Diego Natural History Museum; and Michael Weber of the Museum of New Mexico.

For their careful reading of the manuscript and helpful suggestions, I wish to thank my colleagues and friends Christon Archer, Harry Crosby, and W. Michael Mathes. I also appreciate the work of Carol Schoenherr and Mary Kay Clark in typing the manuscript, and Cynthia van Stralen's assistance in proofreading and checking bibliographic references.

Finally, I wish to express my deepest gratitude to Donald C. Cutter, chairman of my doctoral studies committee, who first suggested this topic and then made it possible for me to pursue my research in Spain and Mexico. His guidance, encouragement, and enthusiasm have been a constant source of inspiration.

Iris H. W. Engstrand

UNIVERSITY OF SAN DIEGO
June 1980

Spanish Scientists in the New World

1

Spain's Scientific Enlightenment

S TUDENTS OF Europe's Age of Enlightenment often overlook the contributions of Spain in the realm of scientific achievement. Although recognition has been given to certain Spanish scholars of the time,[1] the scientists who visited the Americas are scarcely known. These men, trained in the broad spectrum of natural history, carried out experiments; identified and classified innumerable plants, animals, and minerals; and transmitted to Spain extensive collections of rocks, pressed plants, and preserved specimens. They recorded everything they thought significant about Indian life and customs, prepared vocabularies, and gathered artifacts. The results of their labors, however, were not available to the European intellectual community for several reasons. First, it was traditional for Spain to employ secrecy as a means to deny enemies any geographical knowledge, and, second, the political crises after 1792 caused a shift in priorities and precluded the editing and publishing of scientific papers. Many documents were consigned to archival storage where they remained until well into the twentieth century. As a result, the considerable achievements of Spanish scientists were virtually unknown outside of Madrid.

Spain's extensive territories in the late eighteenth century still made

1. Spaniards notable for their contributions during the Enlightenment included the Benedictine father Benito Jerónimo Feijoó, who criticized the Spaniards for their backwardness in science; Gaspar Melchor de Jovellanos, an economist who asked that education be more practical; and José Cadalso, a writer who supported reforms in education. Others interested in the promotion of science were Casimiro Gómez Ortega in botany, Andrés Piquer in medicine, Fausto Ilhuyar in geology, and Antonio de Ulloa in natural history.

up the largest colonial empire in the world and provided an unparalleled opportunity for exploration, but after the death of Carlos III in 1788 there was no strong monarch to patronize the arts and sciences. The vacillating policies of Carlos IV (1788–1808) and the problems resulting from court intrigues, international disputes, and the Napoleonic invasion, all but insured the obscurity of Spanish scientific efforts, while those of England and France became known throughout the world.

Several decades earlier, however, the story of Spain's intellectual achievement had had a happy beginning.[2] Shortly following his accession in 1759, Carlos III, a most capable Bourbon monarch, began to encourage scientific endeavors by sponsoring several monumental expeditions. For the first time, interest in natural history took its place beside political and commercial considerations. Under a policy of relaxed censorship, channels of communication were opened to allow French writings to cross the Pyrenees. Spanish correspondence with centers of learning in London, Stockholm, Frankfurt, and Philadelphia made possible an international exchange of ideas and a zealous promotion of useful knowledge throughout the Iberian Peninsula and in the Americas.[3]

The whole climate of European thought had its effect on Spain, but most influential in guiding the progress of science was the concept of naturalism—the assumption that the whole universe of mind and matter was subject to and controlled by natural law. Its acceptance caused men of the Enlightenment to turn with enthusiasm to rediscovering their own lands: studying and recording natural resources and noting the customs and history of a region. Ancient authority was no longer sufficient to establish the truth of long-accepted propositions; everything on earth, and even beyond, was submitted to questioning and new investigation. Men broke with Aristotelian tradition and adopted a method of inquiry based upon direct observation and reason. The criti-

2. Although the Spanish crown began to further intellectual pursuits early in the century, the greatest impetus for historical and scientific investigation came during the reign of Carlos III (1759-88). See Pedro Aguado Bleye and Cayetano Alcázar Molina, *Manual de historia de España*, pp. 370–77.

3. The travels of officials, merchants, and scientists between Europe and the Americas allowed a constant exchange of information. Despite some effort at censorship, ideas of the Enlightenment reached the Spanish colonies with almost the same speed as they entered other areas. Further, books and periodicals from the United States influenced Spanish colonial and peninsular thought. Benjamin Franklin achieved membership in the Spanish Academy of History in Madrid and his work was sent to Spanish America. See Arthur P. Whitaker, ed., *Latin America and the Enlightenment*, pp. 5–20.

cal spirit of the age inspired Spanish intellectuals to reevaluate previous knowledge and project a geographical, historical, and statistical survey of the New World—one that would leave no corner of Spain's territories uncatalogued.[4]

This kind of scientific zeal existed in the leading countries of Europe, especially in England and France, and to a lesser extent in Sweden, Russia, Germany, and the Netherlands. The young United States also participated. All had explorers and scientists "in the field" cataloguing and pictorially reproducing the zoological, botanical, and geographical aspects of the New World. Among the English-speaking contributors, the name of Captain James Cook stands out. His artists made hundreds of drawings of the Pacific area during his three around-the-world expeditions from 1769 through 1778. The famous naturalist Sir Joseph Banks, who accompanied Cook's first voyage, endowed a botanical garden and assembled extensive collections. The Forsters, Johann and son Georg, traveled with Cook to collect and catalogue plant life on the second and third voyages. George Vancouver, with botanist Archibald Menzies, studied the Northwest Coast in 1792. The French take credit for the around-the-world voyage of Louis Antoine de Bougainville from 1766 to 1769, when naturalist Philibert Commerson forever enshrined the name of his leader in a purple flowering vine of South America. The Count of La Pérouse sailed to California, Hawaii, and the South Pacific in 1785–86, sending back comments, drawings, and botanical specimens until his ships were lost at sea. In Philadelphia, the American Philosophical Society encouraged the scientific pursuits of Benjamin Franklin; while John and William Bartram toured the continent and wrote their classic journal of botany, *Bartram's Travels.* Jonathan Carver, a Connecticut Yankee, reported his news of nature with untiring detail from the interior of North America.[5]

In Spain, the subject of botany had commanded royal attention since the first Bourbon king, Felipe V, had requested all state officials in the

4. For general works on the participation of Spain and Spanish America in the Enlightenment, see Marcelino Menéndez y Pelayo, *Historia de los heterodoxos españoles* and *La ciencia española;* Vicente G. Quesada, *La vida intelectual en la America española;* Juan Carlos Arias Divito, *Las expediciones científicas españolas;* John Tate Lanning, *Academic Culture in the Spanish Colonies;* Richard Herr, *The Eighteenth-Century Revolution in Spain;* Michael E. Burke, *The Royal College of San Carlos;* and Arthur P. Whitaker, "Changing and Unchanging Interpretations of the Enlightenment in Spanish America."

5. See David Scofield Wilson, *In the Presence of Nature,* for an excellent work on naturalists in America during the eighteenth century.

Spanish empire to watch for unusual specimens of plants, animals, and minerals and send them to Madrid. He also required that two Spaniards, Jorge Juan and Antonio de Ulloa, accompany a French scientific expedition to South America in 1735.[6] Nevertheless, the major reforming efforts of Carlos III were first directed toward removing obstacles to Spain's progress. Aware that he must accelerate the political and economic development of his own country if he were to compete with others, the energetic monarch centralized his administration and appointed capable ministers.[7] He introduced tariff reform, reduced the public debt, constructed roads and canals, encouraged scientific farming, reorganized the army, rebuilt the navy, improved his governments overseas, and fostered emigration to America. By the mid-1780s, Spain had tripled her revenues, increased her population, and assumed a position of renewed prestige among European nations.

To encourage intellectual pursuits, Carlos III sponsored the establishment in Madrid of several academic institutions. These included the Royal Botanical Garden, the Museum of Natural Science, the Royal Academy of Medicine, and an Astronomical Observatory. Staff members of these centers assessed the accuracy of new knowledge and passed judgment on the new truths. They trained scientists for participation in expeditions throughout the Iberian Peninsula, the Canary Islands, and Spain's overseas empire. Encouraged by the work of Swedish botanist Carolus Linnaeus,[8] already famed for his classification of known and new species, and excited by the amount of information contained in Buffon's encyclopedic *Natural History of Animals*,[9] Spanish

6. See Jorge Juan and Antonio de Ulloa, *A Voyage to South America*, pp. 3–19. Ulloa and Juan spent the years from 1735 to 1746 in South America, at times in the company of Louis Godin, Pierre Bouguer, and Charles Marie la Condamine, members of a French expedition to the northern regions of South America.

7. The ministers who played key roles in educational as well as other reforms were the Conde de Aranda (1719–98), president of the Council of Castile; José Moniño, Conde de Floridablanca (1728–1808), minister of state; and Pedro Rodríguez, Conde de Compomanes (1723–1803).

8. Born Carl von Linne (1707–78), his major works on scientific nomenclature were *Systema naturae* (1735), *Genera plantarum* (1737), and *Species plantarum* (1753). The Linnean system, though somewhat artificially contrived, achieved almost immediate acceptance throughout Europe. A student of Linnaeus, Pehr Loefling, promoted his mentor's works in Spain in 1751 and directed a botanical expedition to Venezuela in 1754. See Arthur Robert Steele, *Flowers for the King*, pp. 7–25.

9. Georges Louis Leclerc, Count of Buffon (1707–88), a zoologist, was director of the French Royal Museum and a member of the Academy of Science. His works were trans-

naturalists especially desired to apply new methods of identification to the botanical, zoological, and mineralogical resources of North and South America.

Early in 1768, following a precedent of cooperation established with the French earlier in the century, Carlos III gave official sanction to a combined Franco-Spanish expedition of astronomers destined to observe the transit of Venus in Baja California during June 1769. Responding to the urgings of British scientists who had sent Captain Cook to Tahiti, Spain appointed two qualified naval officers, Vicente Doz and Salvador Medina, to accompany the party of Abbé Chappe d'Auteroche from the Paris Academy of Science. Their destination was San José del Cabo where, with the assistance of Mexican-born astronomer Joaquín Velázquez de León, they set up their observatory, one of seventy-seven stations around the world.

Despite the deaths of Chappe, Medina, and several other participants, results of the observations were successfully transmitted to Paris and coordinated with those of 151 other reporters. English astronomer Thomas Hornsby in 1771 used the information to conclude the mean distance of the earth from the sun to be 93,726,900 English miles, a good estimate for the time.[10]

In 1777, the Spanish crown named an extremely able botanist, Hipólito Ruiz, as chief of an expedition designed to accomplish, in the words of Carlos III,

. . . the methodical examination and identification of the products of nature of my American dominions, not only to promote the progress of the physical sciences, but also to banish doubts and falsifications which exist in medicine, painting, and other important arts, and to foster nature, describing and making drawings of the plants found in these, my fertile dominions, in order to enrich my Museum of Natural History and the Botanical Garden of the Court.[11]

Accompanied by José Antonio Pavón, a fellow Spanish botanist of nearly equal rank; Joseph Dombey, a well-educated French naturalist with a doctorate in medicine; and two artists, Ruiz made an extensive

lated into Spanish as *Historia natural del hombre* by Alonso Ruiz de Piña (Madrid, 1773) and *Historia natural, general y particular* by Joseph Clavijo y Faxardo (20 vols., Madrid, 1785–1805).

10. See Harry Woolf, *The Transits of Venus,* pp. 150–97; and Iris Wilson Engstrand, *Royal Officer in Baja California.*

11. Quoted by Steele, *Flowers for the King,* pp. 57–58.

examination of plant life throughout the viceroyalty of Peru and parts of Chile.[12] Returning to Madrid in 1788, Ruiz and Pavón brought with them an impressive herbarium of dried specimens and 124 live plants for use in the Royal Botanical Garden. Although plagued by financial difficulties and required to deal with Carlos IV in gaining royal support for their work, Ruiz and Pavón were able to publish three volumes of *Flora peruviana et chilensis.*[13]

In Santa Fe de Bogotá, capital of the viceroyalty of Nueva Granada, another Spanish botanist, José Celestino Mutis, received a royal sanction in 1783 to investigate the fauna and flora of that region. Having periodically requested crown support for botanical studies following his arrival as physician to the viceroy in 1760, Mutis was finally gratified to be appointed director of an official expedition. Commissioned as first botanist and astronomer in charge of one assistant and an artist, he examined extensively the area encompassed by present-day Colombia. Probably the most significant result of Mutis' work was the remission to Madrid of almost seven thousand drawings, the majority in color, of the flora of Nueva Granada. Unfortunately, these illustrations along with four thousand manuscript pages were left unedited at his death and much of the material could not be utilized.[14]

Plans for the Royal Scientific Expedition to New Spain were formulated in 1785, just two years after the crown's sanction of Mutis' efforts. In 1787 the expedition was approved for a six-year term under the direction of Aragonese physician Martín de Sessé. Because of its relatively permanent status in Mexico City, the expedition served as a focal point for all investigations carried out within the viceroyalty of New Spain during the final decade of the eighteenth century. In addition to surveying fauna and flora, members of the group established the Royal Botanical Garden of Mexico and offered professional courses in botany.[15]

12. Ibid., pp. 52–57.

13. Volumes 1, 2, and 3 were published in Madrid from 1798 through 1802; volume 4 was ready for the printer in 1804, but, along with volume 5, which was nearly ready in 1807, had to wait until the late 1950s to be published by the Instituto Botánico A. J. Cavanilles in Madrid.

14. Mutis' works were deposited in the archives of the Real Jardín Botánico in Madrid under the designation *Flora de Santa Fé de Bogotá o de Nueva Granada.*

15. The study of botany had achieved considerable significance as early as the sixteenth century because of the medicinal properties of plants. Those interested in pursuing botanical studies were often licensed physicians or pharmacists desiring to expand their knowledge in the field of "herbal cures." Men of the eighteenth century sought to build upon the groundwork laid by Gonzalo Fernández de Oviedo's *Historia general y natural de*

They trained a number of scientists, including José Mariano Moziño, who accompanied naval or other expeditions to the Pacific Northwest, California, and the West Indies.

Because Captain Cook's final voyage of 1778 had opened the door to large profits in sea otter and other furs, considerations beyond pure science entered into the international scene. After 1789, the matter of sovereignty over the West Coast of North America, and indeed over the entire Pacific Basin, came to a head on the Northwest Coast when England refused to heed Spain's demand for a hasty departure. The controversy arising from the conflict at Nootka Sound needed to be solved. Although Spain had strong evidence for title according to then existing European criteria, her archrival England possessed the naval strength to buttress her weaker claim.[16]

In order to bolster Spain's position, Carlos IV, acting upon the advice of Minister of Marine Antonio Valdés, determined in 1790 that Alejandro Malaspina's expedition, currently sailing off the coast of South America, should proceed as far north as Alaska to map in detail the coastline of the Pacific Northwest. Furthermore, because of renewed speculation, they were to search again for the long-sought passage from the Atlantic to the Pacific. This fabulous strait, known variously as the Strait of Anián, the Strait of Ferrer Maldonado, and the Northwest Passage, had proved elusive; but the Spanish government hoped that discovery of this key geopolitical location would allow Spain to recapture some of her lost supremacy in Europe. The Malaspina expedition, in addition to examining the inland area from Acapulco to Mexico City and its surroundings, therefore expanded its concern to the Pacific Northwest and Alaska. Scientists and artists of the expedition mapped the northern shores, drew coastal profiles, studied local natives, investigated fauna and flora, and described mineral resources.

During the summer of 1791, members of the Royal Scientific Expedition to New Spain worked in Mexico City with the Malaspina scientists who did not accompany the main group to the north. After the departure of Malaspina's flotilla, two botanists and an artist trained at the Botanical Garden were appointed to accompany the 1792 expedition of Juan Francisco de la Bodega y Quadra to the "northern limits of Cal-

---

las Indias in 1535 and the work of Francisco Hernández, palace physician to Philip II, who described plants in six volumes of text and ten of drawings. See chapter 2, note 6.

16. See Warren L. Cook, *Flood Tide of Empire;* William R. Manning, "The Nootka Sound Controversy."

ifornia." Although charged primarily with joining British commissioner George Vancouver to solve boundary questions arising out of the Nootka Sound controversy, Bodega encouraged his scientists to study native customs, examine natural resources, and learn the history of the region. José Moziño's ethnographic study *Noticias de Nutka* resulted from this effort.[17] His fellow botanist José Maldonado accompanied the voyage of Jacinto Caamaño, which left Nootka in the summer of 1792 to map the coastline in the neighborhood of 53° north latitude.

Also in 1792, naturalist José Longinos Martínez of the Royal Scientific Expedition traveled overland from Mexico City to San Blas, crossed the Gulf of California to Loreto, and traversed the entire peninsula from Cabo San Lucas to as far north as Monterey in Upper California. His journal, with accompanying descriptions of Indian customs, plants, animals, and other natural phenomena, provides an early detailed study of the Californias.[18] Longinos and Moziño also explored extensively in regions to the south of Mexico City and in Central America. Finally, Martín de Sessé, the expedition's director, went to Puerto Rico and Santo Domingo on a botanical mission and sent two artists to Cuba to accompany the explorations of the Conde de Mopox y Jaruco in 1796. Although primarily a military enterprise, the count's effort included a study of the island's natural history by Aragonese botanist Baltasar Boldó.

Within the New World provinces, Spanish administrators often supported scientific endeavors. One of the most important governors, the second Conde de Revillagigedo, viceroy of New Spain from 1789 to 1794, maintained the policies of Carlos III after the accession of Carlos IV. An able leader, Revillagigedo personally supervised the many activities of his realm. He firmly believed that the pursuit of nature would yield valuable rewards and continually offered his support to excursions in Mexico, California, and the Pacific Northwest.[19]

On his visit to New Spain in 1803, the celebrated German naturalist Alexander von Humboldt took note of the many scientific activities initiated during Revillagigedo's term in office and commented upon the extent of royal patronage throughout the New World:

17. See Iris H. Wilson, ed. and trans. of José Mariano Moziño's *Noticias de Nutka*.
18. See Lesley Byrd Simpson, ed. and trans., *Journal of José Longinos Martínez*.
19. See José Antonio Calderon Quijano, *Los virreyes de Nueva España en el reinado de Carlos IV*, vol. 1, for a description of Revillagigedo's government. (Revillagigedo appears in much of the contemporary correspondence and records as Revilla Gigedo, but the spelling as one word is generally preferred by authors in Spain and elsewhere today.)

Since the final years of the reign of Carlos III and during that of Carlos IV, the study of the natural sciences has made great progress not only in Mexico, but also in all of the Spanish colonies. No European government has sacrificed greater sums than that of the Spanish in order to advance the knowledge of plants. Three botanical expeditions, that of Peru, New Granada and New Spain, . . . have cost the state nearly four hundred thousand pesos.[20]

Humboldt also reported that botanical gardens had been established in Manila and the Canary Islands, and that the commission sent to Cuba, under the Conde de Mopox y Jaruco, to survey the Güines canal was accompanied by persons charged with examining natural resources. He concluded that Spanish research during the previous twenty years had "not only enriched the domain of science with more than four thousand new species of plants," but had also "contributed greatly to the progress of natural history among the inhabitants of the country."[21]

Unfortunately, these earnest efforts resulted not in fame or lasting contributions, but only in the collection of a mass of unpublished data read by a few contemporaries in the scientific world. The dynamic intellectuals under Carlos III who thought their country could be revitalized and who worked to bring about Spain's resurgence as a great power were destined to fail. The palace despotism of Manuel Godoy, reactionary developments stemming from the French revolution, and finally the disruption of Spanish life by Napoleon's invading armies brought ruin to their ambitious plans. Although some effort had been expended to promote scientific endeavors, several expedition members were banished from Spain, while others were ignored or refused facilities for organizing or printing their reports. The inability of many to make known their observations and conclusions prevented justly deserved recognition in current journals. Worse yet, manuscripts and drawings became scattered or lost during the civil strife that followed the French takeover.

Consequently, the scientific momentum achieved by Spain during the Age of Enlightenment came to a standstill for a generation. Once the continuity was lost, there seemed to be no one to pick up the pieces of a previous investigation. Nevertheless, many of the documents preserved in Spain and throughout the world have now been found and form the basis of several major works on eighteenth-century Spanish

20. Alexander von Humboldt, *Ensayo político,* p. 80. Humboldt in fact utilized much of the materials gathered by his Spanish counterparts during the previous decade.
21. Ibid.

science.[22] As a result of recent scholarship, clearly formed personalities are slowly emerging from partially obscured figures.

22. For example, Harold W. Rickett, "The Royal Botanical Expedition to New Spain," pp. 1–81; Donald C. Cutter, *Malaspina in California*; Cutter, "The Return of Malaspina," pp. 4–19; Simpson, trans. and ed., *Journal of José Longinos Martínez*; John Tate Lanning, *The Eighteenth-Century Enlightenment*; Steele, *Flowers for the King*; Arias Divito, *Las expediciones científicas españolas*; Wilson, trans. and ed., *Noticias de Nutka*; Cook, *Flood Tide of Empire*; and Edward J. Goodman, *The Explorers of South America*.

2

The Royal Scientific Expedition to New Spain: The Formative Years, 1785 to 1789

THE ROYAL Scientific Expedition to New Spain—unlike the botanical surveys of Mutis in Nueva Granada (Colombia) and of Ruiz and Pavón in Peru—was not initiated by the crown. The plan to extend a new investigation to Mexico was conceived and promoted by a quietly determined Aragonese physician, Martín de Sessé y Lacasta, who directed the expedition's activities for almost fifteen years.[1] In designing his program, Sessé solicited the help of Casimiro Gómez Ortega, director of the Royal Botanical Garden in Madrid, who took an active interest in promoting Spanish investigations in the New World.[2] Without Gómez Ortega's cooperation in gaining the approval of Carlos III, Sessé could not have put his ideas into action. Of this there is ample evidence in the correspondence maintained between these two men.[3]

Sessé thought of establishing botanical studies in New Spain while practicing medicine in Havana, though he had become acquainted with the new Royal Botanical Garden ten years earlier when he worked in Madrid with court physician Antonio Flamenco in 1775 and 1776. With Gómez Ortega's support, he believed that Spanish botanists, caught up in the spirit of the times, would be receptive to a survey of Mexican

1. Sessé, son of Agustín Sessé and María Lacasta, was baptized in the parochial church of Baraguas in Aragón on 11 December 1751. He received his degree in medicine from the Real Academia de Medicina Teórico-Práctica de Nuestra Señora de Gracia in Zaragoza and began his career in Madrid in 1775.

2. Sessé to Gómez Ortega, Mexico, 26 October 1785, 4ª división, legajo no. 19, Archives of the Real Jardín Botánico of Madrid, hereinafter referred to as ARJB.

3. Papeles de Sessé y Moziño, 4ª división, legajo nos. 19 and 20, ARJB.

plants, especially those with medicinal properties. The South American cinchona and coca plants had certainly been received with enthusiasm.

Sessé had spent his early medical career with the Spanish Army in Gibraltar and from there had been transferred to Cuba during the American Revolution. He first served under the command of General Victoria de Navia and later with Count Bernardo de Gálvez, former governor of Louisiana who commanded Spanish troops in aid of the Americans at Mobile and Pensacola. After the war, in June 1784, Gálvez had become the captain general of Cuba so Sessé chose to remain on the island as a private physician. He achieved some success but his scientific curiosity led him toward plant research. He might have remained in Cuba, but when he learned that Matías de Gálvez, viceroy of New Spain, had died suddenly and that his son Bernardo was being considered to replace him, Sessé began to work on a transfer to Mexico.[4]

When the appointment of Bernardo de Gálvez was assured, Sessé submitted his proposal for a scientific expedition to the viceregal capital. His ideas included founding a botanical garden with a chair of botany at the University of Mexico and establishing an academy of pharmacy and medicine. For the latter purpose, he offered six thousand pesos of his own, which he had "on deposit with Sr. Francisco Borda in Cádiz and which could be used to purchase necessary equipment and supplies."[5] He also suggested the completion of the work of Francisco Hernández (1514–78), a Spanish physician/scientist who had directed an expedition to New Spain under orders of King Philip II. Hernández had forwarded six folio volumes of text and ten of drawings to Spain during the sixteenth century, but these had suffered various misfortunes, including a fire. A rescued portion of the manuscript, without the drawings, formed the basis of Gómez Ortega's interest in Mexico's flora; a number of Spanish botanists were anxious to know more.[6]

4. Sessé to Gómez Ortega, Havana, 30 January 1785, 4ª división, legajo no. 19, ARJB.
5. Ibid.
6. Hernández and his son Juan studied the vegetable, animal, and mineral kingdoms of New Spain from 1570 to 1576. Upon his return to the Spanish peninsula, Hernández prepared sixteen volumes of his findings for publication, but they were left unprinted in the archives of El Escorial near Madrid, where most of them were destroyed by fire in 1671. Six volumes were later discovered and published in 1790 under the editorship of Casimiro Gómez Ortega, director of the Royal Botanical Garden of Madrid. Those concerning New Spain are: De historia plantarum novae hispaniae (3 vols. published in Madrid in 1790); "Historia natural de Méjico," MS; "De Pisce Tiburona," MS; "Corografía de la Nueva España," MS; "La materia medicinal de Nueva España," MS; "Tabla de mal

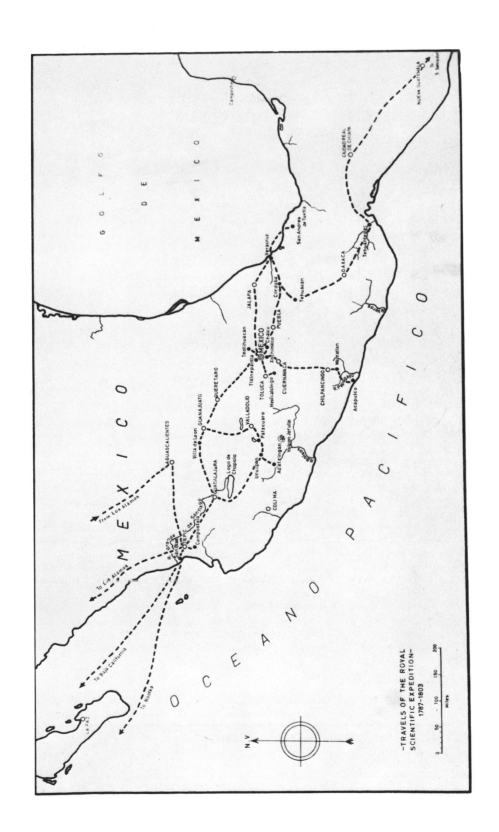

—TRAVELS OF THE ROYAL
SCIENTIFIC EXPEDITION—
1787-1803

Finally Sessé promised that upon his return from Mexico, he would offer the Botanical Garden of Madrid the plant *Lobelia,* known in Nahuatl as *tlauchinoli,* "which Dr. Kalm took from the Savage Indians and gave to the Academy of Stockholm in the year 1782."[7] He would also bring back the *Yerba de Pollo,*[8] known for its balsamic virtue, and the *Palo de la Flecha* or *Arbol de la Margarita*[9] that had newly been discovered to be a miraculous antidote to rabies. Medicinal plants able to "cure the major infirmities with almost complete certainty" were long known to the Aztecs and Sessé wanted above all to enrich the Botanical Garden of Madrid with these extraordinary Mexican species.[10]

Gómez Ortega approved the proposal and issued a commission on 10 May 1785, encharging Sessé, who was by then already in Mexico City, "to survey the plants and herbs that could be cultivated in the Royal Botanical Garden and the possibilities for a scientific expedition."[11] It is not surprising that Gómez Ortega and his fellow botanists in Madrid were immensely interested in New Spain since the botanical features of the area had attracted attention from the days of the earliest explorers. By the eighteenth century it was known that the tropical areas of Mex-

y remedios de Esta Tierra," MS; and "De expugnatione novae hispaniae," MS. See José Luis Benítez Miura, "El Dr. Francisco Hernández," pp. 367–405. See also three-volume Hernández work, edited by Germán Somolinos d'Ardois, *Obras completas,* Mexico D.F., 1959–60.

7. Pehr Kalm, a student of Linnaeus, traveled through North America in 1748–51, seeking plants adaptable to the Swedish climate. He apparently visited Mexico in 1781–82 where he saw the numerous native lobelias. *Lobelia laxiflora angustifolia* is used in medicine as an emetic, expectorant, vomitive, and antiasthmatic, but is considered dangerous because of its paralyzing effect on the respiratory system.

8. *Hierba del pollo,* also called *rosilla,* is of the Spiderwort family and could be either *Commelina tuberosa* L. or *Tinantia erecta.* Its flowers are blue or violet and a juice made from the leaves was recommended for the eyes. The mashed leaves and stems of *Commelina coelestis* were used to make poultices that stopped the flow of blood in hemorrhages.

9. *Palo de la Flecha* is more commonly the name for *Sebastiana pavoniana* Muell. because its poisonous milky juice was used by Indians for their arrows, whereas *Arbol de la Margarita* is probably *Karwinskia humboldtiana.* The seeds of this small tree are oily and contain some principle that paralyzes motor nerves; they are employed in Mexico as an anticonvulsive, particulary in the case of tetanus. An infusion of the leaves and roots was used locally for fevers. See Paul C. Standley, *Trees and Shrubs of Mexico,* vol. 23, pp. 648, 717.

10. Sessé to Gómez Ortega, Havana, 30 January 1785, 4ª división, legajo no. 19, ARJB.

11. "Título de comisionado que a consecuencia del capítulo 26, del reglamento del Real Jardín Botánico, se despacha a Don Martín Sessé, vecino de Mexico," 4ª división, legajo no. 19, ARJB. This document was signed in Madrid by Josef Perez Cavallero, Antonio Paláu, Miguel Tomás Paris, and Gómez Ortega.

ico were extremely productive and it was thought that few regions of the globe possessed a richer flora. Almost every conceivable plant community could be found in the wet tropical forests of the southern lowlands, the temperate deciduous and coniferous forests of the central plateau and ranges of the Sierra Madre, the alpine zones of the high peaks such as Orizaba, Popocatepetl, and Ixtaccihuatl, and the great barren or cactus deserts of the northern provinces.[12] The Spanish scientists hoped that the viceroy of New Spain would give his full support to Sessé's project.

Sessé had a genuine dedication both to serve his king and to advance the cause of science in general. He believed himself qualified to make a valuable contribution since he was well acquainted with the works of scientists throughout Europe and had kept himself fully aware of the progress made during the eighteenth century. He had studied thoroughly the surviving material of the Hernández expedition and recognized that to understand all that Hernández wrote, as well as to be a productive member of the botanical expedition, he would have to study the Aztecs and their language. Because he knew Latin well and hoped to learn the Nahuatl tongue as soon as possible, he could work in the same manner as Hernández and continue at once to catalogue the staggering number and variety of Aztec medicinal plants.[13]

Sessé searched diligently for Hernández' manuscripts in Mexico. He scoured archives, libraries, and countless bookstores without encountering a single letter of Hernández' work. There seemed to be no other solution than to put a notice in the *Gaceta de México* asking for help in locating a copy of the work and assuring the "good intention of the Sovereign."[14]

On 12 August 1785 he petitioned the new viceroy, Bernardo de

12. As late as 1926, Paul Standley could still write: "Many botanists have visited the country [Mexico] in the last hundred years, yet the flora is still but imperfectly known. Almost every collector at the present day makes discoveries of remarkable species previously unknown to science, and some plants are still unknown botanically although their supposed medicinal properties, or their products, such as fruit, lumber, fiber and gum are well known locally. . . . [A]way from the Sierra Madre are innumerable isolated masses of mountains and hills, still unvisited by a botanist, which must yield a host of localized species" (*Trees and Shrubs of Mexico*, pp. 1–2).

13. According to Gordon Schendel, *Medicine in Mexico*, "the approximately two thousand different species of medicinal plants growing in the imperial botanical gardens when Cortés arrived in Tenochtitlán in 1519 comprised by far the largest such collection in the world" (p.62).

14. Sessé to Gómez Ortega, Mexico, 26 July 1785, 4ª división, legajo no. 20, ARJB.

Gálvez, for local approval of his proposed scientific expedition throughout New Spain.[15] While awaiting a response, Sessé remained in Mexico
acting as physician to the Holy Office (Inquisition) and giving medical
service in prisons.

Back in Madrid, Gómez Ortega continued his efforts to lay the
groundwork and assemble personnel for the expedition. Because he had
been chief botanist at the Royal Botanical Garden since 1772, he knew
people who were well qualified to serve the crown. In September 1786,
Gómez Ortega proposed the following names to the viceroy of Mexico:
Juan Diego del Castillo, then employed as director of the pharmacy of
the hospital of Puerto Rico; Vicente Cervantes, a "student of Medicine,
a good Philosopher, a good Chemist and Pharmacist, and a possessor of
the French language,"[16] and José Longinos Martínez, a surgeon.
Gómez Ortega selected the latter because the "work of Dr. Hernández
. . . included the other Kingdoms of Nature, the Animal and Mineral," and he deemed it necessary to name a person competent in these
two branches. Longinos' ability in anatomy and in preparing and
stuffing birds, fish, and other genera of animals was well tested and
"the Museum of Madrid could assure itself of copious additions, as
could the said work of Dr. Hernández."[17]

As a result of the combined efforts of Sessé and Gómez Ortega, a
royal order of 27 October 1786 called for the establishment of a botanical garden and an expedition to survey and examine the natural
resources of New Spain. This was followed by a second royal order on
13 March 1787, issued to Alonso Nuñez de Haro, archbishop of Mexico
and recently appointed viceroy of New Spain,[18] confirming those who
were to take part: Sessé was named director; Cervantes, professor of
botany with the help of Castillo and Longinos; and Jayme Sensevé, a
resident of Mexico, was appointed to join them as professor of pharmacy. Two artists would be sent from Spain if no satisfactory illustrators could be found in Mexico. All would be assisted by two or three

15. Referred to in a letter from Eugenio de Llaguno to the viceroy of Mexico, Aranjuez, 27 April 1786, Historia 527, Archivo General de la Nación (Mexico, D.F.). Hereinafter referred to as AGN.

16. Gómez Ortega to the viceroy of México, Madrid, 21 September 1786, Flora
Española—1786, Archivo del Museo Nacional de Ciencias Naturales (Madrid). Hereinafter referred to as AMCN.

17. Gómez Ortega to the viceroy, Madrid, 21 September 1786, Flora Española—1786,
AMCN.

18. Archbishop Nuñez de Haro became interim viceroy of Mexico following the death
of Bernardo de Gálvez on 30 November 1786.

Negro servants, or helpers, paid out of the account of the royal treasury.[19]

A third royal order on 20 March 1787 outlined more completely the purposes of the expedition. Essentially, the participants were to follow the example of royal orders already issued with regard to scientists in Peru and Colombia. They were "to examine, draw and describe methodically the natural products of the most fertile dominions of New Spain" and to "banish the doubts and uncertainties then existing in medicine, dyeing and other useful arts."

The scientists were to illustrate and catalog natural resources and put the results of Hernández' work into a useful form. The order contained a promise by Carlos III that the Botanical Garden of Mexico and publication of all manuscript work would be supported.[20]

As director, Sessé would serve under guidelines issued from the Council of the Indies and signed separately by the secretary of state. The instructions provided, first, that Sessé would remain in New Spain with the commission for six years; second, that he would earn a salary of two thousand pesos annually from the day on which he commenced the expedition, the salary to be paid by the nearest royal treasury if he should be away from the capital; third, that during his trips throughout the kingdom he would be paid a double salary to compensate for expenses incurred in the field; and fourth, that upon his return to Spain he would be paid one-half his salary "for the purpose of formalizing and presenting his complete work—the fruit of his career." Finally, Sessé was assured that he would be able to obtain the books and instruments necessary for his profession at the expense of the treasury.[21]

Carlos III specifically charged the viceroy of New Spain to support and protect Sessé during his efforts, to provide him "with the honors and preeminences necessary for his success" and to pay him, through the royal treasury of Mexico, his salary and additional expenses. Registration of the order was completed in the Office of the Indies on 21 March 1787, and Cervantes and Longinos, the two members of the expedition living in Madrid, made preparations to leave for New Spain.[22]

19. Real Cédula (Royal Decree), 13 March 1787, Flora Española—1787, AMCN; Historia 527, AGN.

20. Real Cédula, 20 March 1787, Flora Española—1787, AMCN; Historia 527, AGN; 4ª división, legajo no. 20, ARJB.

21. Real Cédula, 20 March 1787, Flora Española—1787, AMCN.

22. Petition signed by Longinos, Cervantes, Gregorio Baca, and Andrés Cuellar, 5ª división, legajo no. 6, ARJB.

Sessé's assistants were well prepared for scientific research. Vicente Cervantes, born in 1755 in Safra, Badajoz, in the province of Extremadura, had wanted to study pharmacy at the University of Madrid, but lacking the necessary funds had become a pharmacist's clerk. In his spare time, he studied botany, getting the lessons from a friend who was studying under Gómez Ortega. Later, Cervantes petitioned the director of the Botanical Garden for admission to the examination for pharmacists, an unprecedented request. To the amazement of Gómez Ortega, Cervantes passed the examination and received the degree in pharmacy. He afterwards entered botany classes and accompanied the director on a number of excursions. After qualifying for a degree in botany in 1784, Cervantes competed successfully for the post of pharmacist at the general hospital of Madrid, but eventually gave up this position to go to Mexico as professor in the new botanical garden.[23]

Little is known about the early life of José Longinos Martínez, naturalist of the expedition, except that he was a native of Calahorra on the upper Ebro River.[24] Longinos studied botany in Madrid under Gómez Ortega, although his recommendation as "naturalist" and his designation as "surgeon" implied that his specialty lay in the study of animals rather than plants, and particularly in their dissection. Longinos and Cervantes were classmates and Gómez Ortega apparently felt he had chosen wisely. Unfortunately, however, the botanical expedition was to be plagued from its beginning by friction between the irreconcilable personalities of Longinos and Sessé.

Many of the supplies that were to be used by the members of the expedition were assembled in Madrid and shipped from Cádiz. In May 1787, a royal order directed that thirteen boxes be sent to the port city for immediate transshipment to New Spain. The boxes, which weighed approximately 1,650 pounds, contained the following:[25]

Paper from Holland for the drawings of plants and animals, a specimen of
which brand was shown by Prof. Vicente Cervantes—Six reams
Ordinary good paper for writing—18 reams

23. José García Ramos, "Elogio histórico del farmacéutico Don Vicente Cervantes," p. 753.

24. Declaration of José Longinos Martínez as godfather to an Indian child baptized at Mission San Fernando Velicatá, Baja California, by Fr. Jorge Coello, 1 July 1792, Libro de Bautismos, St. Albert's College, Oakland, California. Nicolás León, *Biblioteca botánico-mexicana*, p. 172, lists Longinos Martínez as a native of Logroño.

25. Flora Española—1787, AMCN.

Blank notebooks in folio encased in parchment for writing observations—1 dozen

Two thousand black pins for mounting insects

Four saws of various sizes

Hammers

Chisels

Little hoes for rooting up plants

Iron spades

Eight hatchets

Eight machetes

Two compasses for governing oneself in the forest

Six little tin flower pots called "dilenianas" in which to grow plants

Three presses in which to dry plants

The medicines, both simple and in composition, most necessary to fill the medicine chest that is now empty, to be used for curing while traveling and for examination of mineral waters

One-half pound of vermillion for the artists or painters

Additional items included some forceps and other instruments, one-and-a-half dozen cartons, different classes of paint, writing paper and pens, a sharp black pencil, and two barometers. A notation referred to a separate paper entitled "Books for the Director of the Expedition," although there is no record of books having been sent to New Spain at this time. It apparently took Gómez Ortega some months to assemble the works considered most valuable for the expedition since the final list was not dated and signed until 21 June 1788. The seven volumes of Carolus Linnaeus were among the most significant to which the members of the expedition eventually had reference.[26]

Cervantes and Longinos arrived in Mexico during the latter part of July or early August 1787, since the expedition was formally incorporated in Mexico City on 4 August of that year.[27] Finding appropriate quarters for their work was difficult. Sessé at first acquired use of the former Jesuit College of San Pedro y San Pablo, but this later proved to be unsatisfactory because its adjoining garden had been given to the Seminario de San Carlos de Naturales in 1770. The director then discovered what he believed to be a suitable piece of land; it was called the Potrero (pasture) of Atlampa. The property, although slightly swampy,

26. A document entitled "List of Books sent to Mexico in two boxes for the use of the Botanical and Natural History Expedition of that Kingdom," dated and signed more than one year later by Gómez Ortega, is contained in Flora Española—June 1788, AMCN. See Appendix A.

27. Sessé to Gómez Ortega, Mexico, 28 October 1787, 4ª división, legajo no. 20, ARJB.

was situated within the city limits and was large enough to support a botanical garden and the necessary buildings. Mexico City officials ceded use of the land to the crown for the purposes of the expedition.[28]

In October 1787, Sessé petitioned to have plans drawn for a building that would contain a hall for instruction, space for an herbarium, a museum, a library, and sufficient living quarters for the professor and his staff. He requested that an architect be commissioned by the royal treasury for this purpose.[29] The viceroy appointed Miguel Costansó to survey the site and present a list of necessary expenses so that a cost estimate could be made.[30] After several revisions, Costansó submitted his completed figures in September 1788, with construction of the garden placed at 46,060 pesos and an additional 651 pesos for a greenhouse. He estimated the cost of the building at 21,636 pesos and 5 reales.[31]

Meanwhile, in May 1788, Sessé had officially commenced the activities of the expedition. A special inauguration of classes in botany, accompanied by an elaborate ceremony, was held in the Hall of Dissertations at the Royal and Pontifical University of Mexico. The *Gaceta de México* reported the event in great detail and praised Carlos III for "promoting in his vast American dominions" a scientific expedition to collect, identify, and describe the products of the three kingdoms of nature. The king's Mexican subjects also appreciated the creation of a botanical garden similar to that of Madrid, where the results of the expedition might be preserved and studied under a chair of botany.[32]

Sessé delivered an address in which he expounded the usefulness of botany and its relationship with commerce, agriculture, economy, and other arts. He particularly emphasized its value in medicine and urged young men to dedicate their lives to the study of natural history. The audience included members of the Royal Audiencia, professors from

28. Sessé to Viceroy D. Manuel Florez, Mexico, 14 September 1787, 4ª división, legajo no. 20, ARJB. Comunicaciones con el Virrey de Méjico, Mexico, 27 August 1789, Flora Española, AMCN.

29. Sessé to Viceroy D. Manuel Florez, Mexico, 3 October 1787, Historia 461, AGN.

30. Miguel Costansó had come to New Spain in 1764 with the expedition of Juan de Villava; he served as engineer and cartographer with José de Gálvez in 1768 at San Blas and La Paz, and accompanied the Portolá-Serra expedition to California in 1769 with the Catalonian Volunteers commanded by Pedro Fages. Upon returning to Mexico in late 1770, he participated in a number of projects including a plan to drain the lakes of Mexico. He continued his cartographic works and taught mathematics at the University of Mexico. See Janet R. Fireman, *The Spanish Royal Corps of Engineers*.

31. Costansó to the viceroy of Mexico, Historia 462, AGN.

32. *Gaceta de México*, vol. 3 (6 May 1788), pp. 75–77.

the university, clerics of all orders, civil officials, military officials, and other important members of society. Viceroy Manuel Antonio Florez was unable to attend, but had designated Francisco Xavier Gamboa, regent of the Royal Audiencia, to preside in his place.[33]

At seven in the evening the balconies of the university were illuminated, and after a brief musical interlude, a magnificent display of fireworks, "ingeniously executed by the pyrotechnic artist, Joaquín Gavilán," lit up the stage.[34] The vivid and imaginative nature of the ceremony reflected the significance given to the study of botany at this time. Three specially designed *papayo* trees, which bear the papaya fruit, were placed on a stage as follows: two female trees, decorated with their respective flowers and fruits, on each side a male tree that, as such, was without fruit. Sparks of fire from the male tree blew toward the females—representing the transfer of pollen through the air to fertilize the female flowers. At the foot of the male tree, lighting effects suggested a growing garden and illuminated the plaza with brilliant and changing colors. As the display of the three trees disappeared, an inscription in letters of fire—*amor urit plantas*—appeared in their place, to demonstrate "what the illustrious Carolus Linnaeus held in his ingenious dissertation *Sponsalia plantarum.*"[35] On the following day, courses in botany opened under Cervantes' direction and plantings in the botanical garden were officially commenced.

Still lacking suitable housing, members of the expedition were given the use of a house and garden belonging to New Spain's chief architect Ignacio Castera, located on the Calle Victoria adjacent to the Potrero of Atlampa. Both the small area of land belonging to the house and the adjacent pasture, an area of 20,000 square yards, were cultivated. Workers built a picket fence to enclose the area and, following a practice common in Europe at the time, formed the earth into raised beds edged with boards. A system of pipes and troughs provided for the distribution of water and the entire cost was kept at 1,781 pesos. Gardeners planted seeds brought from Spain and transplanted a number of native species from the surrounding country. From the beginning, however, they grappled with problems of frequent flooding and soil conditions

33. Viceroy Florez (1787–89) to Francisco Gamboa, Mexico, 30 April 1788, Historia 461, AGN.

34. *Gaceta de México,* vol. 3, p. 76.

35. Although the Latin phrase indicated that "love" inflames plants, they were actually showing the sexual nature of plant reproduction.

that were apparently unsuitable for the cultivation of many kinds of plants. Nevertheless, having no alternative, they continued their plantings for the next four years.[36]

Because the botanical garden was to be self-supporting and was even to reimburse the crown for expenditures on its behalf, Sessé, not unlike modern fundraisers, came up with various proposals. He first planned a *plaza de toros* seating 15,000 people to be conveniently located near the center of town between Calle de Victoria and Paseo de Bucareli. He estimated construction costs at 70,500 pesos, annual upkeep at 8,196, and revenues from twelve bullfights at 56,358 pesos. When Costansó presented Sessé his final drawings, complete with a model bull ring, costs had jumped to 150,000 pesos. A second idea was to use the proceeds from the state lottery, but these had already been spoken for by the hospitals. A third plan was for staff members from the garden to inspect pharmacies and help them comply with current drug laws. Even though the cost would be only 50 pesos each every two years, the Royal College of Physicians, already jealous of the new institution, protested that the public would suffer from added drug costs. The university was then asked to support the chair of botany, but, being slightly hostile to the Spanish group, it said there was no money. Finally, Sessé thought that perhaps vagrants, drunkards, and other delinquents could be used as cheap manual labor to carry dirt and fertilizer, but this plan would only save—and not make—money.[37] The botanical garden never did pay its way.

Despite problems with the garden, Sessé lost no time in getting men into the field. Beginning in October 1787, Sessé, Sensevé, and Longinos explored the Valley of Mexico and, by mid-June 1788, had extended their efforts as far as six leagues (about fifteen miles) from the capital. As a result, they had placed about two hundred plants in the herbarium, had artists prepare sketches, described new species, and made notes on species already known. They had stayed for a time in the picturesque suburb of San Angel since it provided an appropriate place from which to explore nearby mountains. Because they had not left anciently settled areas, the travelers thought the majority of plants might

36. Harold W. Rickett, "The Royal Botanical Expedition to New Spain, 1788–1820," pp. 7–10. Rickett, bibliographer of the New York Botanical Garden, spent several months in Mexico investigating sources in the Archivo General de la Nación and gives an excellent description of the garden's founding and certain other activities of the expedition. This work will be hereinafter cited as Rickett, "Royal Botanical Expedition."

37. Ibid., pp. 10–11.

already be known and cited "by the botanists who had traveled by way of the Cape of Good Hope, through Canada and into Virginia."[38] Sessé lamented the lack of these botanical descriptions to compare with his own observations which were nevertheless fairly complete for the time.[39]

In his search for illustrators, Sessé had interviewed Jerónimo Antonio Gil, director of the Royal Art Academy of San Carlos in Mexico, who had suggested two excellent students—Vicente de la Cerda and Atanásio Echeverría. Sessé incorporated the two young men into the expedition at an annual salary of 1,000 pesos each while traveling and 500 pesos while in the capital. Both artists were capable, but Sessé felt that the eighteen-year-old Echeverría greatly surpassed Cerda in ability. He sent Gómez Ortega a painting of a butterfly that Echeverría rendered "so completely enchanting that it appeared to want to escape from the paper." The artists were not only talented but agreeable and easygoing, an assurance of uninterrupted peace during botanical journeys.

Sessé employed two other men part-time at the garden at annual salaries of 190 pesos each. They distributed plants to botany students and supplied duplicate drawings of those on which Cerda and Echeverría were working. These assistants also depicted plants that had bloomed or gone to seed while other expedition members were out of the capital. In this way Cervantes or Sessé could determine the nature of such plants when they returned. The work went smoothly, but Sessé still lacked some necessary books, principally the volumes of Paláu, Rumphio, and Plumier, that were supposed to have been shipped to New Spain.[40]

Juan del Castillo, the second official botanist, finally arrived in Mexico on 17 July 1788 and joined the expedition on 10 August. Born in Jaca, Aragon in 1744, Castillo had studied Latin and completed the course in pharmacy. At age twenty-seven he was sent to Puerto Rico as chief pharmacist of the Royal Hospital and remained at that post from 1771 until his assignment to New Spain. After a lengthy delay in settling the pharmacy's accounts to official satisfaction, he sailed for Mex-

38. Sessé to Gómez Ortega, San Angel, 26 June 1788, 4ª división, legajo no. 20, ARJB.

39. Rogers McVaugh, in *Botanical Results of the Sessé and Mociño Expedition*, p. 123, indicates that the botanists collected between 550 and 600 species of plants, and the artists made paintings of 187 species as a result of the first excursion, even though it "was hardly an excursion in the modern sense."

40. Sessé to Gómez Ortega, San Angel, 26 June 1788, 4ª división, legajo no. 20, ARJB.

ico. As soon as he found lodgings, he left the capital to work with the group in the mountains.[41]

During the summer and early fall of 1788, the expedition had covered the most fertile of the surrounding territories, but severe frosts began to hamper their efforts. They were having trouble finding the plants that Hernández had described because of "the loss and distortion of the Mexican idiom" and because "his descriptions or sketches supplied little or no light" on the search.[42] Nevertheless, they had found enough to assemble a shipment of plants, drawings, and animals that "were rather good considering the little bit the nearby places had to offer."[43]

On 30 November 1788, the botanists returned to Mexico City because winter weather made collecting difficult. They had spent the preceding month in the more temperate climate of Yacapixtla where Sessé and his companions found plants more plentiful. The total number of species that they collected in the rugged mountainous region surrounding the eight-thousand-foot-high Valley of Mexico had reached 550, "without counting the more common ones found in the irrigated lands in the proximities of the capital." Cervantes, in charge of local plant gathering, was preparing a separate notice of those found nearby. Staff members occupied their time arranging collections and "classifying the herbarium, the drawings, and the seeds according to the order which is found in the translation of Sr. Paláu."[44]

Sessé wanted to make the first shipment of specimens to Spain before they departed on a second excursion. The group planned to leave in mid-February or early March and head for the "hot climates" to the southwest. Sessé, Castillo, and perhaps Longinos would explore the tropical regions and make the city of Cuernavaca their temporary base of operation. Sessé was particularly excited by this area because he knew it to be one of the most fertile and most thoroughly covered by Hernández.[45]

As the year 1788 drew to a close, Longinos began to have difficulty

41. Vicente Cervantes, "Discurso pronunciado en el Real Jardín Botánico de México."

42. Steele, *Flowers for the King,* comments that even though Hernández classified plants according to unscientific Aztec standards and his descriptions are vague, "he preserved a body of ethno-botanical lore that probably otherwise would have been lost" (pp. 6–7).

43. Sessé to Gómez Ortega, Mexico, 27 October 1788, 4ª división, legajo no. 20, ARJB.

44. Refers to Antonio Paláu y Verdera, *Parte práctica de botánica del caballero Carlos Linneo,* which is based on Reichard's 1779–80 edition of Linnaeus' *Systema plantarum.*

45. Sessé to Gómez Ortega, Mexico, 5 January 1789, 4ª división, legajo no. 20, ARJB.

in complying with Sessé's policy that members of the group stay together while traveling. Because Longinos was to study fauna rather than flora, he insisted that it was not always possible to encounter desired animals when the rest of the expedition was searching for plants. Therefore, and apparently with the consent of the director, Longinos and the artist Echeverría stayed behind in Mexicalzingo to stuff animals and make drawings until 7 December 1788.

While Sessé and the others were exploring the area near Mexico City, Cervantes had remained in the capital to fulfill his professorial obligations. The first course in botany given under the auspices of the Royal Scientific Expedition was, therefore, successfully completed before the end of the year. Sessé enthusiastically reported the affair to Antonio Porlier in Madrid in January 1789:

> On the 20th day of December last, the first exercises in Botany were celebrated in this Royal and Pontifical University with more applause than might have been expected because of the short epoch of this study, the lack of a Garden, and the many other obstacles capable of hindering its advancement. . . .
>
> With this good beginning, which conforms to the general Jubilee which attended the opening of the school . . . one is persuaded that with the planting and enriching of the Garden with the abundance of plants produced on this Continent Botany will progress rapidly in these Dominions, and the Sovereign will gain satisfaction in seeing his pious intentions bearing fruit.[46]

In the absence of the viceroy, Regent Francisco Gamboa again presided. Many important dignitaries representing the University of Mexico, the church, the military, and the local citizenry attended the affair.[47]

As the new session began in 1789, classes were continued in the Ignacio Castera home. The undaunted botanists made further, although for the most part futile, attempts to establish a respectable garden in the pasture of Atlampa, popularly called *El Sapo,* the Toad, because of its wetness. While Cervantes planned his classes and the improvement of the garden for the coming year, Sessé assembled his shipment of plants for Madrid and made preparations to leave on a second major excursion.

On 27 January 1789, the six official members of the exploring expedition joined together in petitioning the king for funds to pay the three servants who had been promised according to the royal order of

46. Sessé to Antonio Porlier, Mexico, 7 January 1789, Flora Española—1789, AMCN.

47. *Gaceta de México,* vol. 3 (6 January 1789), p. 214.

13 March 1787. The scientists asked for speedy payment, arguing their need for help during their continuous travels through isolated locations. There is no indication that they received the funds for servants before setting out for Cuernavaca in early March 1789, but apparently the fifty-mile trip was made with little difficulty.[48]

Upon reaching Cuernavaca on 19 March, Sessé examined some items that had been sent or brought into the capital by others and would be included in the first shipment to Spain. Two boxes had been left with Cervantes that contained the following products and drawings:[49] the first box "contains thirty-five birds and three quadrupeds which inhabit the Lagoon and immediate surroundings of Mexico. . . ." The second box

Contains the herbarium and drawings of the animals and new, rare plants encountered in the proximities of this Capital. In the same box go six tin boxes with the following products:

Number 1. Enclosed is *Mangle* and *Sangre de Drago* of this Kingdom.[50] *Mangle* is a gum which is used in medicine for sicknesses of the chest. According to what the natives say, it is produced by the plant of the same name [*Rhizophora mangle*]. This will be explained as it should be when we see the plant that produces it, which is indigenous to the tropics. *Sangre de Drago* is a resin well known in Europe because of its powerful astringent virtue. It is produced in abundance in this Kingdom and is of a much purer class than another of the same name which is currently sold commercially. They bring the resin to this Capital from the tropical regions; and for this reason it has not been possible to examine the plant from which they extract the resin, nor inquire into all that corresponds to its history, which we note remains necessary to be done, such as how to propagate it and remit it to this Garden.

Number 2. Contains the fruit, seeds and fiber of a tree known by the Indians by the name of *Pochotl* [*Bombax ellipticum*].[51] If it can be produced easily, as we are assured was done by the Ancient Mexicans, it would be of much economic and commercial utility because it is an extremely abundant plant, which grows spontaneously in these Provinces without meriting the appreciation of the natives.

48. Sessé, et al., to Antonio Porlier, Mexico, 27 January 1789; Sessé to Porlier, Cuernavaca, 24 March 1789, Flora Española—1789, AMCN.

49. This list in Spanish is annotated by Enrique Alvarez López in "Noticias y papeles de la expedición científica mejicana," pp. 77–79.

50. The *mangle rojo,* or red mangrove, is a tropical shrub found in marshy areas and tidal mudflats. It is listed in *Plantae novae hispaniae,* p. 71. There are a number of dragon's blood plants, but the *Croton draco* Schlecht. is best known for its astringent properties. The blood-red sap is bitter and gives a red dye.

51. A large variety of the cotton-tree family, also called *xiloxochitl* (cornsilk flower) because of its long-tasseled pink flowers. A tea of the flowers is used against fevers and coughs.

Number 3. Contains the resin *Copal,* of great use in medicine, which the pharmacists use in place of *Goma de Limón.* It grows in great abundance and spontaneously in trees which have the same name [*Hierba de Copal.*][52]

Number 4. Lacca and Succino, the first gum from a tree called *Tzina cancuitla-quahuitl,* by the Mexicans and *Croton Lacciferum* by the botanists. It is also abundant in this Kingdom, and better than that currently sold in Spain. The second is also a product of a plant which, according to what the *Gaceta de Literatura* of the Kingdom informs us, grows in the roots of a tree called *Quapinole,* native to tropical lands.[53]

Number 5. Contains another product called *Axin* by the Natives, which is equivalent to *Unto* [ointment]. They assure us that it is efficacious for the nerves, and a strengthener when dissolved in oil and smeared on the affected part. We will give a more extensive account of it when we arrive where it is produced.

In the same box is included a gum known here as stone of the *Yerba governadora* or *Hediondilla,* which plant we examined from a dried specimen sent to us. We determined it to be a species of *Xara* or *Cistus.*[54] It is very celebrated as an excellent nerve medicine and antiparalytic; thus the gum, like the plant, is cooked with a fine wine and applied to the affected part.

Item . . . another gum called *Texcalama,* which comes from a plant called *Higueron,* is an admirable astringent and is used in relaxations with as good success as that of the celebrated *Ocuje of Havana.*[55] This plant has just arrived alive, so we will be able to describe its natural character.

Number 6. Contains the flowers of a plant called *Yerba del Pollo* and by others *Rosilla,* and known among the botanists by *Commelina erecta.*[56] Besides the medicinal virtue which Dr. Hernández, who distinguished it by the name *Matlaliztic tetzcocana,* has given it, it supplies an excellent blue color, which was used to draw this same plant and some of the animal sketches remitted. Its brilliance cannot be imitated by the best *ultramar* [bright blue] that we have. One should clean out the calixes and nectars and employ only the leaves of the flower in order to obtain the most perfect color. One can easily propagate it by

52. *Elaphrium jorullense* H.B.K. is known both as *copal* and *goma de limón.* Maximino Martínez in his *Catálogo de nombres vulgares y científicos de plantas mexicanas* (Mexico, 1937), pp. 112–13, lists ten different species of *copal* and many more varieties of the *Burseraceae,* or Torchwood, family. They all commonly exude a resin.

53. *Plantae novae hispaniae,* p. 153; the name *cuapinole* or *guapinole* or even *succino del pais* is common for *Hymenaea courbaril* L., p. 63. The gum exuded from its trunk is used in making varnish and incense. See Standley, *Trees and Shrubs of Mexico,* p. 413.

54. *Cestrum roseum* H.B.K. is given by Standley, *Trees and Shrubs of Mexico,* p. 1280. *Hierba governadora* (*Larrea tridentata*) or creosote bush is also called *hediondilla,* which could be translated as "little stinker." See Jeanette Coyle and Norman Roberts, *A Field Guide to the Common and Interesting Plants of Baja California,* p. 104.

55. A black fig tree (in Nahuatl, *texcalamatl,* meaning lava-fig) reported by Sessé as *Ficus nymphaefolia,* a similar South American species. It is given by Martínez, *Catálogo de nombres vulgares,* p. 464, and Standley, *Trees and Shrubs of Mexico,* p. 210, as *Ficus petiolaris. Ocuje of Havana* is the Calaba tree.

56. *Commelina tuberosa* L. or *Tinantia erecta.*

the root, or, in case this is not accomplished, by the seed, which we sent by post to Sr. Ortega.[57]

The boxes reached Madrid some time during the latter part of 1789 and the thirty-five birds and three animals were sent to the Museum of Natural History to be cared for separately. All animal and mineral species sent to the museum were to be catalogued and kept for examination by the botanists upon their return to Spain. The plants would remain in the care of the Royal Botanical Garden of Madrid.[58]

Activities of the second excursion centered upon the fauna and flora found between Cuernavaca and Acapulco. Principal localities visited were Tixtla, Chilapa, Chilpancingo, Mazatlán (in the present state of Guerrero), and Acapulco. The expedition followed approximately the main route between the capital and its west coast port.[59] It is difficult to pinpoint the amount of time spent examining plants in each of these locations, although a long letter written by Longinos sheds some light on the journey. This letter also indicates some of the difficulties the naturalist was experiencing under Sessé's directorship.[60]

Longinos complained that because Sessé still insisted that the expedition travel and work as a group, he had spent five months in Mazatlán collecting plants since there were no zoological specimens to examine. In Cuernavaca, on the other hand, where the expedition remained a little more than a month, Longinos had too much to do rather than too little. In Acapulco he was forced to complete three months' work in ten or twelve days by working through the siesta and at night, and by employing servants and fishermen, because the director insisted upon the presence of everyone in Cuernavaca by a certain date.[61]

Even though the second excursion did not please Longinos, Castillo found the trip rewarding. He carefully prepared eleven folios of descriptions in Latin of some forty-two species of plants found on the

57. Sessé to Porlier, Cuernavaca, 24 March 1789, Flora Española—1789, AMCN; another copy in 4ª división, legajo no. 20, ARJB.

58. Porlier to Sessé, Madrid, 20 July 1789, 4ª división, legajo no. 20, ARJB; Conde de Floridablanca to José Clavijo, Aranjuez, 27 March 1790, legajo no. 3, carpeta 5ª, AMCN.

59. McVaugh, Results of the Sessé and Mociño Expedition, p. 129.

60. Longinos Martínez to Viceroy Revillagigedo, 25 May 1790, Historia 464, AGN. This letter is in answer to a request for an explanation as to why he had refused to accompany the expedition when it left for Michoacan and Sonora in May 1790.

61. Ibid. Longinos also complained in this letter that Sessé kept all the books and supplies to himself in his own house and required the others to come "like schoolboys" to use them, and then made the others submit to him all their collections in order to enhance his own glory.

way to Acapulco. About one-third were native to Mazatlán and were seen in bloom in October. Several were given Acahuitzotla as their natural habitat, and two others were listed as native to Cuaxiniquilapa. Castillo described the remainder as inhabiting the region around Acapulco and as blooming in October, November, and December.[62]

The major result of the second excursion was the general classification of 372 plants, which were compiled and listed in the *Index herbarii secundae excursionis.*[63] In addition, the members of the expedition also gathered and remitted a collection of seventy-seven different kinds of seeds.[64] In a report entitled "Plants and Grasses found in Cuernavaca," they described seventeen common plants in terms of their native designations.[65] One of these, *Tzina cancuitlaquahuitl,* had been previously described and sent in the 1789 shipment to Spain. A few of these plants are included in either *Plantae novae hispaniae* or *Flora mexicana,* although the majority are not.

The second excursion also produced a list of thirty types of woods, with their uses, which were native to the surrounding territory.[66] This list was prepared for and sent, complete with specimens, to Josef de Flores, a wealthy resident of Acapulco who kept a small museum in his home.[67] Although unsigned and undated, it is in the same handwriting as other works of the expedition and includes sixteen kinds of woods known for their color, such as the black ebony, greenish-yellow mulberry, and yellow lysiloma (*quiebra-hachas*) used for inlays; the *orejón,* or

62. "Plantas descritas por Don Juan del Castillo en el viaje a Acapulco," 4ª división, legajo no. 14, ARJB. McVaugh, *Results of the Sessé and Mociño Expedition,* p. 129, indicates that the list of about forty-two species is written up "in the form of a *florula* complete with descriptions, citations of synonymy, specific localities and dates of flowering." The list begins with twelve species from Mazatlán, four from Acahuizotla, twenty-four from Acapulco, including such maritime species as *Conocarpus erecta, C. racemosa, Hippomane mancinella, Rhizophora mangle, Guilandina bonducella,* and *Chrysobalanus ycaco.* Most are included in *Plantae novae hispaniae.*

63. The complete list of plants is given in Enrique Alvarez López, "Las tres primeras campañas de la expedición científica," pp. 98–125.

64. "Semillas colectadas en la 2ª excursión" (Seeds collected on the second excursion and sent to the court on 29 November 1789), 4ª división, legajo no. 15, ARJB.

65. Plantas y hierbas que ay en Cuernavaca, 4ª división, no. 14, ARJB. See Appendix B.

66. See Appendix C (List of woods). "Lista de las maderas, cuyas muestras se dirigen del Curato de Chicontepec, del Obispado de la Puebla de los Angeles, al Señor Capitán Dn. Joseph de Flores, Castellano del Puerto de Acapulco; con expresión de sus colores y propiedades respectivas, y de los usos, a que se aplican," 4ª división, no. 15, ARJB.

67. Nicolás León, *Biblioteca botánico-mexicana,* p. 335.

ear-drop tree (*parota*),[68] described as coffee-colored, but becoming darker and more beautiful with use; and the dark purple *xaltzapotl*, from which night sticks, canes, billiard cues, and staffs used by Indian officials were made. Five medicinal woods (including some previously examined), four dyewoods, and three aromatics were also given, with their uses. Finally, two special woods were mentioned: el *Chijol,* or *Nexquahuitl,* a very hard wood that seemed to turn almost to stone when formed into pillars; and the *Lixa* (sandpaper) tree, whose leaves were so rough they could be used for sanding wood.

During the excursions of Sessé and the others, Cervantes, as always, continued the courses in botany. The session of 1789 had been attended by some outstanding students, especially one José Mariano Moziño, a young scholar who would soon join the expedition as a botanist on its third venture. At the graduation exercises on 21 November 1789, Moziño, whose later fame would exceed that of his professor, delivered an opening address that competently defended the Linnean system of nomenclature.[69] Moziño concluded his discourse by describing four native plants— *Plumeria alba, Loranthus americanus, Serapis mexicana,* and *Bignonia stans*—and received recognition as the year's outstanding pupil. With the addition of this energetic and capable individual, the Royal Scientific Expedition to New Spain entered upon a new and more vigorous epoch of exploration.

68. *Enterolobium cyclocarpum* also called *guanacaste, cuanacaztle,* and other variations from the Nahuatl *cuau-nacaztli,* "ear-tree." Its dark, durable wood is well known throughout Mexico. See Standley, *Trees and Shrubs of Mexico,* p. 391, and chapter 3 herein, p. 36.

69. *Gaceta de México,* vol. 3 (22 December 1789), p. 439.

3

Moziño's Botanical Surveys of Central and Northern Mexico

MEXICAN HISTORIAN Alberto M. Carreño believed José Mariano Moziño to be one of the most conspicuous scientific personalities that New Spain produced in the eighteenth century.[1] He was born of Spanish parents in the pueblo of Temascaltepec in the present state of Mexico on 24 September 1757.[2] First educated in his native town, Moziño was a hardworking and promising student. At age seventeen, because his family could not afford to pay for continued studies, Moziño applied for and won a scholarship to enter the Seminario Tridentino in Mexico City. Just two years later, in 1776, he was graduated in philosophy, but decided to continue on for a degree in scholastic theology and ethics, which he received in 1778. Because of his extraordinary talent, Moziño was recognized as one of the seminary's most outstanding scholars.[3]

During his years at the seminary, Moziño shared a room with his uncle, Dr. Luis de los Ríos, who had helped him obtain the scholarship. The two men lived in the home of María Rita Rivera y Melo Montaño,

1. Carreño, *Noticias de Nutka,* p. v. See also Iris Higbie Wilson, ed. and trans., *Noticias de Nutka,* pp. xliv–xlvii.

2. Carreño, *Noticias de Nutka,* p. vi. Moziño was baptized on 24 September 1757 with the name Joseph Mariano. He was listed as Spanish (*Español*), legitimate son of the legitimate marriage of Juan Antonio Mosiño and Manuela Losada, "old Christians, without mixture in the blood nor dishonor in the line [cristianos biejos, sin mezcla en la sangre, ni infamia en linaje]." The three most common spellings of the name are Moziño, Mociño and Mosiño, with the first being that most commonly used by Moziño himself. The second spelling has been used in a number of printed works concerning the Mexican scientist. Such phonetic liberality in spelling was characteristic of the time.

3. Ibid., pp. vi–xi.

an attractive young woman whose charms captivated Moziño at a vulnerable time in his life. He gave up his plans to enter the clergy and married María. The date of the wedding is not certain, but when de los Ríos went to Oaxaca as official theologian, he was accompanied by José Mariano and his bride. In Oaxaca, Moziño became a professor of ecclesiastical history at the local seminary and at times taught theology and ethics.[4]

During the next four years, Moziño tried to settle into his career as a provincial college professor, but his life lacked challenge. Always fascinated by the mysteries of nature, he expressed a desire to study further in the fields of natural science and medicine. Despite his wife's protests, Moziño returned to Mexico City in 1784 and enrolled in the university's school of medicine. María could not understand his abandoning a professorial position in exchange for three more years as a student. Bishop José Gregorio of Oaxaca agreed with her that Moziño was being irresponsible and called him a "misguided young man, without property and nothing more to lean on than his great God-given talent and ability for writing."[5] María accused her husband of leaving her in Oaxaca without support, but Moziño, who by this time regretted his marriage, maintained that she had stayed of her own accord.

Moziño pursued the course in medicine at the Royal and Pontifical University of Mexico by studying physics, mathematics, botany, chemistry, and anatomy. He also wrote essays challenging scholasticism, composed poetry in Latin, and discussed the latest ideas in philosophy with local literary lights.[6] He received his degree of Bachelor of Medicine on 30 April 1787. Instead of going immediately into medical practice, Moziño chose to enroll in Cervantes' course in botany that was due to begin just five days later on 4 May 1787.

Moziño demonstrated such amazing aptitude for this science that he was quickly singled out by Sessé for special assignments. By this time the director was having trouble with Longinos, who refused to accompany the expedition on its travels, and with Sensevé, who Sessé believed was poorly qualified for the study of natural history and was better suited to laboratory work. A solution proposed was for Moziño to accompany the expedition on its excursions while Sensevé remained in the capital dissecting specimens. Since members of the expedition were

4. *Diccionario universal de historia y geografía* (1854)), vol. 5, p. 582.

5. Bishop Gregorio to María Rita Rivera, Oaxaca, 14 August 1790, Historia 465, AGN.

6. Carreño, *Noticias de Nutka,* pp. xv–xvi.

Yellow-headed blackbird (Xanthocephalus xanthocephalus), *drawn by Vicente de la Cerda, Royal Scientific Expedition.* Museo Nacional de Ciencias Naturales, Madrid

Tuberous begonia (Begonia gracilis), *drawn by Francisco Lindo in Mexico, Malaspina Expedition, 1791.* Real Jardín Botánico, Madrid

Golden-cheeked woodpecker (Centurus chrysogenys), *drawn by José Cardero, Malaspina Expedition, 1791.* Museo Naval, Madrid

Porehead blenny (Labrisomus multiporosus *Hubbs*), *drawn by José del Pozo, Malaspina Expedition, 1791.* Museo Naval, Madrid

Butterflies of the genera Anartia, Adelpha, Eurytides, *and* Hesperocharis, *drawn by Atanásio Echeverría in Mexico, Royal Scientific Expedition, 1789.* Museo Nacional de Ciencias Naturales, Madrid

paid double for time spent in the field, Moziño would receive the extra 1,000 pesos that Sensevé forfeited by staying at home.[7] The Conde de Revillagigedo, viceroy of New Spain since 1789, supported the group's endeavors and accepted this plan on 24 March 1790.[8] Preparations were then made for Moziño to accompany the third excursion scheduled to depart in May.

Before leaving the capital, Sessé sent four boxes containing the most significant results of the previous year's work to Pedro Vertiz in the port of Veracruz. They were to be placed on the next ship departing for Spain.[9] In the first box were three smaller tin containers, one of which held an herbarium of 385 rare and unclassified plants, drawings of 180 of the most interesting, and thirty-six sketches of birds and other animals unknown in Europe. The second box carried a duplicate herbarium of plants previously shipped, and the third contained some special products. These included eight pounds of the cortex of a tree called *Copalquin* that could be used effectively in mitigating a fever in the same manner as Peruvian *quina* or *cinchona*.[10] It also held samples of *Tacamahaca* just as it was gathered from "a tree known among botanists as *Amyris sylvatica*" (possibly a kind of tea). *Tacamahaca* was also the name of a resinous material used in medicines as well as paints and varnishes.[11] The final items were samples of *lacca,* probably a kind of lacquer or gum-arabic that had come from a new species of mimosa called mesquite, and "fruits of a *bignonia* worthy of being in the Royal Museum because of its particular form."[12]

The second box contained twenty-two stuffed birds, two rare lizards,

7. "Testimonio del expediente sobre haverse resuelto que el botánico Don Jaime Sensevé quede en México y que en su lugar salga con la expedición el médico Dn. José Mosiño, nombrando para la disección de los animales al cirujano Maldonado," Flora Española—1790, AMCN. José Maldonado was a fellow student of Moziño's and was graduated in the same class in botany.

8. Revillagigedo to Sessé, Mexico, 24 March 1790, Flora Española—1790, AMCN. Later Gómez Ortega sought royal approval of the plan in a letter to Antonio Porlier (Marqués de Bajamar), Madrid, 19 December 1790, Flora Española—1790, AMCN.

9. "Razón de lo contendio en quatro caxones, que remite para el real gavinete y jardín botánico la expedición de Nueva España," Flora Española—1790, AMCN; Sessé to Marqués de Bajamar, Tepic, 13 August 1791, Flora Española—1791, AMCN.

10. quinine

11. Martínez, *Catálogo de plantas mexicanas,* p. 446, gives *Elaphrium tecomaca* DC. The resin exuded from most of the species of Elaphrium is called *copal.* Francisco J. Santamaría, *Diccionario de Mejicanismos,* p. 992, discusses the various meanings for *tacamahaca.*

12. There are several possibilities in the bignonia family including the flowering willow (*Chilopsis*), the trumpet flower (*Bignonia capreolata*), and the jacaranda (*Jacaranda*). Moziño had described the attributes of *Bignonia stans* at his graduation exercises in 1789.

and a special kind of bat native to the Americas, probably *Vespertilio spectrum* Linn., as drawn by one of the artists of the expedition. The third box held seeds and fruits of rare and virtually unknown plants. It also included three pounds of *guapinole,* the resin previously shipped. They had found great quantities on the roots of a tree of the same name, which they had recognized as a new species of *Cynometra (Hymenaea courbaril,* the locust tree or carob tree). *Guapinole* was "of excellent use for all kinds of varnishes."[13]

They were also sending bark from a tree called *Bálsamo,* either Balsam of Peru or Balsam of Tolu, because of healing virtues in the fragrant, dark red liquid it secreted. Its medicinal properties were well known to early inhabitants of Mexico who regularly gave jars of the resinous substance to the emperor as tribute. The first Spaniards sent it back by way of Peruvian ports, hence the misleading name, and it sold at prices ranging from twenty to two hundred dollars per ounce. Since the balsam was used by the clergy in preparing sacramental ointments, destruction of the tree was prohibited by papal bulls of 1562 and 1571. An infusion of the fruit in alcoholic liquors was taken internally as a stimulant, diuretic, and anthelmintic (dewormer), and used as a lotion to remove freckles. A powder from the tree's bark could cure ulcers of the skin, although its primary use was for animal wounds.[14]

Box number four contained the head of an elephant's femur and a petrified jaw-tooth of another, which, according to information received from an excavation next to the Pueblo of Santa Fe, was found with the rest of its toothless skeleton two leagues distant from the capital. With these were enclosed a "monstrous ram's horn weighing 8 pounds 5 ounces brought from the Interior Provinces by a shepherd from San Miguel el Grande," and a petrified piece of *ligno aloës* (a kind of aloë). Some wood from a tree called *parota* in Guadalajara or *guanacaste* in other areas gave an example of beautiful hardwood used in construction and cabinet making. Pods from the tree were used for cattle-feed and a syrup made from the bark provided a remedy for colds.[15] The contents of the fourth box, including a piece of unknown wood that could throw off sparks with steel, were a donation from Lt. Col. Josef de Flores for the Royal Museum.

13. See chapter 2, note 53.

14. Balsam of Tolu is given by Santamaría as *Myroxylon pereirae* or *Toluifera pereirae* Baill. in *Diccionario general de Americanismos,* pp. 180–81. See also Standley, *Trees and Shrubs of Mexico,* p. 434.

15. *Enterolobium cyclocarpum;* see chapter 2, note 68.

After shipping the boxes, Sessé outlined the proposed range of the third excursion. It would last considerably longer than previous journeys and the scientists would make a northwesterly circuit.[16] Longinos had again refused to accompany the expedition, but other members felt this was for the best. By 19 May 1790, they had reached Tlalnepantla, a town just north of Mexico City. The party included botanists Sessé, Castillo, and Moziño; artists Cerda and Echeverría; several servants; and necessary pack animals.[17]

Descriptions of plants made on this trip verify that the group moved north through San Juan del Río to Querétaro, which they reached just prior to the first of June.[18] This mountainous region, cut by various rivers to form long green valleys, offered a pleasing view to the collectors. They described some fifteen species of plants in the vicinity and set off again. Their route took them through the Bajío by way of the Hacienda de Ixtla, and through San Miguel el Grande (now Allende). They visited the hot springs of Atotonilco and then traveled west by way of the mountain road that passed near the pueblo of San Damián and continued on to Guanajuato, arriving there in mid-June.[19] Impressed by the beautiful churches and productive mines, they toured the city but did little botanizing, probably because of the dryness of the season. Sessé did, however, take time out to write a short note to Spain warning that Longinos' descriptions of birds were probably erroneous.[20]

From Guanajuato, where they remained about a month, the scientists turned southward passing through Temascatío and Salamanca and somewhat to the west of Valle de Santiago into the mountainous region of Puruándiro before reaching Valladolid (now Morelia) in early August 1790.[21] After remaining several weeks to explore the proximities of this city, which yielded few new species, they decided to examine the thick pine forests covering the mountains of southwestern Michoacan. Botanizing was definitely better after the onset of midsummer rains had caused the ground to be covered with luxurious natural vege-

16. See McVaugh, *Results of the Sessé and Mociño Expedition,* p. 130, and the map of travels on p. 15.

17. Sessé to Revillagigedo, Tlalnepantla, 19 May 1790, Historia 460 AGN.

18. Sessé to Revillagigedo, Querétaro, 28 May 1790, Flora Española—1790, AMCN.

19. "Descripciones de los géneros de plantas de Nueva España," 4ª división, legajo no. 3, ARJB; McVaugh, *Results of the Sessé and Mociño Expedition,* p. 130.

20. Sessé to Antonio Porlier, Guanajuato, 20 June 1790, Flora Española—1790, AMCN.

21. Sessé to Revillagigedo, Valladolid, 9 August 1790, Historia 462, AGN.

tation. They spent enough time in Pátzcuaro to visit the lovely cres-
cent-shaped lake set in its amphitheater of high hills, witness Tarasco
fishing activities, and describe twenty local plants.

The botanists then proceeded to Uruapán, a town just over 5,200 feet
in altitude that today has a beautiful arboretum and botanical garden.
The fields and hillsides yielded twelve new species and the travelers
continued on to rugged lava beds in the vicinity of the still-active volcano of Jorulla.[22] To the north they saw the pine-covered front of the
Sierra Madre rising several thousand feet above the intervening country, and to the south a succession of irregularly grouped hills gradually
descending to the valley of the Río Balsas. They reached Apatzingán in
late October and decided to make this city their headquarters for several
months. Within days Sessé reported to Revillagigedo that all were sick
with fever from an epidemic in that part of the country.[23] They were
out of danger in about two weeks although Sessé was suffering some
difficulty because of an ulcer on his right leg.[24]

The three months that began with their arrival in Apatzingán proved
to be the most productive period of the third excursion. They studied
and described more than 140 plants in the area. Sometime in January
1791, the expedition crossed into present-day Jalisco through the mountains toward Coahuayana. Resting very little, they must have reached
the Pacific Ocean during the next two months since several plants were
cited as being collected next to the "Mar del Sur."[25] They visited
Colima, Zaptotlán, and Sayula in February and March.[26]

In the spring the scientists departed for Guadalajara, second colonial
city of Mexico. Collecting plants in the intervening localities, they
reached their destination in April and remained there for several months
to explore the surrounding territory. Enjoying the temperate climate,
they visited Lake Chapala, the largest Mexican lake, and other areas of
natural beauty. Sessé arranged materials to be shipped to Madrid, while
Moziño worked on plant descriptions.[27]

The third excursion, the longest and most extensive, officially ended
in Guadalajara. The significant botanical results were sent to Spain

22. McVaugh, *Results of the Sessé and Mociño Expedition*, p. 131.
23. Sessé to Revillagigedo, Apatzingán, 10 November 1790, Historia 460, AGN.
24. Sessé to Revillagigedo, Apatzingán, 24 November 1790, Historia 460, AGN.
25. "Descripciones de los géneros de plantas," 4ª división, legajo no. 3, ARJB.
26. McVaugh, *Results of the Sessé and Mociño Expedition*, p. 132.
27. Sessé to Revillagigedo, Guadalajara, 22 June 1791, Historia 464, AGN.

under the title of *Herbarium tertiae excursionis hispaniae missum julio mense an. 1791*.[28] The index, although containing only 172 species of plants, reflected the botanists' greater selectivity and the fact that only species new to the collectors were included. The first excursion had yielded 583 species and the second 372.[29] On the 1790–91 trek, the artists produced slightly over one hundred botanical sketches.

The most important result of the third excursion was the completion of the manuscript *Plantae novae hispaniae*. The work treated 1,383 plants, of which more than 700 were credited to previous authors and the remainder described as new species. Unlike *Flora mexicana,* which contained descriptions or brief references to some 1,500 miscellaneous species,[30] *Plantae novae hispaniae* formed a definite unit and seems to have been chiefly Moziño's work, since the entire Latin manuscript is written in his hand.[31] It was intended basically as a field report and not for publication as such, so criticisms leveled against it at a later date have resulted from poor editing as well as the one-hundred-year delay in its appearance. It should also be kept in mind that Sessé and Moziño were attempting to identify Mexican plants solely with the aid of Linnaeus and other European authors who were generally unfamiliar with

28. 4ª división, legajo no. 16, ARJB; Flora Española—1791, AMCN. The complete list is printed in Arias Divito, *Las expediciones científicas españolas,* pp. 380–82.

29. In the list of plants collected on the second excursion, only 2.4 percent were listed previously on the first one, and in the third only 6.5 percent correspond to species already found on the two preceding ones.

30. McVaugh, *Results of the Sessé and Mociño Expedition,* p. 117, points out that the manuscript *Flora mexicana* in the Royal Botanical Garden in Madrid contains approximately one thousand unnumbered leaves bound in three folio volumes with no title page or introduction. The first eight pages are in Moziño's hand and include the genera *Amomum, Costus, Maranta,* and *Alpinia* through *Bicalyculata* of the printed text. They contain references to *Icones* and herbarium numbers. Beginning with the ninth page, according to McVaugh, "the manuscript ceases to be an organized flora; from that point on it consists of a series of plant-descriptions and notes assembled roughly in systematic order, but from a variety of sources."

31. Ibid., p. 112. Enrique Alvarez López, in "Las tres primeras campañas de la expedición dirigida por Sessé," p. 40, has prepared the following distribution of citations giving the percentage of plants from each excursion included in *Planta novae hispaniae* and *Flora mexicana:*

	1st. Exc.	*2nd. Exc.*	*3rd. Exc.*
Cited in *PNH*	66 %	80 %	72 %
Cited exclusively in *PNH*	54	60	26.5
Cited in *PNH* and *FM*	14	20	45.5
Cited exclusively in *FM*	2.5	1.3	6.5
Not cited in either work	29	12.9	7.5

tropical American plants. The two men actually succeeded fairly well in making reasonable identifications and in assigning hundreds of new species and genera a place in the Linnean system.[32] Some additional results of the expedition included thirty-seven unidentified drawings of plants, undoubtedly those of Cerda or Echeverría, as well as eighty-seven labeled drawings under the classification "Flora Mexicana," presumably by the same artists.[33] None has been included in any published work.

After working in Guadalajara, members of the expedition separated. Sessé explained that the trip for the year 1791 was designed to allow re-examination of any of the provinces that, because of their different altitudes and climates, offered a variety of natural products. It was agreed that Moziño, Castillo, and one of the artists would cover the skirt of the Sierra Madre on the west as far as Alamos. By crossing the range at the scenic Puerto de Canelas, they would be able to explore in Nueva Vizcaya. In the meantime, Sessé, the other artist, and Moziño's classmate José Maldonado, an anatomist who had recently joined the expedition, would explore the provinces of Sinaloa and Ostimuri as far north as the missions of the Yaqui River. The entire expedition would then reunite in Aguascalientes "because the ruggedness of the Sierra and the dangers of enemies would not permit it to be in another more convenient point."[34]

Sessé again attempted to get Moziño officially incorporated into the expedition with a salary commensurate with his ability and sufficient to purchase necessary supplies. The difficulties of traveling in mountainous regions or through remote pueblos were compounded because of the scarcity of food. The expeditionaries had to carry provisions equal "to the commissary taken on sea voyages" so as to "prevent death from hunger even on the best trodden roads." The "scant and wretched fare which the frugal and semi-barbarous Indians of these parts used for food" barely met local needs, much less those of visitors. Moziño, without the small salary he enjoyed with the expedition, would have no way to pay for the food and clothing that he had to buy prior to departure.[35]

32. McVaugh, Results of the Sessé and Mociño Expedition, p. 114.
33. 4ª división, legajo nos. 5 and 22, ARJB.
34. Sessé to Revillagigedo, Mexico, 9 May 1793, Historia 527, AGN; Carreño, Noticias de Nutka, pp. xlvii–lii.
35. Sessé to Revillagigedo, Mexico, 9 May 1793, Historia 527, AGN.

While Moziño, Castillo, and one of the artists set out for the north, Sessé went with the others to Tepic in August 1791, before heading for the coast. While in this city he wrote to Porlier, now Marqués de Bajamar, to report that "by the weekly post of the 22nd of June," he had sent to the viceroy a box containing descriptions of 1,383 plants in two volumes in folio (*Plantae novae hispaniae*) and drawings that were listed in the catalogue attached. Sessé hoped they would not "be too excessive in their volume" to be shipped by the first maritime post.[36] He advised that he still did not know if the marqués had received the four boxes placed with Pedro Vertiz in Veracruz in May 1790, which should have left the port in late June of that year.

Sessé thought the boxes might have disappeared and thus was sending duplicates of all drawings of animals made on the two preceding excursions. He could not do the same with the plants because he had left them with Cervantes, who would send the herbarium of the latest collections and two boxes of stuffed animals "of whose species I am ignorant because the Naturalist [Longinos] is traveling separately from the Expedition without giving me, up until now, the least notice of his observations."[37] The itinerant Longinos had, however, sent Revillagigedo another box containing "exquisite stuffed birds dedicated to Our Lady the Queen" to be included with the shipment.

To emphasize Longinos' "insubordination," Sessé complained that drawings of birds remitted by Longinos in 1789 "had for the major part been found in error in their labeling" and would certainly bring discredit to the expedition if they were seen by knowledgeable scientists.[38] He urged that the drawings be examined by qualified persons in Madrid so corrections could be made in the manuscripts. Sessé thought that when Longinos realized the consequences of his actions, he would be humbled sufficiently to submit to Sessé's authority in the future.

Cervantes placed all the boxes in the care of the ministries of the army and royal treasury in early October 1791, and Revillagigedo ordered that they be conducted to Veracruz. The superintendent of the port was to meet with the captain of the ship transporting the boxes to assure their secure and safe passage.[39] With such explicit instructions

36. Sessé to Marqués de Bajamar, Tepic, 13 August 1791, Flora Epañola—1791, AMCN.

37. Ibid.

38. Ibid.

39. Revillagigedo to Marqués de Bajamar, Mexico, 8 October 1791, no. 316, Flora Española—1791, AMCN.

having been issued to those in Veracruz, all seemed to be in order. As late as 30 November 1791, Revillagigedo complained that the governor of Veracruz had not yet confirmed departure of the shipment. He thought the boxes must still be in the plaza, detained in customs because of an error by the ministers of the royal treasury. The viceroy therefore sent duplicate instructions and expected shipment to be made at once.[40]

Even though delays through official Spanish channels at times were interminable, the bureaucracy did function. The two boxes arrived in good condition in the port of Cádiz aboard the frigate *La Astrea*.[41] The one with the stuffed birds was presented to Queen María Luisa, "to whom they were destined by the Naturalist Don Josef Longinos," and were well received. The other, with drawings, two volumes of manuscripts, and the herbarium was examined by Carlos IV "with pleasure" and the sketches found to be "exact, well drawn, and beautifully colored." The Spanish monarch expected that the "application, attention and endeavor" of the scientists would "correspond to the generosity with which assistance had been imparted."[42]

Once the necessary shipments to the Court of Spain had been arranged, Sessé, with Moziño, Castillo, Cerda, Echeverría, and perhaps Maldonado, continued his explorations along the coast in Sinaloa as far north as the Yaqui River. The men drew their salaries at Alamos on 21 October 1791, and at Durango on 2 January 1792. Except for these locations, their exact whereabouts during the fall and early winter cannot be determined with certainty. Longinos and Sensevé spent the latter part of 1791 on the "South Coast," that is, in Nayarit, most likely in the area of San Blas.[43]

Meanwhile, Revillagigedo had faced another problem. His previous order of 24 March 1790, which had approved the substitution of Moziño for Sensevé, had been disallowed by an apparently unreasonable action of Carlos IV, who had succeeded his enlightened father Carlos III in 1788, or one of his advisors. Royal instructions ordered that Sensevé and Longinos join the expedition in the field at once and that Moziño

40. Revillagigedo to Marqués de Bajamar, Mexico, 30 November 1791, no. 333, Flora Española—1791, AMCN.

41. Manuel Gonzáles to Marqués de Bajamar, Cádiz, 16 March 1792, Flora Española—1792, AMCN.

42. Orden del Rey Carlos IV [1792], 4ª división, legajo no. 15, ARJB.

43. McVaugh, *Results of the Sessé and Mociño Expedition*, pp. 132, 134.

and Maldonado be discharged. The king's order, dated in Madrid on 22 March 1791, was not received in Mexico until 4 June 1791.[44] Revillagigedo took no immediate action.

44. Historia 462, AGN.

4

The Malaspina Expedition: Personnel and Organization, 1789 to 1791

B Y MID-1791, members of the Royal Scientific Expedition in New Spain had realized several important goals and were optimistic about the future. Their extensive excursions from the capital had yielded abundant results, while their colleague Cervantes continued the successful training of young botanists in Mexico City. In late spring they had been joined by scientists from the Malaspina expedition. Plans for this global enterprise had reached fruition in 1789, shortly after Sessé's group began work in New Spain. Its scope was immense—instead of limiting scientific exploration to merely one kingdom or even one continent, it was designed to encompass all of the Americas plus the Pacific Islands.

The man who conceived the idea of this large-scale effort was Italian-born Alejandro Malaspina, a brilliant Spanish naval officer who had served in Gibraltar, the Philippines, and India.[1] Having circumnavigated the earth in 1786–88 in command of *La Astrea,* Malaspina formulated a plan of exploration that would follow approximately the same

1. Malaspina was born in Mulazzo in the Duchy of Parma, Italy, 5 November 1754, of noble parentage. His mother, Catalina Melilupi, belonged to the family of the princes of Soragna. Malaspina enlisted in the marine guard of Cádiz in 1774 and rose rapidly in rank until, at the age of thirty, he apparently received command of the *Astrea.* See Pedro de Novo y Colson, ed., *Viaje político-científico alrededor del mundo por las corbetas* Desubierta y Atrevida, p. viii. This work is hereinafter referred to as Malaspina, *Viaje político-científico.* Malaspina's career is summarized in "Antiguedades de los oficiales de guerra de la Armada," MS 1161bis, Archives of the Museo Naval, Ministerio de Marina, Madrid, hereinafter referred to as AMN. The expedition did not actually circumnavigate the globe, but returned from the Philippines, Australia and New Zealand by way of South America.

westward route. Tireless in his attention to detail, dedicated to the welfare of his men, and committed to the advancement of science, Malaspina always presented an example to be followed. He selected as his partner fellow officer and friend José Bustamante y Guerra, a native of Santander who had also enjoyed great success in the navy. Bustamante had risen swiftly to a frigate command at age twenty-seven in 1784. Together, on 10 September 1788, they submitted a "Plan for a Scientific and Political Voyage around the World" to Spain's Minister of Marine Antonio Valdés.[2] The plan's introduction reflected the expansive enlightened thinking of these late eighteenth-century Spanish naval officers:

For the past twenty years the two nations of England and France, with a noble rivalry, have undertaken voyages in which navigation, geography, and the knowledge of humanity have made very rapid progress. This history of human society has laid the foundation for more general investigations; natural history has been enriched with an almost infinite number of discoveries; and finally, the preservation of Man in different climates, on extensive journeys, and among some almost incredible tasks and risks, has been the most interesting acquisition of these navigators.

The voyage which is being proposed is particularly directed toward the completion of these objects; and the aspect which is being called the Scientific Part will certainly be carried out with much care, continuing with effectiveness the paths of Cook and La Pérouse.[3]

Malaspina emphasized his idea that a voyage made by Spanish navigators should include two other special purposes: the making of hydrographic charts for the most remote regions of America and oceanic charts for the "little-expert mercantile navigation"; and the investigation of the political state of America with regard to Spain, foreign nations, commerce, manufacturing, natural resources, and defense. The general public would benefit from the gathering of historical informa-

2. "Plan de un viaje científico y político a el rededor del mundo remitido a el Exmo. Sr. Bailío Fray Antonio, Valdés de Madrid en 10 de Sept. de 1788," MS 316 AMN. Valdés, knight of the prestigious Order of Malta, *Caballero del Toisón de Oro*, captain general of the Royal Armada, and minister of marine from 1782 to 1795, was an enthusiastic supporter of scientific endeavors. Admiral Julio F. Guillén, *Indice de la colección de Fernández de Navarrete*, calls him "the promoter of the most brilliant epoch of the Royal Navy."

3. Ibid. Captain Cook's voyages and major works are discussed in chapter 5, p. 89, notes 30 and 31. Jean François Galaup, Comte de la Pérouse, sailed from Brest in 1785 as commander of a geographic, scientific, and commercial expedition around the world. After visiting the Northwest Coast and Monterey, the expedition was lost north of New Hebrides in 1788. La Pérouse's journal, previously forwarded to Paris, was published as *A Voyage around the World in the Years 1785, 1786, 1787, and 1788* in the first English edition.

tion and all possible curiosities for the Royal Museum and Botanical Garden, while the crown would benefit from the hydrographic studies and political speculations.[4]

Malaspina believed that the Royal Navy would be able to supply nearly all individuals necessary to carry out the various aspects of the commission. He lacked only two botanists or naturalists and two artists whom he believed might be found in Madrid. The corvettes required for the journey, designed especially for scientific research, were to be completely equipped and ready to depart from Cádiz in July 1789. The 109-foot *Atrevida* would be commanded by Bustamante and the identical *Descubierta,* by himself.[5] Malaspina estimated that the voyage would take approximately three and one-half years.

Minister of Marine Valdés, a man of truly long-range vision, provided Malaspina all necessary official assistance, yet permitted him free rein to organize the expedition as he saw fit. Accordingly, Malaspina began to select his personnel, carefully screening possible candidates to fulfill the obligations of the "scientific part." In October 1788, he informed Valdés that he knew an ideal person to serve on one of the two ships as chief of natural history—First Lieutenant Antonio Pineda y Ramírez of the Royal Spanish Army.[6] Malaspina described this officer as possessing "not only all the intelligence and capacity necessary for that science, but also an admirable energy and disposition, and that true love of new studies and new honors which can be the only motive and reward of such enterprises."[7]

Valdés recommended the appointment of Pineda to the king and received royal confirmation in December 1788.[8] Having prepared the corresponding official order to the minister of war, Valdés reported the news to the commander of the expedition, and Malaspina wrote his friend Pineda that he was officially in charge of "Natural History in all of its branches" on the forthcoming expedition.[9]

Although born in Guatemala in 1753, Pineda, like some wealthy

4. Malaspina, "Plan de un viaje científico y político," MS 316 AMN.

5. The two ships, or *corbetas,* were especially constructed for the voyage according to Malaspina's specifications; each was 120-feet long and displaced 360 tons. Christened the *Santa Justa* and *Santa Rufina,* they traveled under aliases of *Descubierta* and *Atrevida* (Cutter, *Malaspina in California,* p. 2).

6. See Iris Higbie Wilson, "Antonio de Pineda y su viaje mundial," pp. 49–64.

7. Malaspina to Valdés, Cadiz, 31 October 1788, MS 583 "Correspondencia relativa al viaje de Malaspina," AMN. These documents are drafts of the letters sent by Malaspina.

8. Valdés to Malaspina, Madrid, 12 December 1788, MS 278, AMN.

9. Malaspina to Antonio Pineda, Madrid, 29 December 1788, MS 427, AMN.

young men of pure Spanish parentage, was sent to the peninsula for military service. During his stay in Madrid, he actively pursued his hobby of natural history. In 1788, while serving in the Royal Spanish Guards, Fifth Battalion, he obtained a special assignment at the Royal Museum of Natural Science. He completed a study of the birds that were on deposit in the museum and apparently had experience in all of the natural sciences.[10]

Pineda's brother, Arcadio, also a lieutenant, but in the Royal Navy, was selected by Malaspina to serve in the expedition as one of the officers on the *Atrevida*.[11] In addition to his naval duties, Arcadio was responsible for the organizing and recopying of many of Antonio's scientific observations, which he did very well. Upon his brother's untimely death in the Philippines in 1792, Arcadio took charge of natural history, but did not have the broad experience to achieve the same measure of success.[12]

Named to assist Pineda was French-born Luis Neé, a man well known to Gómez Ortega. Neé, a naturalized Spaniard, had worked for many years on a number of projects for the Royal Botanical Garden in Madrid. In 1784 he established a botanical garden in Pamplona and gathered plants throughout the historic Basque country. During 1785 and 1786, he sent to Madrid more than twelve hundred species from the region of Navarre; and before his departure with the expedition from Cádiz in July 1789, Neé submitted a report on the vegetation of southern Spain.[13] Upon receiving the King's approval of Neé's appointment, Valdés forwarded the necessary official order to the Conde de Floridablanca.[14]

In July 1789, Valdés informed Malaspina that the king had deemed it advantageous to gain the services of Tadeo Haënke, a brilliant Bohe-

10. Miguel Colmeiro, *La botánica y los botánicos*, p. 182. "Historia de las aves, que se guardan en el gavinete de historia natural," Madrid, 27 October 1787, papeles de Antonio Pineda, AMCN.

11. "Libro de guardias de la corbeta *Atrevida,* con un plano de señales y orden de disciplina," MS 755, AMN.

12. At the termination of the expedition, José Bustamante believed Arcadio Pineda to be of little talent and of limited application in all branches of his profession (Bustamante to Valdés, Madrid, 6 January 1795, informes reservados, miscelanea 6, doc. 4, AMN).

13. Colmeiro, *La botánica y los botánicos*, p. 182. In a letter to Valdés, Cádiz, 5 December 1788, MS 583, AMN, Malaspina wrote that Luis Neé was "well versed in theoretical and practical botany, was indefatigable in his investigations, and twenty years before had traveled through the mountains of Asturias. He was then working in the garden of the Royal Pharmacy."

14. Valdés to Malaspina, Madrid, 12 December 1788, MS 278, AMN.

mian-born scientist offered to the expedition by the ambassador from Sardinia. Valdés obtained permission from the Austrian government for Haënke to serve the Spanish crown in the capacity of botanist and naturalist, for which he would be paid an annual salary of twenty-four thousand reales plus food allowance.[15] Haënke, though only twenty-eight years old, had traveled through Syria, Corinth, and Tyrol; knew Spanish, French, Latin, Italian, and German; had earned his doctorate from the University of Prague; and was well qualified both in natural history and botany. Because of transportation difficulties, he arrived in Cádiz two hours after the corvettes had sailed for South America; he finally caught another ship to Buenos Aires only to have it wrecked near Montevideo. With a copy of Linnaeus in his nightcap, he swam ashore sans baggage and instruments, only to miss the expedition once again. This resourceful scientist hired some native guides and crossed overland to the Chilean coast, making botanical notes and collecting twenty-five hundred specimens along the way.[16] He joined Malaspina in Santiago de Chile in April 1790.[17]

Antonio Pineda, upon learning of his appointment to the expedition, began to itemize the books and instruments he considered necessary for the scientists during the voyage. Pineda's list, like the one proposed by Gómez Ortega for the Royal Scientific Expedition, serves as an index of the best-known scientific works of that epoch. It is even more complete because it included a separate section for zoology and mineralogy in addition to botanical works.[18] Because all the books were by foreign authors, including the works of Linnaeus, Forster, Plumier, Forskael, Pallas, and Buffon, it can be assumed that Pineda did not list the Spanish works that were undoubtedly readily available.[19] This is confirmed by a letter from the Conde de Floridablanca to José Clavijo, vice-director of the Royal Museum of Natural History in Madrid, stating that "Don Antonio Pineda may carry for his use the books belonging to the

15. Valdés to Malaspina, Madrid, 29 July 1789, MS 279, AMN. Haënke was born in Kreibitz, Bohemia, 5 October 1761.

16. Cutter, *Malaspina in California*, p. 5; see also Laurio H. Destefani and Donald Cutter, *Tadeo Haënke y el final de una vieja polémica* and Josef Kühnel, *Thaddaeus Haënke, Leben und Wirken eines Forschers*. A number of Haënke's botanical drawings from the Americas were edited by Karel B. Presl and published in a large two-volume work *Relinquiae Haenkeanae*.

17. Nicolás Arredondo to Malaspina, Buenos Aires, 19 February 1790, MS 278, AMN; Malaspina to Valdés, Santiago de Chile, 2 April 1790, MS 583, AMN.

18. "Lista de libros e instrumentos," Malaspina Papers, YALE.

19. Aranjuez, 13 June 1789, legajo no. 4, carpeta 3, ACMN.

Royal Museum that he now has in his possession, with the obligation of returning them upon his return from the voyage."

Pineda concluded with a note that certain other books and instruments were not requested because he either had them or could acquire them in Madrid or Cádiz. He also suggested that any items unavailable in Paris could probably be obtained in London, but time was of the essence since all had to arrive in Cádiz before the end of April. Pineda hoped that the Conde de Fernán Nuñez, a patron of the sciences, would help them with their purchases in Paris or London. At the conclusion of the expedition the foreign collection could be placed in public libraries, because the books were not then available in Madrid. The chief of natural history listed thirteen additional items concerning mineralogy, astronomy, and natural history.[20]

Finally, Pineda wished to acquire a work of M. de Puisegur of the French navy explaining new methods used in charting the island of Santo Domingo. He also felt that Mayer's lunar tables, recently perfected by MacKelyne, were necessary for calculating the distances from the moon to the sun to release them from dependence during a long voyage "upon reports of conditions that might or might not be available at the places of arrival."[21]

Numerous other books, major items of equipment, and ample provisions were requisitioned by Malaspina and other expedition members. Food consisted of bread, soup (including gazpacho), salted meat, rice, beans, lentils, oil, vinegar, and wine. Sauerkraut was taken along for the treatment of illness. Malaspina favored the use of coffee and tea because he believed sugar to be antiscorbutic, but he also ordered a good supply of lemon and orange juice. By July 1789, it appeared that all necessary preparations had been completed. The *Descubierta* and *Atrevida* set sail from Cádiz on 30 July and headed for the Canary Islands. During their Atlantic crossing they were surprised to find the ships' biscuits infested with caterpillars. Antonio Pineda checked the bread with his microscope and concluded that the heat had caused eggs already in the bread to hatch. His assurance that the caterpillars were not toxic made them no easier to eat.[22] The expedition reached Montevideo in September, after weathering some severe storms, and surveyed the Río de la Plata area for two months.

20. See Appendix D.
21. Malaspina Papers, YALE.
22. Goodman, *Explorers of South America*, p. 211.

They finally sailed on 10 November for the Patagonian port of Deseado where they stopped briefly for scientific study, then continued on to Port Egmont in the Falkland Islands. Departing from the coastal waters of Argentina in December, the expedition rounded Cape Horn as the new year began and arrived in the Port of Valparaiso de Chile in February 1790. Haënke, after completing his trans-Andean trek, joined the scientific corps in Santiago, much to their surprise and delight. The group spent several months along the coast cruising northward, visiting the ports of Coquimbo and Arica during April and May. The "winter" months were spent in the port of Callao (Peru) and the month of October in Guayaquil (Ecuador). Pineda reported, after visiting the city of Guayaquil, that they wanted "to again visit the Cordilleran Mountains and Volcanos . . . and to examine the plant life of the interior lands." He and Luis Neé decided to journey to Chimborazo and the Volcan de Nicaragua.

Pineda explained how they had examined the base of a nearby volcano and then climbed to its peak where they could perceive the noise of a deep flame "as if it were a great oven of grain." The party made some meteorological observations, gathered specimens of volcanic material, and collected several kinds of plants. They also examined a hot spring from which the natives extracted an excellent purgative salt. They were unable to reach the 20,577-foot-high mountain of Chimborazo because of rains and snow. Pineda observed that the immense forests contained many precious drugs and vegetable products that were unknown to the natives and of whose existence even the Spanish were ignorant.[23] One of these was the *Goma elástica* used in making varnishes. In Peru, he noted, this product was called *xebe,* after the tree from which it was extracted:

In order to obtain the gum, knife-cuts are made in the bark; from these wounds is secreted a juice like fresh milk, which is gathered on the wide leaves of the banana tree. In a short while it hardens and becomes black. It manifests the same properties as the elastic gum which is brought from Portugal and sold in Madrid, in ignorance of the fact that it is produced in our colonies. The natives of the provinces of Quito liquify it over a fire and with it varnish linens, obtaining excellent and flexible oil-cloths, which are used in the making of rainproof caps, boots, and hat-covers.

Pineda also reported having made a collection of birds and animals in Guayaquil amounting to eighty species, but that it was completely de-

23. Pineda to Valdés, Panama, 10 December 1790, Malaspina Papers, YALE.

Cornsilk or shaving brush flower (Bombax ellipticum), *drawn by Vicente de la Cerda or Atanásio Echeverría, Royal Scientific Expedition in Mexico.* Conservatoire Botanique, Geneva

Tacamahaca, a resinous tree, described by Sessé as Amyris sylvatica (Bursera tecomaca), *drawn by Cerda or Echeverría, Royal Scientific Expedition in Mexico.* Conservatoire Botanique, Geneva

Blue-throated hummingbirds (Lampornis clemenciae), *drawn by Cerda or Echeverría, Royal Scientific Expedition.* Museo Nacional de Ciencias Naturales, Madrid

Greater roadrunner (Geococcyx californianus), *drawn by Cerda or Echeverría, Royal Scientific Expedition.* Museo Nacional de Ciencias Naturales, Madrid

New World leaf-nosed bat, drawn by Echeverría, Royal Scientific Expedition. Vespertilio spectrum, *Linnaeus' designation, has been assigned to the vampire bat of Mexico.* Museo Nacional de Ciencias Naturales, Madrid

Red-shafted flicker (Colaptes cafer), *drawn by José Cardero, Malaspina Expedition in Monterey, California.* Museo Naval, Madrid

"Badger" *of Acapulco* (*Coati,* Nasua nasua), *drawn by Tomás de Suría,*
Malaspina Expedition. Museo Naval, Madrid

Opossum (Didelphis), *drawn by José Guío, Malaspina Expedition in Mexico.*
Museo Naval, Madrid

Cortez angel fish (Pomacanthus zonipectus), *Acapulco, drawn by Tomás de Suría, Malaspina Expedition.* Museo Naval, Madrid

Century plant or maguey (Agave), *found in Atotonilco and Ixmiquilpan, Mexico, drawn by Francisco Lindo, Malaspina Expedition.* Real Jardín Botánico, Madrid

Alejandro Malaspina. An 1885 engraving by B. Maura from Novo y Colson, Viaje político-científico

Model of the Atrevida, built by M. Monmeneu, Madrid. Los Angeles County Museum of Natural History

Chief of Mulgrave and his delegation greet Malaspina's corvettes, seeking peace.
Sketch probably by José Cardero, 1791. Museo de América, Madrid

Frame of a seasonal winter house, Port Mulgrave (now Yakutat Bay), by José Cardero, Malaspina Expedition. Museo de América, Madrid

Hat worn by the chief of Mulgrave, by José Cardero. Museo de América, Madrid

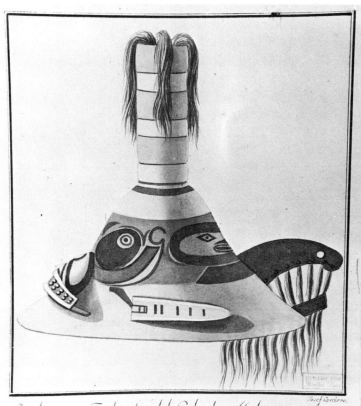

Sombrero ò Turbante del Gefe de Mulgrawe...

Woman of Mulgrave, showing labret, drawn by Tomás de Suría,
Malaspina Expedition. Museo Naval, Madrid

Pyre and sepulchres of the family of Chief Anakau, Port Mulgrave, drawn by José Cardero, Malaspina Expedition. Museo Naval, Madrid

Presidio of Monterey, California. Sketch of soldiers and Indians working in the fields by José Cardero, Malaspina Expedition. Museo Naval, Madrid

Plaza inside the Presidio of Monterey, by José Cardero, Malaspina Expedition. Museo Naval, Madrid

Indian woman of Monterey, drawn by José Cardero, 1791.
Museo Naval, Madrid

Atrevida among the icebergs, rounding Cape Horn, 28 January 1794. Engraving by B. Maura in Madrid, 1885 from Novo y Colson, Viaje político-científico

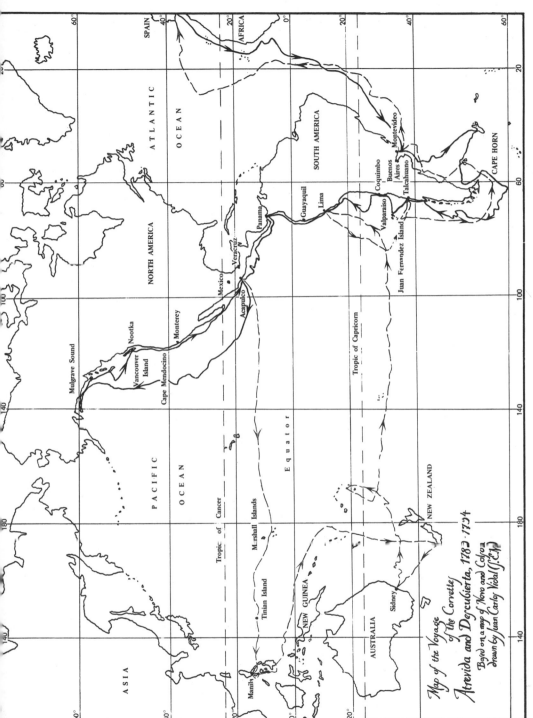

Map of the Voyage of the Corvettes
Atrevida and Descubierta, 1789-1794
Based on a map of Novo and Colron
drawn by Juan Carlos Vidal (J.C.V.)

The solid line traces the first phase, and the dashed line represents the second phase of the Malaspina Expedition of 1789-1794.

stroyed by the "multitude of insects in this hot country" on the short crossing to Panama. He explained that, according to Captain Cook's diary, the English scientists experienced similar accidents, which were very difficult to prevent.[24]

From Panama the two corvettes followed separate routes northward. The *Descubierta* made a stop in the port of Realejo (Nicaragua), while the *Atrevida*, commanded by Bustamante, sailed directly to the port of Acapulco and arrived in 2 February 1791.[25] The scientists of the *Atrevida* included botanist Neé, artist and taxidermist José Guío, and physician Pedro María González, who served as a part-time naturalist. Originally proposed by Pineda, Guío was described as an excellent young botanical artist who, because of his poverty, "would not make many demands and would be very useful in carrying out the obligations of this branch." Guío's drawings exhibited extreme precision and were characterized by a black and yellow border with a monogram in red ink. González was the official surgeon (*cirujano*) on board the *Atrevida*, but was described as desiring "instruction in botany in order to contribute to the progress of this science."[26]

Finding Acapulco abundant with plant life, Neé collected, studied, and wrote up descriptions of more than thirty new species of native plants during February. Arcadio Pineda recorded on 29 February that "today Luis Neé retired aboard extremely satisfied with his excursions in these proximities . . . having discovered as many new plants as have been described by botanical writers since Hippocrates to the present time."[27] During the same period Guío made expert drawings of a number of these species, including several of the genera *Bauhinia, Jacquinia, Aristolochia,* and *Polygala.*[28]

While the *Atrevida* lay in the port of Acapulco, its captain received on board Tomás de Suría,[29] a young artist from the Academy of San

24. Ibid.

25. Lorenzo Sanfeliú Ortiz, *62 meses a bordo,* p. 119; MS 583, AMN.

26. MS 583, MS 92 bis AMN. Approximately two hundred samples of Guío's work are contained in the Real Jardín Botánico in Madrid and numerous other drawings can be found in the Museo Naval. While in Acapulco, González described a number of zoological specimens, and his report is contained in the Museum of Natural Science in Madrid.

27. "Diario desde Panama a Acapulco," MS 94, AMN.

28. Luis Neé, "Dibujos de plantas," vols. 1, 2, and 4, ARJB.

29. Born in Valencia in 1761, Suría traveled to Mexico in 1778 with Jerónimo Gil, his professor at the Royal Art Academy of Madrid, when Gil was appointed founding director of the Royal Academy of San Carlos of Mexico. Suría was working as an engraver for the Casa de Moneda [mint] when he joined the Malaspina expedition. See José Torre

Carlos in Mexico, who had been sent by Revillagigedo to replace temporarily José del Pozo, the artist of the *Descubierta* who had remained in Lima.[30] Because the *Atrevida* was preparing to set sail within a few days for San Blas, the port of supply for Alta California, Bustamante instructed Suría to remain in Acapulco until Malaspina's arrival with the other members of the expedition.[31]

During the *Atrevida*'s stay in San Blas, Neé was able to examine the flora of the vicinity. Some of these plants were drawn by Guío. Arcadio Pineda obtained a list of the various kinds of woods available in the immediate area from Josef María Monterde, head of the Department of San Blas.[32] This was the same list used a few months later by José Longinos Martínez to compile (with a number of additional explanations) a document called "Trees of the Hot Country of San Blas." Some of the woods having uses of particular medical interest were: mezquite (*Prosopis juliflora*), a solution of its wood used for sore eyes; pochote (*Ceiba acuminata*), its bark used as an antidote for poisonous stings of insects; guamuchil (*Pithecollobium dulce*), its pods boiled to make a mouth wash; tepeguaje (*Leucaena* sp.), a decoction of its bark effective for tightening the teeth; guapinole (*Hymenaea courbaril*), a solution of its resin used for making ether; quautecomate (*Crescentia alata*), a syrup made from its fruit used for contusions and injuries from falls; hobo (*Spondias* sp.), a decoction of the whole plant beneficial in treating cholera; zorrillo (*Petaveria alliacea*), employed against jaundice; guayabo (*Psidium guajava*), its fruit (guava) used to treat scurvy; higuera (*Ficus carica*), appropriate for difficulties of the spleen; bálsamo (*Toluifera pereirae*), yields a balsam effective for any kind of wound; and margarita (*Karwinskia humboldtiana*), used against rabies.[33]

Revello, *Los artistas pintores* and Justino Fernández, *Tomás de Suría y su viaje con Malaspina, 1791*.

30. Revillagigedo to Malaspina, Mexico, 19 January 1791, MS 279, AMN. Pozo, a native of Sevilla, was described as an excellent artist of perspective and of very good education (Malaspina to Valdés, Cádiz, 30 June 1789, MS 583, AMN), but apparently exhibited an extreme opposition to work, which he attributed to sickness. Pozo eventually died in Lima in 1821.

31. "Diario de Arcadio Pineda," MS 94, AMN.

32. "Relación de las maderas que se remiten del corte de San Blas, sus largos y diámetros en Píes de Burgos, San Blas," 20 April 1791, MS 127, AMN. The complete list of trees appears in Simpson, *Journal of José Longinos Martínez*, pp. 83–89; these have been classified by Professor H. S. Reed of the University of California, Berkeley.

33. The scientific designations are taken from Martínez, *Catálogo de nombres vulgares,* based generally upon use of the common name in the San Blas region. Some local variations may exist.

The officers of the *Atrevida* compiled charts of the port of San Blas and its vicinity as far south as Cabo Corrientes, although they were unable to locate a certain reef near the cape, which had been indicated to Bustamante by a merchant captain anchored in San Blas. Setting sail on 13 April, the *Atrevida* arrived in Acapulco seven days later to join its sistership.[34]

Having departed from Panama on 15 December, the *Descubierta* had directed its course toward Realejo, Nicaragua. Taking advantage of the time spent at sea, Antonio Pineda collected and studied a number of fish, mollusks, and other species of marine life. He described numerous varieties of *Salpa* and *Medusa,* using the work of Danish scientist Pehr Forskael as a guide.[35]

While the *Descubierta* lay at anchor in Realejo for ten days, Pineda and Haënke investigated the surrounding territory. Traveling to the Volcán del Viejo, the two scientists disproved a popular native belief that the volcano did not give off smoke, explaining that the smoke was merely hidden from the inhabitants of the plain. Deep inside the crater, Pineda discovered piles of excellent crystalized sulfur that could replace the amount being imported into the country. One of the ship's officers, Cayetano Valdés,[36] "not indifferent to natural history," made a detailed examination and collected a number of samples from the Volcán de Tetica. In regard to natural resources, Pineda reported that Realejo produced, besides valuable woods, many medicinal plants, gums, and precious resins like that of cedar, sangre de drago, liquidambar, and menjui [Benjamin], and that

. . . their extraction, developed by means of rewards, could give vigor to this port, a part of which is now very decadent and poor. [Realejo] also produces ginger and a plant of the genus of the *Sidas* that can be substituted for hemp. They call it *escobilla* and it grows everywhere in the country in abundance; from it they make coarse linens, and they could make finer ones. Those who have more time will discover many other balsams besides that of the *Palo de María,* and other dyewoods that are still unknown and would be appreciated in Europe.[37]

34. "Diario de Don Juan Vernacci," MS 94, AMN.

35. *Descriptio anamalium, avium, amphiborium, piscium, insectorum, verminium quae in itinere orientali observatit.*

36. Nephew of the minister of marine, Cayetano Valdés was later given command, along with Dionisio Alcalá Galiano, of a smaller exploratory enterprise that visited the Pacific Northwest Coast in 1792. See chapter 8.

37. Pineda to Valdés, Acapulco, 14 April 1791, YALE.

Sailing from the Nicaraguan port on 30 January 1791, the crew of the *Descubierta* sighted the landmarks of Acapulco after almost two months at sea, dropping anchor in its welcome harbor on 29 March. Antonio Pineda commented that Acapulco presented an abundant wealth of precious resins, particularly the *copal* and the *suchicopal,* as well as many of the products that were found in Realejo. The plentiful sea-life included varieties of madrepores; gorgonias (sea fans) resembling nets; sponges; and two species of purple murex that would be a "great source of wealth if one could find a way of conserving their tinctorial juice." Pineda and his assistants were able to replace the collection of birds and fish previously destroyed by insects and tropical heat and Pedro González, physician on the *Atrevida,* had skillfully prepared and described some local birds before leaving for San Blas.

Pineda also reported that José Cardero, a talented servant of Cayetano Valdés, had applied himself with "considerable success to drawing the products of nature."[38] Most likely as a result of José del Pozo's departure in Lima, Cardero began drawing in Guayaquil. His early efforts reflected a lack of formal training, but his sensitivity and natural dexterity enabled him to show a steady improvement. From that time on he sketched general scenes in addition to preparing zoological plates. Pineda used Cardero to depict a number of new species, including a detailed study of a "tortuga verde del Mar del Sur."[39] While in Acapulco, Cardero drew several views of the port and the city.[40]

Suría, the artist from the Mexican academy who was instructed to await Malaspina's arrival, made a number of drawings that were sent to Madrid from Acapulco.[41] Those completed under the guidance of Pineda were the following:

38. Ibid. Cardero was born and reared in Ecija in the Andalusian province of Sevilla and enlisted in the Royal Navy as a cabin-boy to the officers of the expedition. He was just twenty-three years old in 1791. His service record is found in Joseph Cardero, "Expediente matrimonial," Archivo General Militar, Segovia. See Donald C. Cutter, "Early Spanish Artists on the Northwest Coast," pp. 150–51.

39. Vista de la tortuga berde, anatomía de la tortuga, partes interiores de la tortuga, folios 20–24. Vol. 2, "Figuras y animales" (Depósito Hidrográfico de Madrid, Ministerio de Marina), AMN.

40. Cardero's drawings are contained both in the above collection in the Museo Naval and in a private collection held by the family of Felipe Bauzá; photocopies of the latter are also in the Museo Naval.

41. "Lista de los dibujos concluidos entregados a Dn. Alexandro Malaspina para la remisión desde Acapulco dibujados por Suría," MS 563, AMN. These zoological sketches, plus a "View of the Bay and Port of Acapulco from the Hospital of the Hipolites," are preserved in Depósito Hidrográfico, vols. 1 and 2, AMN.

Species of bear called *Tejón* [badger]
Garza Tigre [tiger heron] of Acapulco and other parts of the Pacific Coast
Snake called *Coralillo* [coral-snake]
Entrails of the *Tetraodón* or Frog-fish *Coztotl icterus,* Cazique of New Spain or
Brison

Fish

Algarropa [grouper] of Acapulco
Chetodón with the fin along the back *Azul Ultramar*
Jurel of Acapulco or *Scomber hippos* Linn.
Pargo Flamenco [red snapper] of Acapulco
Salmonete of Acapulco
Yellow *Chetodón*—commonly called Pámpano of Acapulco

Suría later received an appointment to sail with the *Descubierta* on its journey to the Pacific Northwest and accepted, despite protests from his wife and mother-in-law. He was given an increase in salary over his wages as an engraver in the Mexican mint and was allowed certain expenses as well.[42] Since the young artist was eager to embark on such a prominent voyage of exploration, his family was forced to reconcile itself to his absence.

Malaspina remained in Mexico City for some days arranging for Pineda and several other members of the expedition to make excursions throughout New Spain when circumstances permitted. They planned to cover as wide a circuit as possible including the religious shrine of Guadalupe, mining towns, Indian pueblos, and agricultural regions. Pineda vowed that they would, "while forces permit, allow no corner of Nature to remain unscrutinized."[43]

On 19 April, Malaspina returned to Acapulco from Mexico with the news that he had received orders from Carlos IV to search for the "Pass to the Atlantic of Ferrer Maldonado," the famous Northwest Passage, according to new theories recently reported to the Royal Academy of Science.[44] This supposed waterway, still being sought by both English and French navigators, had been one of the important motives for several Spanish expeditions to the north beginning in 1774.[45] Its discovery

42. Donald C. Cutter and Mercedes Paláu de Iglesias, "Malaspina's Artists," p. 22.
43. Pineda to Valdés, Acapulco, 14 April 1791, YALE.
44. Diario de Don Juan Vernacci, MS 94, AMN.
45. Juan Pérez, Esteban José Martínez, Ignacio Arteaga, Juan Francisco de la Bodega y Quadra, and others had been involved in the search since 1774.

at this time would be a grand finale to scientific investigation. In addition, Malaspina was to investigate the controversy at Nootka Sound over Spanish and English territorial rights. With these ends in view, he made plans for a systematic survey of the northern coasts.

5

Malaspina in Alaska, the Pacific Northwest, and California, 1791

IN VIEW of his orders to search for the Strait of Anián and because of the controversy touched off by the seizure of British ships at Nootka Sound in 1789, Malaspina abandoned his original plan to spend three months of 1791 in Hawaii and began preparations to sail for the Pacific Northwest. As arranged with Revillagigedo, he left Antonio Pineda and several officers and scientists in Acapulco to make the previously planned examination of the coastal and inland regions during the next six months.[1] The *Descubierta* and *Atrevida* set sail from Acapulco on the first of May 1791, while the overland group departed for the capital a few days later.

The personnel on board the two corvettes, in addition to assessing the political situation, were charged with examining the natural history of the area, so important to the Spanish crown. All had proven their skills in botany, zoology, cartography, astronomy, and artistic reproduction. Felipe Bauzá, chief of charts and maps, had previous experience in general mapping of the Iberian Peninsula,[2] while botanist Haënke was by this time well versed in American specimens. González, the surgeon on board the *Atrevida,* had spent his time in Acapulco identifying and describing zoological specimens.

---

1. See chapters 6 and 7.

2. Before sailing with Malaspina, Bauzá had been an instructor of art at the Naval Academy, MS 94, AMN; numerous examples of his charts, coastal profiles, and perspectives are in the Museo Naval. See also Juan Llabrés Bernal, *Breve noticia de la labor científica del Capitan de Navío Don Felipe Bauzá y de sus papeles sobre América (1764–1834)* (Palma de Mallorca, 1934).

The two artists were Suría, of the Mexican Art Academy of San Carlos, and Cardero, the amateur whose work had improved steadily since he first started sketching in Nicaragua. While on the expedition, Suría kept a journal in which he recorded daily events, his observations about Indian customs, and a considerable number of sketches.[3] Cardero drew zoological plates as well as general scenes showing the ships at anchor or under sail, geographic features of the coasts and bays, and Indians at work or play. In contrast to Suría, Cardero was careful to identify most of his contributions with a signature in the right corner.[4]

After coasting along the shores north of the Queen Charlotte Islands, Malaspina's first major stop was on 27 June 1791 at Port Mulgrave (Yakutat Bay) in the vicinity of 58°30′ north latitude. Here he hoped to find the elusive Northwest Passage, referred to in the manuscript of Lorenzo Ferrer Maldonado who had allegedly marked the strait at this latitude as he passed through it during the late sixteenth century.[5] Lieutenant Antonio de Tova Arredondo, second in command of the *Atrevida,* graphically described the arrival of the corvettes and their reception by the Tlingit Indians:[6]

> We were scarcely within a league of it [Port Mulgrave] when two canoes came out, one of which headed for the *Descubierta* and the other toward us. The natives who managed them, whose number could not have been less than thirty, quit rowing, and being near stood up with arms outstretched, and sang a song full of harmony and cadence.

The men of the *Atrevida* tried to imitate the Indians as best they could as a sign of peace. Their chief insisted upon taking some hostages, but finally came aboard even when the request was denied. A short while later another quite different type of vessel appeared with only two men in it. One was a very old man called Ankau who quickly boarded the *Atrevida.* After walking about the quarterdeck "with feigned timidity," he uttered a long, enthusiastic speech, directing his voice alternately to

3. Suría's journal, the original of which is in the Yale University Library, is translated in part by Henry R. Wagner and published as "Journal of Tomás de Suría of His Voyage with Malaspina to the Northwest Coast of America in 1791." Apparently there were two or more parts since the outside was marked notebook (*cuaderno*) 1. Wagner's translation is hereinafter referred to as "Suría Journal." A Spanish version containing a brief biography of Suría was published by Justino Fernández, *Tomas de Suría.*

4. Donald C. Cutter, "Early Spanish Artists," pp. 150–57.

5. Suría Journal, pp. 246–47.

6. Yakutat Bay natives belong to the Tlingit linguistic family of the Northwest Coast, being the northernmost branch. See Aurel Krause, *The Tlingit Indians.*

the sky, to the sea, to the Spaniards, and to his own people. Ankau confirmed that he was the head chief and that the first chief who had appeared was his son. He indicated this by placing his arms in the position of holding a child and then rocking it. The aged chief was an expert in sign language and answered many questions about the anchorage sites and nearby natives. He indicated his desire that the Spaniards anchor near his town at Mulgrave, where they would find everything to satisfy their needs, and not in the opposite direction where the "inhabitants were ferocious and would kill [them] unmercifully."[7]

According to Suría, the Tlingit were dressed in well-tanned skins of various colors which seemed to come from bears, tigers, lions,[8] deer, and marmots. Their thick hair hung loose with a great abundance of red ochre and grease, which had a distinctive odor. They continued their show of friendship and singing of songs while the Spaniards searched for an appropriate place to anchor.

The morning of the twenty-eighth dawned with a thick fog and the corvettes were surrounded by Indians who wanted to trade little objects or simply to board the ships to look around. They were guilty of some pilfering, but in general the exchange of goods was pleasant. The Indians brought fishing implements, domestic articles, or apparel they had made to trade for old clothing, nails, buttons, and other similar articles that they prized. Successful negotiations were accompanied by song. Suría drew the chief's portrait, who in turn was very pleased and insisted that he be drawn with a helmet won in combat. By the twenty-ninth the weather had improved and the sun was out; during the next few days wood and water were taken on board and some skins were exchanged.[9]

Lieutenant Tova's journal describes another aspect of the trade relationship. "The chief showed other lines of trade with little luck. At first we believed that only the lower class women prostituted themselves, but we soon learned that even the most complacent member of the royal family would have sold her greatest favors for very little."[10]

The news of Malaspina's arrival spread throughout the vicinity. The Tlingit traders visiting the ships warned that two foreign canoes were

7. Journal of Antonio de Tova Arredondo, translated by Donald C. Cutter in "Malaspina at Yakutat Bay," p. 42. Cutter's translation is hereinafter referred to as "Tova Journal."

8. The skins were probably from mountain lions or cougars.

9. Suría Journal, pp. 247–49.

10. Tova Journal, p. 45.

coming and asked that a shot be fired. The newcomers in the canoes, about fifty in each, answered the gunfire with a song, which was taken as a sign of peace. Afterwards the "strangers" viewed with curiosity the "nails and bells" of the Spaniards and did not seem impressed by the size of the corvettes.[11]

At a clear moment on the afternoon of the thirtieth of June, Mount St. Elias, first seen by Vitus Bering in 1741,[12] appeared in the distance. The Spaniard's calculations of its height were only a hundred feet off.[13] Malaspina and Suría then went to the river at the channel entrance to examine the burial place of which Captain George Dixon had spoken.[14] Suría "drew a picture of that structure without any opposition from the natives." They put aboard a box

. . . adorned on the outside with shells and inside there was another small [box] in which there were found wrapped in a basket some calcified bones, mostly pulverized. It was learned from the natives that these were the sepulchres set aside only for the ruling family, there being no doubt about the cremation of bodies around the great figure, which is represented in the drawing with great exactness.[15]

At dawn, on the second of July, Malaspina, Bauzá, and Tova set out to find the Strait of Ferrer Maldonado. They sailed northward to 59°51' and established with certainty at the head of the inlet that no strait existed. After prolonged and disappointing searches in other areas, Malaspina finally declared that "modern navigators, disdaining to pursue longer so useless a project, will direct all their efforts to the inspection of the few points that have not yet been examined or to the successful profits and development of . . . commerce.[16] The three explorers performed a symbolic act of sovereignty by placing a coin beneath a bottle that contained the words: "The Corvettes of His Majesty, *Descubierta* and *Atrevida,* commanded by Don Alejandro Malaspina and Don José Bustamante discovered this port on the 20th of June, 1791, and called it Desengaño [Detection] taking possession of it in the name of his Catholic Majesty."[17]

11. Ibid.

12. Vitus Bering, the Danish navigator, first explored the Alaskan area at the head of a Russian expedition in 1741.

13. The Spaniards calculated it to be 6,507.6 *varas castellanas,* which, at approximately thirty-three inches to the *vara,* puts them off 112 feet. MS 169, AMN.

14. See George Dixon, *A Voyage Round the World.*

15. Tova Journal, p. 45.

16. Malaspina, *Viaje político-científico,* p. 190.

17. Tova Journal, p. 46.

After rejoining the main force, the Spaniards found pilfering still to be a problem; the theft of some clothing had created a major standoff. Malaspina and Bustamante prohibited further trade until the Indians showed signs of remorse. They did this by singing on the beach and offering the return of some missing underwear. Malaspina accepted the gesture of peace and allowed the trade to continue.

On 4 July, with wood and water supplies completed, they prepared to depart. The Tlingit of Mulgrave continued their warm friendship and tried to find any overlooked item to trade. The Spaniards planned to leave on the fifth, but, because of the wind, did not clear the port until the sixth. Both Tova and Suría described the Indians in detail. They agreed that they were robust and strong and of medium stature. Tova commented that "they have generally a round face, a large mouth, large tightly-spaced teeth, a wide nose, and small but black and brilliant eyes. Their hair, which they ordinarily wear tied with a cord around the crown of the head or loose drawn down their backs, is lusterless and thick." The color varied between black, its natural color, and a kind of brown, depending upon the amount of materials mixed into it. Normally young men to the age of twenty-five or thirty had absolutely no facial hair, whereas after that time they wore long and thick beards. Tova, knowing that nature observed "a regular progression" in all its works, ascribed the sudden change to the process of pulling out each hair until a time of life when authority no longer required it or when "efforts at beauty" ceased.

The Tlingit also painted themselves red, black, and other colors in common with other Indians whom the Spaniards had observed. Although Tova felt the use of so much paint increased "their normal ugliness," it perhaps preserved "the face from the rigors of the winds and the sun to which the Mulgraves are continually exposed." When some of the Indians washed their faces completely, their skin was "as white as the people of south Europe," but their bodies were much darker.[18] Tova continued his narrative with a classic description of the labret used by the native women of Mulgrave:

Among all customs that have been introduced by the caprice and extravance of women in their desire to look good, there is none more unique than a special one of the Tejunenses [Tlingit] women. They make an incision inside the lower lip parallel to the mouth and of the same length, and in it they place an elliptical shaped piece of wood, the length of which could not be less than two

18. Ibid., pp. 48–49.

inches by one inch wide. Once in place, by its own weight it assumes a horizontal position, and forcing the lip to separate from the mouth, all of the teeth of their lower jaw are left uncovered. One cannot exactly imagine how much an adornment that adds a thousand charms in the eyes of the Tejunenses disfigures the face of these women. How different are the opinions of men concerning beauty.[19]

Suría agreed that "the size of it appears incredible as well as the custom of wearing it."

Suría commented that the women tatooed their arms and hands with various designs which "remained forever." Their dress consisted of a robe of tanned skin that modestly extended from their throat to their feet and covered their breasts and arms down to the wrist. They also wore a cape of skin over the right shoulder, held in place by a piece of leather. The men generally wore some kind of animal skin, but some went "entirely naked." Warriors wore a breast-plate, back armor, and a helmet with a visor made usually from a piece of wood. They fought with lances, bows and arrows, knives, and hatchets. The latter they had obtained by trade with the English.[20]

During their nine-day stay among the Tlingit Indians, the group gathered native weapons, articles of dress, manufactured items, and other artifacts; and attempted to learn the language, compiling a vocabulary that consisted primarily of words used in trade. They also explored the nearby glacier, later named for Malaspina. Haënke prepared a summary of available wood in the area; González scientifically described a number of animals, birds, and plants;[21] and Cardero and Suría illustrated what they saw.

Following their departure from Yakutat Bay, the corvettes cruised westward along the coast exploring various inlets, and then turned south. Suría continued his narrative of events despite difficulties in writing. Upon embarking at Acapulco he had thought it would be fairly easy to keep a daily diary since "the commander had allotted a cabin to the second pilot and himself." What he did not anticipate, however, was the cramped space. He lamented that "while stretched in

19. Ibid., p. 49. The labret, used by the Tlingit, Kitimat, Tsimshian, Haida, and northern Kwakiutl at Bella Bella was described by almost all early travelers (La Pérouse, Portlock and Dixon, Moziño, and others).

20. Suría Journal, pp. 255–56.

21. "Relación de maderas de Mulgrave, de Nutka, de Monterey in Pacifico América," MS 126, AMN. and "Descripciones del Sr. Gonzáles hechas en el viaje a los 60°N," in AMCN.

my bed with my feet against the side of the ship and my head against
the bulkhead . . . the distance is only three inches from my breast to
the deck, which was my roof. This confined position does not allow
me to move in my bed and I am forced to make a roll of cloth to cover
my head and, although this suffocates me, it is a lesser evil than being
attacked by thousands of cockroaches."

Therefore, because of his tight quarters, he often had to wait until a
later time to confirm information about Spanish activities with others.
Regarding the Indians, however, he felt qualified to observe and record
all their actions and movements personally, since his thirteen years' residence in Mexico had given him a great interest in them and helped him
understand their character.[22]

After cruising southward for some time, the corvettes reached Bucareli Sound. Malaspina and Bustamante recognized the entrance,
"marking all the most interesting points" and confirming the maps of
"Don Juan Bodega y Quadra, and [Francisco] Mourelle, his pilot, who
laid the bases for this port."[23] They did not examine the area carefully
since they could see by their charts "the care and exactness with which
those deserving officers worked out this interesting point of geography." They agreed it might be the port most worthy of fame in the
world for its size and "the incredible number of sheltered ports, large
and small, which surrounded it."[24] The Spaniards were surprised to see
no canoes coming out to trade with them or any signs of habitation or
smoke as on the rest of the coast.

The corvettes continued sailing southward off the Queen Charlotte
Islands when they were hit by a tremendous storm. According to Suría,
"the wind kept getting stronger every instant with rain and a very
heavy sea. The rolls were tremendous and the darkness terrifying." The
ships had to run east-southeast before the wind for six days. "There
was not a man who could keep his footing, simply from the violence of
the wind." Mountains of water and foam swept over them like a copious rainfall and "the roaring noise of both elements was horrible and
terrifying. The confusion and shouting on the ship, along with the

22. Suría Journal, p. 260.
23. Juan Francisco de la Bodega y Quadra and his pilot Francisco Mourelle had visited
the area aboard the tiny schooner *Sonora* in 1775. Bodega y Quadra later returned to the
Northwest Coast in command of the frigate *Favorita,* along with Ignacio Arteaga commanding the *Princesa,* in 1779.
24. Suría Journal, p. 269.

maledictions of the sailors," who, Suría noted politely, by breaking into blasphemy, "augmented the terror to such an extent that it seemed as if all the machinery of the universe was ready to destroy us." During the six days no one could get more than a few moments rest and all were so worn out that Malaspina did not ask them to repair the sails, "some of which had been blown to pieces," and simply ordered that they continue their course.[25] Tova called the storm "a veritable hurricane, the likes of which we had never experienced on the whole voyage," adding that they decided against entering Dixon canal.[26]

The next stop on Malaspina's projected itinerary was the Spanish settlement at Nootka Sound on the west coast of Vancouver Island, 49°35' north latitude. They passed Cabo Frondoso, or Woody Point, about midday on 11 August and when they were about a mile distant from the entrance to the sound, the wind died and prevented their entrance into Friendly Cove, site of the Spanish fort. Two canoes of Indians came alongside and some of the occupants clambered aboard. They spoke some Spanish and indicated that they knew the ships were from Spain. A launch from the frigate *Concepción* came out to be of assistance. At eight o'clock the next morning they entered the port and dropped anchor. Captain Ramon Saavedra of the *Concepción* and Lt. Colonel Pedro Alberni, commandant of the Nootka garrison of Mexicans and Spaniards who belonged to the First Company of Catalonian Volunteers, came aboard to offer greetings.[27]

To place the Malaspina visit to Nootka Sound in proper perspective, some background information is helpful. The first brief European contact with the Indians at Nootka had been made in 1774 by the Spaniard Juan Pérez, commander of an expedition instructed to explore the Pacific coast to 60° north latitude and take possession of those lands for Spain. Illness, fog, and contrary currents forced Pérez to turn his ship, the *Santiago,* southward short of his goal. Having reached a north latitude of 54°40', the Spaniards coasted along the western shores of Queen Charlotte and Vancouver Islands. Pérez did not land at Nootka, which he called San Lorenzo, but anchored offshore while twenty-one canoes containing nearly 150 amazed Indians approached his ship.[28] Several of

25. Ibid., p. 271.

26. Lorenzo Sanfeliú Ortiz, *62 meses a bordo,* p. 162.

27. Ibid., pp. 162–63; Suría Journal, pp. 272–73.

28. "Viaje de la navegación hecha por el Alférez Graduado D. Juan Pérez de ord. del Sr. Bucareli a la altura de los 55 grados donde está situada la entrada y bahía de su nombre en la fragata *Santiago,* álias la *Nueva Galicia,* San Blas 3 de Noviembre de 1774,"

the more courageous Indians boarded the *Santiago* and took part in a friendly exchange of gifts; they pilfered some silver spoons, which were found in their possession by Cook's expedition four years later.[29]

On his third voyage of exploration in 1778, the intrepid Captain James Cook entered Nootka with his two ships *Resolution* and *Discovery* and called the inlet King George's Sound. He later changed the name to Nootka, believing that to be the name used by the natives. Visiting the Indians at what Cook called Friendly Cove, the English explorers remained in the sound for nearly a month. Cook's prolonged visit allowed him to describe the inhabitants and surrounding country in some detail. He also compiled a vocabulary of Nootkan words that served as a basis for subsequent studies of their language.[30] The journal of John Ledyard of Connecticut, who sailed with Cook on the *Resolution,* devoted several pages to the Indians and their activities at Nootka. He described the fortuitous sale of beaver and other skins—obtained from the Nootkas for trinkets—for one hundred dollars apiece in China.[31] As a result, American and other merchants became interested in the possibilities of the Northwest fur trade.

The Spaniards, who had claimed possession of the entire north Pacific coast since 1774 as a part of the viceroyalty of New Spain, became alarmed about the number of foreign vessels operating in the area. In a desire to strengthen Spanish interests, Viceroy Manual Antonio Florez sent Esteban José Martínez to Nootka in June 1789, to take formal possession of the port and establish a military post. The new commandant

---

AGN, Historia 62; MN, MSS 331, 575 bis. See also Manuel P. Servín, "Instructions of Viceroy Bucareli to Ensign Juan Pérez," p. 239.

29. Cook wrote that "what was most singular, two silver tablespoons were purchased from them, which, from their peculiar shape, were judged to be of Spanish manufacture. One of these strangers wore them round his neck by way of ornament" (M. B. Synge, ed., *Captain Cook's Voyages Round the World,* p. 430; hereinafter cited as Synge, ed., *Cook's Voyages).*

30. Cook's description of Nootka and its inhabitants is found in his principal work, *A Voyage to the Pacific Ocean Undertaken by the Command of His Majesty, for Making Discoveries in the Northern Hemisphere in the Years 1776, 1777, 1778, 1779, and 1780* (3 vols. and Atlas; London: G. Nicol and T. Cadell, 1784). Upon returning to the Sandwich [Hawaiian] Islands, which he had discovered, Cook was killed by natives on 14 February 1779. Volume 3 of Cook's work was written by Capt. James King. See also J. C. Beaglehole, *The Life of Captain James Cook,* pp. 591–636.

31. James K. Munford, ed., *John Ledyard's Journal of Captain Cook's Last Voyage,* pp. xxx–xlix, 69–76. In 1779, James King reported: "A few prime skins, which were clean and had been well preserved, were sold for one hundred and twenty [dollars] each" (quoted in Frederic W. Howay, ed., *The Dixon-Meares Controversy,* pp. 17–18).

Plaza Mayor de Mexico, drawn by Fernando Brambila, 1791, Malaspina Expedition. Museo Naval, Madrid

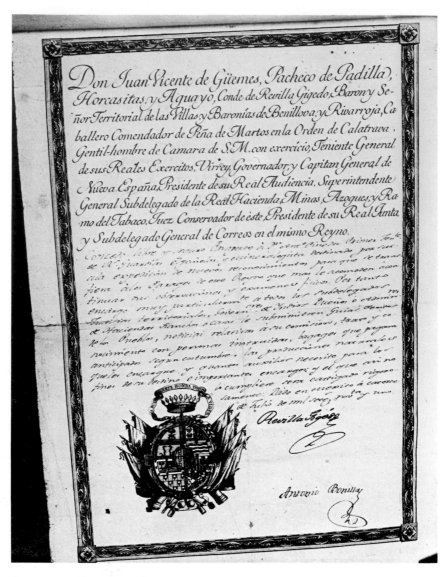

Passport issued to Antonio Pineda on 14 July 1791 by Viceroy Revillagigedo to travel freely throughout Mexico

Mexican Indians [artist unknown], Malaspina Expedition.
Museo de América, Madrid

Clachiquero [*man who extracts honey-water from the* agave],
drawn by José Guío, Malaspina Expedition

CLACHIQUERO.
ONBRE QUESACA EL AGUAMIEL DEE MAGEI N.ᵉ E.ᵃ

Guío

View of the bay and port of Acapulco from the Hospital of the Hippolites, by Tomás de Suria, Malaspina Expedition. Museo Naval, Madrid

Cockfight in Acapulco, drawn by Tomás de Suría, Malaspina Expedition.
Museo Naval, Madrid

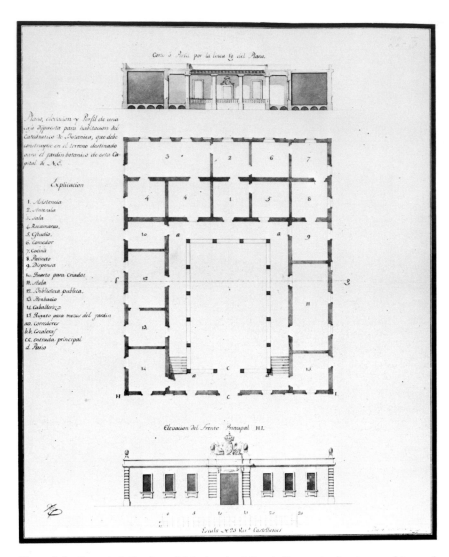

Plan of the Botanical Garden of Mexico, by Miguel Costansó, showing working and living quarters for scientists and professors. Archivo General de Indias, Sevilla

Crater of the volcano of Tuxtla seen from the east in 1793
A, B: diameter of the column of smoke, 23 September 1793
C: site where first bottle with inscription was buried

D: site for second bottle with inscription
Drawing by Echeverría at San Andrés de Tuxtla, Mexico, Royal Scientific
Expedition. Archivo General de Indias, Sevilla

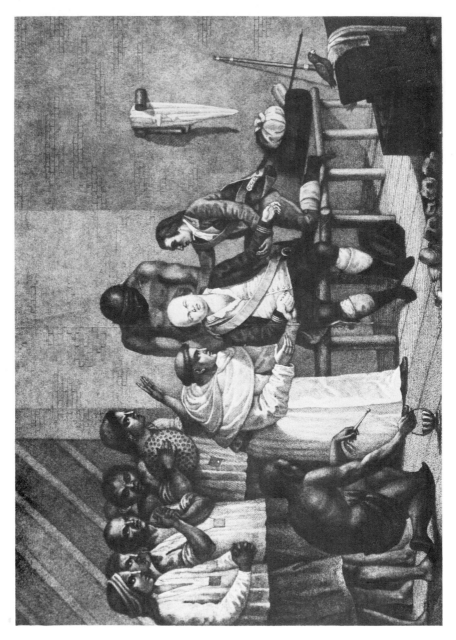

Antonio Pineda dies in Luzon, Philippines. Engraving by José Vázquez, 1795, Malaspina Expedition

attempted to maintain his nation's exclusive rights of ownership in the face of British, American, and French trading activities, but it proved difficult. His arrest of British Captain James Colnett after an argument about the ownership of some land caused a serious breach. When Martínez seized Colnett's ship, *Argonaut,* and sent it with Colnett and his crew as prisoners to San Blas, Mexico, there was no turning back. Although Colnett and his ship were released and an agreement was reached for the return of the *Princess Royal,* another ship seized by the Spanish at Nootka and impressed into service, the British refused to ignore the incident. The events set into motion a controversy that would take the courts of Madrid and London five years to settle. Nootka Sound thus became the focal point of a full international crisis and required Malaspina's analysis of political as well as scientific matters.[32]

On the first day at Nootka, Malaspina's scientists set up an observatory on shore to make astronomical and geodetic calculations. Crew members were sent to gather wood and replenish water supplies. They were impressed by the wooden buildings serving the Spanish troops, the bakery that supplied them with fresh bread daily, the blacksmith forge, and the gardens cultivated by the soldiers. Captain Alberni had a green thumb, much to the delight of the members of the expedition, who had been without fresh vegetables for some time.[33] They reported that the plantings cultivated by the soldiers included cabbage, garlic, onions, lettuce, chard, radishes, turnips, carrots, parsley, and artichokes. Squash was small but good; the tomatoes, also small, did not ripen well. Beans and peas were produced in abundance, although the chickpeas, wheat, and corn did not mature; barley and potatoes thrived. Everything needed a great deal of care because either the abundance of water caused the plants to rot or they were attacked by worms. The livestock fared well and they counted two cows, one bull, one calf, one goat, one sheep, and twenty pigs. There were sixty hens and some four hundred chickens that "multiplied in the same seasons as Europe despite the rain and cold."[34]

On the morning of 14 June, a chief from a nearby village, Tlu-pana-nutl, came to welcome the expedition and assure them of his loyalty.

32. Warren Cook, *Flood Tide of Empire,* pp. 146–99; Wilson, *Noticias de Nutka,* pp. xxviii–xxxiii.

33. See Wilson, *Noticias de Nutka,* pp. 77–80, for a discussion of Alberni's efforts.

34. "Noticia de las semillas que se da en Nootka" (appears to be in the hand of José Bustamante), MS 330 AMN.

Suría presented him with a portrait that he had sketched, thereby cementing their friendship. Tlu-pana-nutl reported that Maquinna, chief of the Nootkans, could not be trusted and "was crafty and overbearing" and that he looked upon the Spaniards "with hatred and abhorrence." Tlu-pana-nutl warned that Maquinna was about to dislodge the Spaniards, but that they had nothing to fear since Tlu-pana-nutl "being experienced in this double-crossing game will know how to oppose it."[35]

Nevertheless, Malaspina was not dissuaded from his original intention to establish a solid relationship with Maquinna. He sent various messages to the chief, but received no reply. After four days, José Espinosa and Ciriaco Cevallos set out in two longboats to examine the interior channels and seek out Maquinna at his headquarters at the head of Tahsis Inlet. They passed several villages and finally reached the chief's temporary lodging place. Upon seeing the strangers, Maquinna came to the shore with some four hundred men and received the Spaniards with an expression of fear. He took out a box of fifteen muskets as a show of strength, while Cevallos offered gifts in return.

The exchange of trinkets created an atmosphere of cordiality and Maquinna introduced his four wives to the officers. Cevallos, wanting to correspond in some way, took out a small portrait of his own wife and showed it to the Nootkan chief who immediately passed it to the favorite of his wives, a young woman of twenty or twenty-one years with beautiful features.[36] A bond of friendship established, Espinosa and Cevallos continued their explorations and returned to Friendly Cove. A few days later Maquinna appeared at the Spanish presidio with his retinue of wives and servants and called upon Malaspina on board his corvette. He accepted gifts of window glass, a sheet of copper, some blue cloth, two sails, and some hardware.

The Malaspina expedition spent a total of two weeks at Nootka Sound. The artists sketched local inhabitants and their activities while Haënke gathered samples of flora and fauna. He could not find many that were distinct from those of Europe but did discover several that he classified as antiscorbutic.[37] He prepared a list of various kinds of pine trees suitable for ship construction and discussed a kind of moss growing on rocks and in shady places at higher altitudes that could be used as

35. Suría Journal, p. 274.
36. Sanfeliú Ortiz, 62 meses a bordo, pp. 166–67.
37. Suría Journal, p. 275.

caulking. After the moss "is dried, it is put between the planks and when water enters it swells up naturally." The planks "remain as firm and the caulking lasts longer than that used in Galicia."[38]

They learned about the customs of the Nootka Indians, noting that adultery was a grave offense carrying severe punishments. Tova commented that, in Nootka, "the chiefs look upon adultery with such horror that they assured us that it occurred very rarely among them." He continued that "homicide is punished the first time by ten days in prison and with some corporal punishment, but upon repetition of this crime, punishment is irremissible death. Robbers are marked by incisions in the face and cutting the hair (which is the maximum insult) and the fingers of the hands and afterwards he is shunned forever by all society."[39] Tova also mentioned the elaborate funeral ceremonies and talked at length of the commerce carried on between the natives of Nootka and the Nuchimanes. Their favorite items of trade were muskets, abalone shells, iron, cloth, and copper.

Cordial relations with the Indians continued during the entire visit. They were able to complete all appropriate maps of the coastal regions and charts of the labyrinth of canals inland from Nootka Sound. When Maquinna heard of their preparations to depart on 27 August, he visited aboard the *Atrevida,* having several cups of tea. He apologized that his weak physical condition had not allowed him to visit more frequently. After a final exchange of gifts, Maquinna reaffirmed the cession of the land upon which the Spanish fort was built.[40] A lack of wind delayed the Spaniards' departure until the night of the twenty-eighth, when they cleared the port. They sighted the Strait of Juan de Fuca on 1 September and noticed a trading vessel from the United States that Malaspina assumed to be active in the fur trade. They had planned to explore the Entrada de Hezeta (Columbia River), first discovered by Bruno de Hezeta in 1775 and later explored by Robert Gray in 1792,[41] but fog obscured the coastline. Malaspina commented sarcastically that there were signs of a river that would doubtless "give support to the adherents of interoceanic communication who are determined to have the two oceans connected by a northwest passage."[42]

38. "Maderas del puerto de Nutka para arboladura de todos barcos," MS 126, AMN.
39. Sanfeliú Ortiz, *62 meses a bordo*, p. 168.
40. Malaspina, *Viaje político-científico*, p. 194; Fernández, *Tomás de Suría*, p. 97.
41. The American Robert Gray named the river for his ship *Columbia Rediviva* and supplanted Hezeta's name on contemporary maps.
42. Malaspina, *Viaje político-científico*, p. 190.

The weather was mild and a steady northwest wind favored their passage to Cape Mendocino. They sighted Point Reyes and the entrance to San Francisco Bay, but the thickening fog made it necessary for them to sail with care as they made their way between the Farallon Islands and the Golden Gate southward. Bad weather caused them to miss the entrance to Monterey and forced them to cast anchor past Point Pinos on 11 September. The two corvettes kept in touch by firing guns since they were invisible in the fog.

The next morning, guided by the sound of breakers on the shore and cannon fire from the presidio, they managed to anchor inside the bay at eight o'clock. When the fog finally lifted and they could see where they were, their spirits rose and their attitudes changed considerably. As they looked toward the Monterey presidio and saw robust and healthy soldiers tending herds, hitching an animal, or mounting a horse, they recalled the pleasures of country life. The view to the west towards the foothills presented them with countless kinds of birds soaring peacefully and numerous squirrels, rabbits, and hares running and leaping about. The view of the sea, serene and unlimited to the north and northwest, "showed the spectator a thousand species of aquatic birds . . . the huge whale, the seal and the otter, applauding, sometimes, the smiling aspect of the air, at other times the perfect peace that they enjoy." The sea animals were not afraid to come up on the beach and rest within close range of the men. Finally, they saw an infinite number of fish "as various as they are savory, run to the seine and the hook," providing the naturalist with inexhaustible studies and the navigator with a continual diversion.[43]

Malaspina commented that the same attractive features of the coast continued from San Diego to the port of Monterey and even to San Francisco, although so did the fogs, which were frequent and dense. He felt that the moisture was necessary for the productivity of the land despite the problems it created for navigation. Malaspina concluded with the observation that

The winds from the northwest, which prevail during almost all the year, are generally clear, gentle and cold, and those from the southeast which bring the rains are generally strong and humid, and rarely occur more than six or eight times during all the winter. Therefore the fog, far from causing real damage, confers a positive benefit, actively conserving the moisture of the soil, mitigating the rays of the sun, and making of autumn a pleasant and new spring.[44]

43. Edith C. Galbraith, "Malaspina's Voyage around the World," p. 221.
44. Ibid.

Upon their arrival in port, Malaspina and Bustamante were greeted by presidio commandant Lieutenant José Darío Argüello, acting governor between Pedro Fages and José Antonio Romeu who was then enroute from Baja California.[45] Although he had been in Monterey only a short time, Argüello was particularly helpful in aiding their scientific investigations. He saw to it that his sixty-three-man presidial garrison provided the visitors with abundant fresh food and wine, recreation in the form of horseback riding, hunting and fishing excursions, and entertainment with a daily *novillada* (bullfight with young steers). After allowing some initial drunkenness, Argüello and the two commanders agreed that the sale of intoxicating liquors had to be restricted.[46]

As soon as the fog had disappeared, the scientists began making astronomical calculations from the beach to determine latitude and longitude. Lieutenant Juan Vernacci took appropriate altitudes of the sun and cooperated in checking the accuracy of their chronometers. On the afternoon of the thirteenth of September one of their crewmen, John Green, an American from Boston who had signed on board in Cádiz, died of dropsy. He had become ill and deteriorated rapidly at Nootka, where he was given the last sacrament. He was buried in Monterey after funeral services conducted by Father Francisco de Paula Anino, chaplain of the *Atrevida*.[47]

Malaspina and Bustamante soon moved on by horseback to Mission San Carlos on the Carmel River and paid the first of several visits to Father Fermín Francisco de Lasuén, president of the Franciscan missions in Alta California, who had succeeded Father Junípero Serra in 1785.[48] Father Lasuén had been supervising the construction of the Santa Cruz and Soledad missions when Malaspina's vessels arrived, but as soon as he learned of their visit he returned to Carmel. The Franciscan superior was hospitable and offered assistance in their scientific collections. Later in a letter thanking Lasuén, Malaspina promised that Spain someday would recognize the work being done in the New World by the zealous Franciscans. Lasuén had instructed the Indians of the mission to hunt

45. Fages served as military commandant from 1769 to 1774 and from 10 September 1782 to 16 April 1791, the date of Romeu's appointment. Romeu served only a few months after his arrival in Monterey, dying on 9 April 1792. Lt. José Dario Argüello remained in California as commandant of the presidios of Monterey, San Francisco, and Santa Barbara, and as interim governor in 1814–15.

46. Cutter, *Malaspina in California,* p. 30.

47. Ibid., pp. 28–29.

48. See Francis F. Guest, O.F.M., *Fermín Francisco de Lasuén.*

and fish, gather botanical specimens, and collect Indian artifacts for the Malaspina group. He had provided information for a thorough report of the country, including what he knew about the visit of La Pérouse in 1786. Lasuén showed them the small grist mill that Viscount La Langle had given Governor Pedro Fages, and pointed out the seeds and fruit trees left for cultivation.[49]

Malaspina noted that the principal seed crops sown and harvested in the missions were wheat, barley, corn, kidney beans, chick peas, lentils, peas, and horsebeans. The missions of San Buenaventura and San Diego produced grapes, and at Santa Clara they were raising fine and abundant pears, peaches, and plums.

In characterizing the inhabitants of Monterey, the Spaniards felt that the Rumsen and Esselen of Mission San Carlos were less advanced culturally than those of the Pacific Northwest. They observed that even though the Indians seemed to lack intelligence and relied upon the seafood that washed up on the shore "in unspeakable abundance," they were, nevertheless, "very skillful hunters" who provided themselves with hares, rabbits, foxes, squirrels, and deer. To kill the latter, the Indians put on a stuffed deer's head and, hiding in the grass, imitated the stance, appearance, and look of a deer with such exactness that other deer were "deceived until attracted within range."[50] The Spaniards noted that the women practiced abortion to preserve their youth and that males practiced polygamy to the extent that some had four wives. Bauzá considered these people "little ready for rapid progress in civilization."[51]

The collection of Indian artifacts included wooden bowls "inlaid with coral or bone," some highly polished narrow-mouthed vessels, and several bows and arrows. These were similar to artifacts acquired at Nootka.[52] The scientists collected local birds, which were stuffed by the sailors and sent back to Spain. Cardero drew a number of them and Malaspina prepared a list including "turtle doves, quail, larks, mocking birds, thrushes, cardinals, humming birds, jackdaws, crows, sparrow hawks, pelicans, seagulls, owls and other maritime birds of prey, with no lack of ducks or geese of different species and sizes." Local quadrupeds, according to Malaspina, included "deer, antelope, hares, rabbits,

49. Cutter, *Malaspina in California*, pp. 36, 51, 59–60. Lasuén's reply, which praises Malaspina highly, is translated by Guest in *Fermín Francisco de Lasuén*, pp. 267–68.

50. Cutter, *Malaspina in California*, p. 53.

51. Ibid.

52. Malaspina, *Viaje político-científico*, p. 444.

squirrels, mountain lions, rats, bears and tigers," and the most common types of California fish were crabs, lobsters, dogfish, sheepshead, porgy, horse mackerel, little bass, cod, mutton fish, dolphins, skates, salmon, and innumerable savory sardines. Malaspina noted that the salmon ascended the Carmel and San Francisco (Sacramento-San Joaquin) rivers to the north in February and March to spawn.[53]

Haënke spent much of his time examining the various rocks and kinds of soil in the Monterey area. He commented that "the earth was fertilized to double strength and was rich and black, having a layer one or two feet deep, consisting of myriads of decayed matter superimposed on a sandy, ash clay," which is generally found in the entire Monterey area, except near the sea. He also found some extremely fragile light-weight whitish or yellowish rock composed of clay-like material very suitable for building. According to the Indians, various petrified testaceans and some dendrites could be easily found even on the highest hills leading from the presidio to the mission. There was an abundance of the seashell called *Alyotis myde* [abalone].[54]

Turning their attention to botany, Haënke and the others were surprised to find a kind of second springtime in Monterey during mid-September. The copious vegetation excited all those who had volunteered to collect specimens and it seemed that at least a hundred plants were in bloom. Haënke found both the ripe seed and the flower beginning to bloom on the laurel tree; and the countryside contained forests of pine, alder, common oak, live oak, and, at higher altitudes, the redwood extending to great heights. The Bohemian naturalist first described the redwood tree and is given credit as its botanical discoverer.[55] In addition there were many medicinal plants, some poisonous and others useful or pleasant, totaling some 250 types.[56]

---

53. Ibid., pp. 438, 440.

54. Ibid.; Cutter, in *Malaspina in California*, p. 56, n. 32, explains that this refers to the California abalone shell, spelled *Haliotis midae* in modern Spanish, which was a major item in the fur trade of the Pacific Northwest until the native demand was oversupplied. See also Robert F. Heizer, "The Introduction of Monterey Shells to the Indians of the Northwest Coast," pp. 399–402.

55. Willis L. Jepson, *The Silva of California*, p. 138.

56. Malaspina, *Viaje político-científico*, pp. 437–38; Malaspina adds a footnote: "Among the medicinal plants this botanist lists the mallow, the tropcolum-majus, the arthemisia-absinthium, the arthemisia-dracumculus, the arthemisia-maritima, scorconera-dentata, solidago-cricetorum, solidago-cinerea, gentiana-centaurium, salvia-frutesceus; sambucus-racemosa, veronica-anagallis, verbena carolina, rhannus maritumus, sichorium, virgetum, melissa prostrata, oxalis prostrata, tumarea achillea, millefolium, etc., and among the poisonous, rhusradicans, rhustoxico, dendron, la cicutasiides, el hippomane discolor."

The first scientific botanical descriptions of California trees actually resulted from the publications of Luis Neé, the botanist who remained in Mexico with Antonio Pineda. Using specimens gathered at Monterey by two officers, Neé described the coast live oak and the white oak, both of which honor his name—*Quercus agrifolia Neé* and *Quercus lobata Neé*.[57] A second listing of California plants is extracted from *Reliquiae Haenkeanae* and several hundred Haënke specimens are housed in the Missouri Botanical Gardens as well as the Botanical Garden of Madrid.[58]

Another document of the Malaspina expedition concerned the usefulness of timber resources of Monterey rather than their scientific classification. The fifteen trees commented upon included the conifers—pine, fir, redwood, and cypress—and others such as willow, poplar, birch, and various oaks.[59] The local walnut trees did not produce abundantly, although the hazelnut, pear, and apple trees yielded fruit as in Spain.

Other items of interest noted by Malaspina's group included a hemp-growing experiment that, despite showing all signs of success, lacked persons motivated to be responsible for its cultivation and care. Much other statistical information was amassed about California's natural resources, native inhabitants, mission production, ship arrivals and departures, weights and measures, and manufactured goods. Cardero and Suría sketched scenes of the Monterey presidio, Mission San Carlos, and local Indians.[60]

Upon completion of their fifteen-day stay in Monterey, the Malaspina expedition prepared for its return to Mexico. They left at nine o'clock on the morning of 26 September, amid the benedictions of the priests and thunderous cannon salutes from the presidio. While noting the principal headlands to the south, they made no further stops in Cali-

57. Neé's description appeared in the *Anales de ciencias*, vol. 3, published in Madrid in 1801. These were translated and published in English in *Annals of Botany*, Konig and Sims, eds., vol. 2 (London, 1806), pp. 106, 111.

58. Thaddaeus Haënke, *Reliquiae Haenkeanae*, 2 vols. (Prague, 1825 and 1827): vol. 1, p. 38 *passim;* vol. 2, p. 3 *passim*. This work was edited by Karel Boriwog Presl. Susan D. McKelvey, *Botanical Exploration of the Trans-Mississippi West*, pp. 22–23.

59. Relación de las maderas utiles para construcción de vagales y servicio de casas que produce Monte Rey, MS 126 AMN. This "Report of lumber produced at Monterey and useful for ship building and for houses" is translated and included in full by Cutter in Appendix A, pp. 78–79, *Malaspina in California*.

60. See Henry R. Wagner, "Four Early Sketches of Monterey Scenes," pp. 213–16; and Cutter, *Malaspina in California*.

fornia. At Cabo San Lucas, on 6 October, the two corvettes separated and the *Descubierta* made an intermediate stop at San Blas. The *Atrevida* sighted the Islas Marías off the coast of Mexico and by mid-October anchored in Acapulco. Malaspina sent Viceroy Revillagigedo a letter addressed generally to the merchants of Mexico advising them to participate in the fur trade. Since Mexico and California produced trade goods that the Indians desired—copper, cloth, and abalone shells—they would have a definite advantage over the English who offered the less appreciated iron. Malaspina believed a private company should be formed and commercial treaties negotiated with Russia.[61]

During November, the men of the two corvettes prepared for the continuation of their journey to the Philippines and beyond. Malaspina learned at this time that the illness of fellow navigator Lieutenant Francisco Antonio Mourelle was about to prevent the latter's northwestern voyage in the schooner *Mexicana*. Mourelle was to prepare the way for Juan Francisco de la Bodega y Quadra, commissioned to meet with the English over settlement of the Nootka question.[62] Malaspina suggested that two of his top officers, Lieutenants Dionisio Alcalá Galiano and Cayetano Valdés, take over command of the expedition on the *Mexicana* and an identical schooner, the *Sutil*. The viceroy accepted the proposal and Malaspina instructed the officers and a portion of his crew to prepare for arrival of their new ships in Acapulco. Meanwhile, he awaited reports from members of his expedition traveling for the previous eight months throughout Mexico under the leadership of Antonio Pineda. When the reports arrived, Malaspina was not disappointed.

61. Warren Cook, *Flood Tide of Empire,* p. 316.
62. Revillagigedo sent Mourelle private instructions about what to observe on his voyage ("Instrucción reservada que ha de observar . . . en el viaje a que está destinado a la costa de California en la goleta *Mexicana*"), Mexico, 9 September 1791, Archivo Histórico Nacional, Madrid, Estado 4289.

6

The Pineda Expedition from Acapulco to Mexico City, 1791

I
N HIS instructions to Antonio Pineda, head of the scientific detachment in Mexico, Malaspina had been careful to cover all possible contingencies. He asked that botanist Luis Neé, painter and taxidermist José Guío, and scribe Julián del Villar cooperate to produce maximum results for science and the king, with a minimum of discomfort and fatigue.[1] He made Pineda responsible for a "tedious comparative examination of the soil and primary core of this Kingdom, with reference to that of Tierra Firme, Quito, Peru, Chile and the Patagonian Coast which you have visited." Malaspina believed that an investigation of the different methods of nature in forming metals, marbles, petrifactions, and topsoil in various countries would give new light to natural history and "the expedition would not be a useless and detestable repetition of the works of other Naturalists who have been, with growing expense to the public treasury, making examinations in first one and then another Province of New Spain."[2]

While in the capital, Malaspina talked with Revillagigedo and received advice from several scientists of the Royal Scientific Expedition. He also spoke with Dr. José Antonio Alzate y Ramírez, a well-known and respected naturalist with interests in medicine, cartography, and astronomy. A native of Mexico, Alzate was a member of and corresponded frequently with the Royal Academy of Science in Paris.[3] An-

1. Malaspina to Pineda, Acapulco, on board the *Descubierta,* 23 April 1791, MS 427, AMN.
2. Ibid.
3. Alzate, born in Ozumba in 1737, was educated in theology in Mexico City and ordained to the priesthood in 1756; his major interests lay, however, in natural science. In

other helpful contact was Juan Eugenio Santelices Pablo, a linguistic expert who, at the request of the viceroy, prepared a small dictionary comparing the four languages of Spanish, Mexican (Nahuatl), Nootkan, and Sandwich (Hawaiian) for Malaspina's use in his travels.[4] Both men agreed to assist Pineda in Mexico.

As a result of his discussions, Malaspina felt that Pineda should, with the least delay, "put himself on the road toward Mexico, examining particularly the primordial, gigantic mountain range" between Acapulco and Chilpancingo or Tixtla.[5] Pineda was to spend the beginnings of the rainy season in Mexico City and then visit the royal mines of Guanajuato. Afterwards the group was to explore Orizaba and neighboring volcanoes and cover generally the rugged, mountainous territory surrounding the capital. Finally, they were to accompany Alzate to the Gulf of Tehuantepec during the month of October, but only if they could return prior to the ship's departure for the Philippines on the first of February.[6] In regard to botanical collections, Malaspina thought Neé should use his own discretion in "extending his natural activity."

Malaspina knew that equipment on this excursion would be limited and collections for the Royal Museum of Madrid correspondingly small. The scientists were to travel by mules and attempt to incur no new expenses, letting "their natural talent and love for the good service of the King dictate which overcharges be just and which could or should be omitted." All the material pertaining to natural history that had so far been gathered, together with the work of Neé and the artists, was to be delivered to Alcalá Galiano, the officer left in charge of remitting these items from Mexico to Veracruz and Cádiz.[7]

As a final note, Malaspina warned that the men should take good care

---

1768 he published the *Diario literario de méxico* and later *Las gacetas de literatura.* See Francisco de las Barras y de Aragón, "Noticia de la vida y obras de D. José Antonio Alzate y Ramirez," pp. 339–53.

4. Santelices Pablo to Josef de Espinoza, Mexico, 16 March 1791 (letter of transmittal and dictionary), Additional MSS., no. 17631, Archives of the British Museum, London. Santelices Pablo also possessed "an average museum with products of the three kingdoms of nature systematically classified" (León, *Biblioteca botánica-mexicana,* p. 335).

5. Malaspina to Pineda, Acapulco, on board the *Descubierta,* 23 April 1791, MS 427, AMN.

6. Should the *Descubierta* and *Atrevida* fail to return to Acapulco from their northern journey before this date, the members of the expedition left in New Spain were to join the others in the Philippines, making examinations in and around Manila until the arrival of the corvettes.

7. Malaspina to Pineda, Acapulco, on board the *Descubierta,* 23 April 1791, MS 427, AMN.

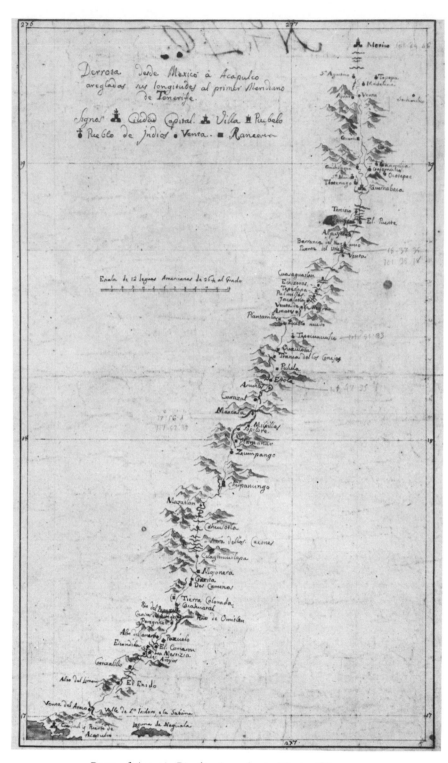

Route of Antonio Pineda, Acapulco to Mexico City, 1791

of their health and "not be so zealous for the Sciences that it exposes the expedition and the nation to the loss of some subjects who have contributed a great asset of useful knowledge, and because of their indefatigable zeal, promise new, helpful and optimum results."[8]

In addition to the scientists and Alcalá Galiano, several other officers were instructed to remain in New Spain. Lieutenant Martín Olavide was to assist Alcalá Galiano in making a series of astronomical observations and geographic studies, and Lieutenant Manuel Novales was "to attend to the cure of his constant and now dangerous dysentery of the tropics."[9] Arcadio Pineda was assigned the task of compiling as many authentic accounts of the ancient and actual state of New Spain as could shed new light on the work of the present investigators and could "contribute to the scientific knowledge of the nation."[10]

The members of the expedition remaining in Mexico witnessed the departure of the two corvettes for the Pacific Northwest on 1 May 1791. They prepared for their journey to the capital by hiring pack animals and purchasing some food. Prior to leaving Acapulco, Pineda decided to entrust a portion of his materials and equipment to one of the officers of the port, Diego Carrillo, in order to lighten the burden of transportation. Included were several boxes of flasks, stills, acids, and earthenware; a portable iron oven; three boxes containing Neé's herbaria and his plant-press; two chests, a leather trunk and a paper-case; two boxes of books; and certain "miscellaneous effects" of natural history.[11] This equipment would not be needed until the group returned to Acapulco.

After making a cursory investigation of the port's immediate vicinity, Pineda and Neé, with Guío and Julián Villar y Pardo, left on 8 May 1791, to follow today's well-traveled route from Acapulco to Mexico City. In his daily journal, Pineda made detailed notes covering all phases of the trip, describing particularly the types of soil and rock formations.[12] Although commenting on various medicinal plants and their

8. Ibid. This warning takes on a special significance in consideration of the unexpected and premature death of Antonio Pineda little more than one year later in Manila.

9. Diario de Don Juan Vernacci, MS 94, AMN.

10. Malaspina to Arcadio Pineda, Acapulco, on board the *Descubierta,* MS 427, AMN. Malaspina added that Arcadio's investigations should be carried out "with moderation, sincerity and true criticism" but that the "results of his talent and application should not offend His Majesty."

11. Account of the royal equipment left in the care of Lieutenant Diego Carrillo, Acapulco, 5 May 1791, Pineda notes, AMCN.

12. "Viaje de Acapulco a México," MSS 562–63, AMN.

uses, Pineda left the majority of botanical descriptions to Neé.[13] His interest in ethnography, however, led Pineda to include a discussion of the inhabitants of each Indian pueblo through which they passed. He noted their customs and modes of dress, commercial activities and medium of exchange, religious and social institutions, and any other aspect of their culture that might be of interest to the expedition. During the trip Guío made drawings of the following:

An *Axólotl,* a species of amphibian
The anatomy of the same; the anatomy of the female
A *Camaleón*
A *Sincoyote* [*Texixincoyotl*—Mexican for lizard]
The same turned on its back
A *Gluaguache* recently born, its natural size
An aquatic insect with all of its separate parts
A quadruped, species of wolf
A *Jilguerito* [goldfinch] of Nueva España
24 drawings of plants [14]

Pineda described the land in minute detail:

Upon departing from Acapulco, one continues along the beach, passing through two thick forests of coconut trees. . . . The road turns to the northeast through some jungle, and everywhere one recognizes great blocks of granite of 4 or 5 yards in diameter. In the Sitio del Muerto there are forms of gneiss composed of little flakes, and others of quartz and feldspath. There are also forms of a schist whose color is that of the hardest *utadina.* All the ground rocks are generally of a granite whose diverse modifications cannot be observed at a distance; one then crosses a patch of red earth whch resembles *bolar* [a reddish clay].[15]

Departing from La Venta del Atajo (literally, the Inn of the Shortcut) on the following day, Pineda, Neé, and the others continued past the pueblo of El Ejido toward El Peregrino. All the terrain, according to Pineda, between Acapulco and the latter pueblo belonged to various subjects of Mexico. The users of the land paid five pesos a year if they had livestock and two pesos if they used it only for planting; there was no limit to the amount of land. Even though the rent was extremely low, they could pay even less by common purchase. A piece of land

13. "Descripciones de plantas por Luis Neé," 2ª división, legajo no. 1, ARJB.
14. "List of the sketches made by José Guío after leaving Acapulco until [reaching] Mexico City [Lista de los dibujos echos por Josef Guio . . .]," MS 563, AMN. The zoological plates are contained in the second volume of the Depósito Hidrográfico in the Museo Naval; a portion of the botanical plates is contained in Luis Neé, *Dibujos de plantas,* vols. 1, 2, and 4 in the Jardín Botánico, Madrid.
15. "Viaje desde Acapulco a México," MS 562, AMN.

four leagues in length by two and one-half in width sold for five hundred pesos, an amount equal to the rent paid by the 115 families who lived on it.

The labor of this country is limited to three operations: clearing out the reeds, weeds and bushes; burning the land; and then planting it two continuous years, leaving it uncultivated during the third year. . . . The plantings of the savannahs are of corn and later cotton in the same year. . . . One-half league of land in the Cerro de la Brea, from whose pines pitch and tar are taken, can yield 700 pesos of capital. One sees here certainly that without the industries to which man directs his hand, the wealth of nature is worth very little and that the true wealth of the state is its people.[16]

On 10 May the explorers stopped at the Pueblo de Dos Arroyos. Continuing from there in a northwesterly direction, Pineda and his companions observed the "spectacle of the desolation, blackened trunks, ashes and reddish earth" caused by the continual burnings of the land. On the following day they climbed El Peregrino, "a luxuriant mountain with rivers and waterfalls bringing an abundant fertility." Among the trees identified by Neé were the *"brasil, drago, bálsamo, palo María, [palo] mulato, morado* (banana), *ambar, granadillo, cuapinol* (guapinole), *roble* (oak), *pino* (pine), *tachicapuchi,* and *palo de ojosí,"* most of which had been described previously by the Royal Scientific Expedition. In addition there were two species of vines and numerous mimosas. The animal kingdom, no less abundant, included "[mountain] lions, jaguars, deer, badgers, black, brown and gray squirrels." The air was populated with "parrots, peroquets, parakeets, magpies, songbirds, gamebirds and other fowl."

Leaving El Peregrino the travelers descended in the direction of the river Papagayo. At mid-day on 11 May they were at the inn of Dos Caminos, where they rested until early the following morning. During the next two days they traveled through the pueblos of Guaximicuilapa, Alcahuizotla, Mazatlán, and Petaquillas. On the thirteenth they arrived in Chilpancingo, the largest town in the district. From here Pineda and Neé made a side excursion to examine the waters of the Río Azul, explore the caves near Tixtlán, and visit various other pueblos. On the road to the "Blue River" Pineda commented upon the local people:

The character of these Indians is to appear humble, but to the person who deals with them, they appear meditative. According to their priest they are very

16. Ibid.

rude and indolent in the matter of religion and unclean (which is readily apparent). They live a long time and among their parishioners is one 120 years old. . . . The Indians are generally poor; their wealth never amounting to more than the possession of a *ranchito* of 5 or 6 cows. This frugal and idle nation, the most humble and suffering of the earth, maintains such an indifference toward what it does not possess that it looks upon luxuries, adornments and conveniences as if they did not exist. Those which might stimulate their work are very few.[17]

After seeing the limited number of priests for such a large area—one for three or four pueblos at a distance of ten or twelve leagues—Pineda found it "very strange that in the Spanish Monarchy where there is so much clergy, where the ministers of religion in the cities are so numerous, that there could be so many destitute vassals in the spiritual pastures." With the impartial eye of the scientist, Pineda summarized his view of the clergy:[18]

These rectors lead, nevertheless, a laborious life. Their customs are generally moderate and they attempt not to create a scandal. They deserve their stipends, which in this Curate are one thousand pesos and the consideration that they can contribute greatly in civilizing the Indians. They are the skillful persons of the country; they possess the language, but it is always necessary to keep after them in order that they do not set themselves up as magistrates abusing the weaknesses of the Indians.

After examining the Río Azul, named for the very blue appearance of its water, the Malaspina scientists passed through the Hacienda of San Miguel, the Pueblo de Mochitlán, and finally reached the Villa de Tixtlán. They then traveled a short distance northeast to visit the Caves of Omiapa or Alpuyeca. Upon entering one of the grottos, Pineda described its ceiling as resembling the paneling of a grotesque chapel formed by extravagant groups of white stalactites. His imagination provided him with outlines of strange animals, shapeless human bodies, extraordinary trees, unknown fruits, and various kinds of pyramids. Some of the hanging stalactites were dripping while others were entirely dry, allowing water to fall only upon being broken. All were composed of a constantly reforming crust, which process Pineda described in detail: "This and similar grottos should be considered as laboratories in which one succeeds in surprising Nature when it is operating secretly . . . but there is always a veil which allows us to see only as a finished work the beautiful stones that adorn the grotto."

17. "Viaje desde Acapulco a México," MS 563, AMN.
18. Ibid.

Leaving the Caves of Omiapa, Pineda and Neé directed their course back to Chilpancingo. They again passed through Tixtlán and the several other intervening pueblos, completing the notes that they had begun previously. In Chilpancingo, a town of approximately five thousand people, Pineda took time to amplify his report. He observed that the houses were ordinarily of straw, although some were covered with tile roofs, and that those occupied by pure Indians were completely bare of furniture. Inside, corn cobs hung from the ceiling, adding to the disagreeable smell of smoke from the constant fire.

Regarding the native dress, Pineda reported that

They wear a small shirt or *cotón* [jacket] that reaches to the navel, with another ordinary shirt underneath. Their breeches are worn over other white ones which are left uncovered at the knees. All the front part of the chest and thigh is covered with an apron of tanned buckskin, which protects them from the branches and brush of the mountains.

The women adorn their heads with two braids which they let fall over their shoulders or pass in front, tying them as if they were an adornment; many do not wear a shirt but a cloth like a mantilla in the form of a scarf, caring little if it covers their breasts, which become elongated and deformed when they are married or are wet-nurses; the single ones have breasts of beautiful conformity.

Pineda noted that the Indian girls had features of great regularity and beautiful black eyes. He felt that if they had better posture the women would not be bad looking, but these "miserable ones pass the majority of their lives over the stone upon which they grind the corn."

The major vices of these Indians are laziness and making love, which are common everywhere. To these are added those which come from the small pueblos—slander and holding grudges. It is said that mothers are disposed to prostitute their daughters, but I have not noted that this custom merits exception in the pueblos of this district. In these lands there are very few who understand the Castilian language, and that of the country is very difficult to pronounce.

From Chilpancingo the expedition headed toward the Pueblo de Zumpango, passing through various mining centers along the way. Departing from Zumpango on 21 May, they traveled to Zopilote and from the latter to the Pueblo de Mescala. While visiting this town, situated on the south shore of the Río Mescala, Pineda observed numerous unusual plants and animals. Of particular interest was a kind of ant called *la arrieta*. The natives used the ants to sew up flesh wounds by applying the head of the ant to the open cut. "With its pinchers the ant clasps it together strongly; its head is cut off and the claw remains attached, never dividing. The application of various others along the length of the wound completes the operation." This ant was large and black in contrast to *la colorada,* a small red one with a painful sting.

Pineda and his companions next stopped at the inn of Carrizal, a building lacking doors, windows, and a covered floor, but abundant in mice. Here the chief naturalist made a list of the most important medicinal plants and their uses. Some of the common remedies included the following:

> The skin of the fruit of the *Cardoncillo* [holly-thistle] prepared with sugar is given for fever; the same preparation with the *Palo dulce* serves for urinary ailments. The cooking of the leaves of the *Capitaneja,* a bush with red flowers, is used to stop cancer. The leaves of the *Sauce* [willow] are eaten as a cure for indigestion; the cooking of the bark of the *Nanz* [nance] is good for headaches; the leaves of the *Schnosquelite,* simply applied, stop tetanus; the bark of the *Quachilate,* cooked, serves to wash the sores of horses and its resin is carminative in the wounds. . . .[19]

Pineda commented that these descriptions were acquired from the Indians only with great effort and would have to be verified when he had an opportunity.

While Neé, Arcadio Pineda, and the others continued directly to Mexico City, Antonio Pineda took a separate and somewhat longer route through the famous mining center of Taxco. He was as impressed with this picturesque pueblo in 1791 as would be an infinite number of tourists of a later day. The outstanding feature of the town was, of course, the church, "which stands out among all and is the best building of the province."[20]

> The principal façade, although orderly, is very elaborately constructed; it has two very high and graceful towers. The Church is composed of a nave with its cross-arch; the altar-pieces are of extremely intricate carvings and there are excellent effigies . . . of the bishops and doctors of the secular state. The sacristy has magnificent paintings which would be conspicuous in whatever collection. . . . Its chapel completes all the work of its founder, the celebrated miner Borda, whose memory is venerated with reason in that country. The construc-

19. "Viaje desde Acapulco a México," MS 563, AMN. Martínez, *Catálogo de nombres vulgares,* gives *Wilcoxia papillosa* for cardoncillo and several species of *Eysenhardtia* for palo dulce. Capitaneja is probably *Verbesina crocata* Nees; sauce, *Salix bonplandiana* H.B.K.; and nanz, *Byrsonima crassifolia* L. Schnosquelite and quachilate may be spelled incorrectly.

20. Ibid.

tion cost him, according to legend, more than 400 thousand pesos, and the adornments are worth an equal amount.[21]

Pineda described the houses of the rich as built of lime and stone with a graceful perspective, while the poor lived in huts of palm leaves. The Indians were of a darker color than those on the coast and were "given to drunkenness." Most of the six thousand inhabitants were involved with the silver mines in some way: "Mining in this country is like a factory; it maintains the farmer and the artisan, consumes the products, and distributes the species with reciprocal benefit." The naturalist reported that miners' wages were paid weekly in silver so that the workers could provide for themselves "without suffering the tyrannical custom of Peru." Every Sunday a fair was held in the plaza in order to give the people of the province an opportunity to purchase their week's supply of food. From Iguala they received corn, meat, vegetables, pepper, and fruit. Wearing apparel was imported from Puebla and Mexico City.

Pineda made a detailed examination of several important mines in the Real de Taxco before continuing his journey toward the capital. He also made side trips to visit the cave of Alpichín on the mountain of Santa María and to explore the nearby Cerro de Huisteco. On 31 May Pineda left Taxco and headed toward the Pueblo de Amistla. From there he traveled on a roadway "that without the beneficial work executed under the patriotism of the Basque Borda would be impassable, but which the imbecilic inhabitants have not cared for in the thirty years since it was made." Despite this lack of care, Pineda described the road as the best he had seen in all of his travels. On it he continued through the pueblos of Aquitlapán, Guapitlán, Alpuyecas, and Xochiltepec, arriving in Cuernavaca on the second of June. The latter appeared as a "very pleasant town, abundant in water, with graceful tree-lined avenues and cultivated lands of fruit trees . . . all forming a beautiful countryside, which, although on a smaller scale, could compete with the luxuriant Granada."

On the following day Pineda left Cuernavaca for San Agustín de las Cuevas, a town of handsome villas and orchards on the outskirts of Mexico City. It was popular as a health resort for wealthy residents of the capital. As proof of its salubrity, Pineda reported having seen the

21. The miner José de la Borda was a native of Jaca, Spain. See Manuel Toussaint, *Taxco: Su historia, sus monumentos,* pp. 86–91.

baptismal record of a native Indian of San Agustín who lived 122 years and 8 months, having been buried in March 1787. Immediately in front of the town was a tract of lava called El Pedregal that extended westward to the mountains.[22]

On 4 June 1791, Pineda completed the final leg of his journey to the viceregal capital of New Spain. On a pillar at the entrance of Mexico City, the Spanish scientist read "a pompous sonnet exalting the excellencies of the roadway . . . which was constructed at the expense of the state under Viceroy Gálvez in order to employ many idle persons who had come to the capital during the famine of 1785."[23] Pineda was to meet his companions, who had reached the city a few days before.

The members of the expedition heading directly to Mexico City from Chilpancingo had arrived during the latter part of May. They immediately assigned themselves to the tasks Malaspina had outlined in his instructions. Arcadio Pineda noted in his diary for 28 May that they were invited by Vicente Cervantes, professor of botany, to attend the opening ceremony of a new course.

The group met at 4:30 in the afternoon in one of the galleries of the Botanical Garden of Mexico, which was in poor condition. Cervantes read a short introduction about the uses of botany and the necessity for its study by doctors and pharmacists, and then gave a lengthy discussion of the many medicinal plants that had been found in New Spain. Pineda commented that the discourse was long because of the professor's earnest desire to make it known "that the expedition of which he was a member had worked very hard, but would not be able to conclude its work because of a lack of time." Pineda also reported that the botanical garden was no better established than the lecture-hall, needing extension and form, but would now be improved by a new head gardener, Jacinto López. López had just arrived from Europe and would negotiate for an appropriate location.[24]

The next few days were devoted to "paying a multitude of bothersome visits," traveling to several pueblos in the vicinity, attending a session of the Royal Academy of History, and looking over reports. Antonio Pineda joined them in the capital on 4 June and they planned their future activities. Several days later the Pineda brothers and Neé

22. San Agustín today is known as Tlalpan and the Pedregal is the site of the University of Mexico.
23. "Viaje desde Acapulco a México," MS 563, AMN.
24. Diary of Arcadio Pineda, MS 562, AMN.

spent the afternoon visiting the "first class museum of natural history" founded by José Longinos Martínez. Arcadio reported that there were few large collections in it because it was still being formed. He thought it surprisingly good, however, "because of its ingenious and methodic placement of the animal kingdom." It lacked birds and quadrupeds, but was abundant in insects, plants, and minerals. The visitors commented that the museum reflected Longinos' prime talent and promised "to become in time one of the best ordered museums." The mountings were done with extreme care and there were "three pillars exquisitely adorned with products of the three kingdoms," and according to Arcadio, Longinos had augmented his collection with some wax figures that greatly enhanced the overall value of the exhibit.

This report on Longinos' museum, the establishment of which was a subject of great controversy between Longinos and Sessé, should have been fairly objective since neither of these men was present in the capital during Pineda's visit.

Two days later the Malaspina group called upon Alzate, with whom Malaspina had made contact. Alzate demonstrated for Pineda the characteristic of a special fish that had previously "been ignored or contradicted by naturalists": his discovery was that a perfectly formed fish, native to Mexico's lagoon, of the genus *Lisas* [mullets], instead of laying eggs, gave birth to live young. Alzate explained that by taking several known to be ready to give birth, one could squeeze them a little bit and force out a bag of eight or ten small fish perfectly packaged.

A little after depositing them in the water they begin to come alive and throw off the tunic or cartilage in which they are wrapped, remaining with the structure and liveliness of small fish; this discovery, so new in the animal system, destroys the principles of some modern naturalists like the Baron de Vernaz, who denies this prerogative to perfect fish, conceding it only to the imperfect or those without gills like the *tamores* and others. . . .[25]

During the remaining part of June and early July, the Pineda brothers gathered local information by searching the archives and personally visiting convents, hospitals, schools, and various government establishments. Neé continued his botanical observations in the company of Cervantes,[26] while the Pinedas worked with Alzate and other local sci-

25. Ibid. Some samples of the fish preserved in alcohol were obtained from Alzate by French astronomers observing the transit of Venus in 1769. See Chappe d'Auteroche, *Voyage en Californie,* plate 1, p. 60.

26. Luis Neé, "De la *Pistia stratiotes,*" p. 76.

entists. In general, they were pleased with all that Mexico City, second only to Madrid in the Spanish empire, had to offer and were favorably impressed by the accomplishments achieved under the royal officials. They marveled at the city's seven causeways, two aqueducts, well-lighted streets, magnificent public buildings, and great university. They also saw miserable slums and beggars and wondered about God's overall plan, but little could they imagine that the movement to over-throw Spanish control was just a few years away.[27]

27. See Timothy E. Anna, *The Fall of the Royal Government of Mexico City,* for an ex-cellent description of these final years.

7

Pineda's Survey
of Mexican Pueblos
and Natural Resources

IN ORDER to facilitate the expedition's work, Antonio Pineda requested an official passport for himself and Neé to examine the Mexican countryside.[1] Revillagigedo complied willingly and issued a document on 14 July 1791, giving the scientists permission to travel to any place in the kingdom they thought desirable for their investigations. The viceroy particularly ordered all district officials, governors of Indians, and those in charge of haciendas, ranchos, or private houses, to supply them with expert guides, written accounts relating to purposes of the commission, and introductions to learned persons. They were also to supply Pineda and Neé with necessary equipment and natural products at the customary price. Anyone not complying with the order would "be rigorously punished."

This passport reflected the ever-present cooperation offered by one of Spain's most enlightened viceroys.[2] Revillagigedo's generous assistance allowed Pineda to obtain a competent and comprehensive picture of life in New Spain. The chief method of gathering information was by asking a particular government official for specific answers of interest to the expedition. For example, Pineda asked the magistrate, the *intendente corregidor,* of Mexico to provide the following:

1. An up-to-date account of the departments of public lands and excise taxes, their values, actual state, ordinary distribution and credits or debits which result

1. Antonio Pineda to Revillagigedo, Mexico, 14 July 1791, Historia 464, AGN.
2. Passport of Antonio Pineda, Mexico, 14 July 1791, MS 562, AMN. See J. Ignacio Rubio Mañé, "Síntesis histórica de la vida del Conde de Revilla Gigedo, virrey de Nueva España," *Anuario de Estudios Americanos* 6 (1949):451–96; and Calderón Quijano, *Los virreyes de Nueva España,* vol. 1.

2. Another of the public establishments of this capital which are for the comfort or diversion of the residents
3. The same of the hospitals and charities with an approximate account of their funds . . .
4. The general state of the city, with an expression of the parishes, convents, chapels and number of houses
5. The general state of the population and the classes into which it is divided . . .
6. Method of policy newly practiced in the various establishments of wax-chandlers . . .
7. An idea of the projects adopted to perfect this beautiful metropolis . . .
8. The maps, reports and accounts which can contribute to the description, natural and geographic, of the different provinces which make up this Intendency . . .[3]

He also encouraged the *corregidor* to talk about the character and customs of the various classes of inhabitants, and to comment on any other point appropriate to the investigation. Other important reports included a general résumé of the assets, products, and effects that were shipped to Spain from America during the reign of Carlos III[4] and a list of all taxes placed on both domestic and imported goods entering the port of Veracruz from European and American ports.[5]

To standardize the information concerning the numerous pueblos, Pineda adopted a uniform procedure of questioning:

1. What is the origin of the pueblo, who founded it and in what year, and what else is known about it?
2. What is the number of families which populate it? What are their classes?
3. What is the number of dependent pueblos?
4. What is the occupation and commerce of its inhabitants?
5. What products are manufactured?
6. What products are introduced into it? What products are extracted?
7. What kind of earth makes up the soil?
8. What quarries are found in the immediate area?
9. What mines are known to be workable?
10. What mineral waters are there?

---

3. "Noticias que desean del Sor. Intendente Corregidor los oficiales de la expedición que viaja alrededor del glovo para el desempeño de ella, en lo tocante al reyno de Nueva España y que lo suplican se sirva comunicarles," MS 563, AMN.

4. "Resumen general de los caudales, frutos y efectos que han entrado en España de la América en el feliz Reynado de Nro. Católico Monarcha Don Carlos III," MS 569, AMN.

5. "Razón de los derechos, que se exigen a todos los efectos así nacionales como extrangeros, que se introducen en este puerto de los de Europa como también . . . de otros puertos de América," MS 569, AMN.

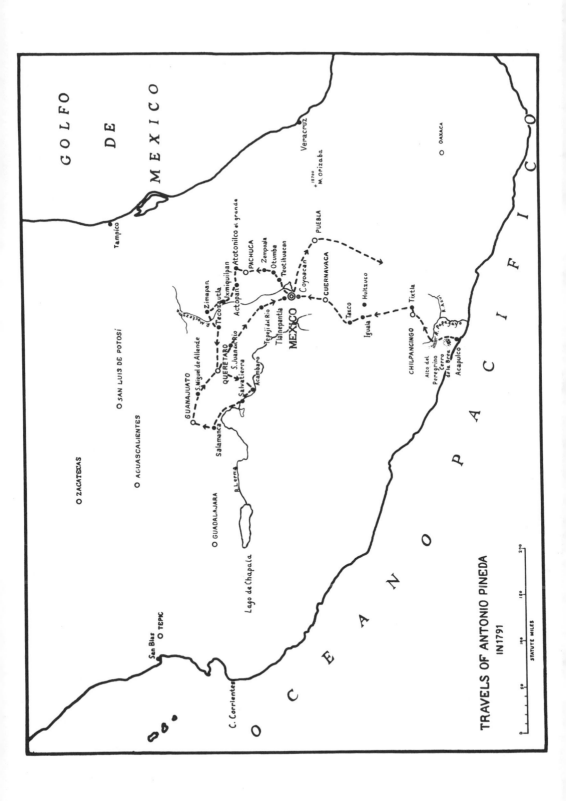

TRAVELS OF ANTONIO PINEDA
IN 1791

STATUTE MILES

11. What particular vegetables?
12. What birds, quadrupeds, etc., are found in this jurisdiction?[6]

For larger cities, such as Guanajuato, Guadalajara and, of course, Mexico itself, full-length reports were made on particular subjects. Officials from the royal mining district of Guanajuato provided a special vocabulary and an explanation of the different kinds of employees in the mines, giving their classifications, duties, responsibilities, and locations.[7] Because of their obvious value to the crown, Pineda made a rather extensive study of mines and their activities throughout New Spain. He collected samples demonstrating hundreds of kinds of mineral ore, which he sent to the Museum of Natural Science in Madrid.

No persons examining the natural resources of New Spain could overlook the famous Mexican plant known as the *maguey,* or century plant, and the Malaspina scientists were no exception. According to one report submitted to Pineda, this plant, called generally *Agave americana,* could produce water, wine, oil, vinegar, honey, syrup, thread, needles, rafters and roofs for buildings, and countless other items.[8] Neé, in his botanical description of the succulent perennial, declared his intention to make it so well known that Spain would not long be without it.[9] He reported that the fibers of the leaves were used in making rope, sacks, burlap bags, blankets for muleteers, small brushes, and many other useful articles. But even with all these products, probably the most important, and undoubtedly the most widely-known, was the popular native beverage of *pulque.*

The liquid extracted from the *maguey* in its natural state was called *agua miel* (honey water), which, when fermented, resulted in *pulque.* From this basic drink many other beverages could be made; for example:

Bingarrote or *Binguí:* Over a barbeque one roasts mature, crushed heads of Magueys; these are placed in a container of Pulque to ferment; afterwards one extracts the liquid which has been distilled over a fire. The first pitcher drawn off is called *Binguí,* and the rest *Bingarrote.*
Pulque de Chirimoia: The Chirimoyas are cut up, without the skin or pits, and

6. "Satisfacción que el juez real de este pueblo de Acámbaro al Sor. Coronel Dn. Antonio de Pineda da sobre las preguntas que le hace, y son las siguientes," MS 562, AMN.
7. "Explicación de varias voces y empleos con que se entienden los mineros de Nueva España tomadas en el real de Guanajuato," MS 562, AMN.
8. "Repuesta que dió el guarda maior a las 35 preguntas que le hace el Señor Superintendente," MS 569, AMN.
9. "Descripciones de plantas por Luis Neé," 2ª división, legajo no. 1, ARJB. Neé believed that it would be very easy to transport it to Spain for cultivation in the ideal terrain of Andalucia. It grows well there at present.

are incorporated into the Pulque; the mixture is passed through a strainer with a corresponding amount of sugar.[10]

Varieties of *pulque* could also be made by using palm leaves, peaches, guavas, eggs, oranges, cactus pears, pineapple, apples, and worms. This last drink was called *tecolio* and was actually made from a variety of worms called *tecolos* that were toasted, reduced to dust, and then mixed with the *pulque*. The resulting beverage was flesh-colored.[11]

To illustrate the amount of *pulque* consumed in New Spain, Pineda recorded a comparison of the entries for this drink during various years between 1780 and 1790 in the archives of the customs office in Mexico. In 1783, during the first four months, 890,313 net arrobas with taxes of 213,304 pesos were entered. The total amount of taxes paid for the entire year was 997,816 pesos.[12] From these figures he estimated that the consumption of *pulque* in Mexico for that year was approximately 4,120,730 arrobas or sixteen and one-half million gallons, considering only that which was legally taxed by the government.

Pineda also requested a report on the various liquid measurements used in the transportation and sale of wine and *aguardiente*.

One *barril* of aguardiente or wine contains 160 *cuartillos* [about 20 gallons]
One regular *pipa* includes 6 *barriles* or 960 *cuartillos*
One *quarterola,* four *barriles* or 640 *cuartillos*
One *garrafón* or *dama juana,* 36 to 40 *cuartillos*
One *frasquera,* which is 18 *frascos* of 4½ *cuartillos* each, contains one-half *barril;* thus 9 *cuartillos* makes one *barril*
One *botella* is 2 scanty *cuartillos*
One *bota* is the same as a regular *pipa*
One *anclote* contains from 2 to 3½ arrobas of 36 *cuartillos* each; but in general it should have from 3 arrobas upward
One *tonel* contains from 13 to 22 *barriles*
One *botija* contains 12 to 14 *cuartillos,* and *perulera,* from 36 to 50
One *cajón de botellas* has from 40 to 50 [*cuartillos*] on land
One *caja,* or *barrica,* on board ship, has no fixed number
One *frasco* has from 4½ to 22 *cuartillos*
One *barvarroja,* "a la vista" [by sight][13]

10. "Explicación del modo de beneficiar cada una de las diversas bebidas, que se usan en el reyno de la Nueva España," MS 335, AMN. See Iris H. Wilson, "Pineda's Report on Beverages from New Spain," pp. 79–90; and Wilson, "Investigación sobre la planta maguey en Nueva España," pp. 501–10.

11. Ibid. There are seventy-seven different recipes given.

12. "Entrada de pulques en la aduana de México," MS 563, AMN, and "Septenio de las cajas reales de México," MS 335, AMN. One arroba equals approximately 4.2 gallons.

13. "Razón de las cavidas de aguardiente y vino, que tienen las diferentes vasijas que se expresaran," MS 563, AMN. This notice was given by "Don Bartholomé Yturriaga, viñatero de México de los de maior crédito, y conocimientos en la materia."

In addition to collecting information from various government officials, Pineda made several excursions to survey the territory surrounding Mexico City. Because of its particular historical interest, he visited the Hill of Guadalupe (Tepeyac) in the company of Alzate, after first stopping at the chapel built in 1709 just below the site of the Virgin's famous evocation to the Mexican Indian Juan Diego in 1531. Pineda recorded in his notebook that the chapel's construction was round, well-executed, and cost more than 100,000 pesos. Inside was enclosed a large natural spring of aciduous water that overflowed into a trough leading to the outside. "The people drink it with devotion, even though they find it tasteless, because it is found in a sacred place." Pineda commented that the apparition of the sainted image to Juan Diego was "based more upon the belief of the faithful than upon historic fundamentals." He added that "in the town one sees fine buildings, and on the crest of the Cerro de Tepeyac, where the miraculous apparition was supposed to have been, there is a hermitage in memory of the event, with its Calvary; a good path with some steps leads to it and one succeeds from this height in obtaining a good view of the Valley of Mexico."[14]

They examined a nearby site where the fossilized bones of a great quadruped had been found. Alzate claimed they were from an elephant, but Pineda remained skeptical, since Santelices Pablo had previously showed him tusks of a sea-cow identified as being from an elephant. "I suspend judgment until I examine them," he wrote, "as one finds the general custom of attributing to that species all the fossilized bones of large quadrupeds that are found, and my experience and observation give proof that it is not such."

The territory they covered on this excursion was, according to Pineda, ". . . adorned with lavas of all kinds as with Pechstein porphyries of the color of flintstone which are used in Mexico for making glassware; here there is a quarry of a milky semi-transparent hydrophane that swells and becomes more transparent beneath the water. This material, so rare and precious in other countries, is so abundant that its quantity cannot be estimated."[15]

Alzate and Pineda then explored the Monte de la Esmeralda, upon which all the objects assumed a greenish color. Pineda attributed this to

14. "Expedición al Cerro de Guadalupe en compañía de Don Josef Alzate," MS 563, AMN.
15. Ibid.

the effect of the disposition of clouds transmitting colored rays, or perhaps to the surface of the bodies reflecting a dominant color. On the Monte de las Cruces they observed lavas and angular fragments of porphyry that were greenish, red, and grey; lavas of solid white ash and other colors with shorlaceous crystals; strata of red ochre with a fine grain and vermillion color excellent for the potter's trade; and an abundance of plant life, including the important pepper tree *Schinus molle*.[16]

During August, Pineda kept busy gathering and coordinating data. He was personally pleased at that time to learn from Revillagigedo that the king of Spain had approved his promotion to the rank of colonel. He thanked Valdés for "the sovereign's gracious favor," knowing that the Minister of Marine no doubt had a part in its influence. Valdés had continued to watch over the expedition during its stay in the New World.[17]

While Malaspina's group resided in the capital, they explored extinct volcanoes, climbed snow-covered mountains, and collected materials from near the Volcán del Fraile. On 26 August 1791, Pineda left for Guanajuato to investigate the various royal mines and other places of interest. Because Guío was suffering from a sickness known as the "tercianas" (fever every three days), Pineda had to employ Francisco Lindo, a young painter from the Mexican Academy of San Carlos. José Gutiérrez, another painter who also taught a course in architecture involving quarries, marbles, and various kinds of stones, offered to accompany the expedition without fee in order to have more influence in the academy.

Pineda's proposed route to Guanajuato was from Mexico by way of Guadalupe to San Cristóbal, "in order to examine the magnificent roadway which passes from the Lagoon of San Cristóbal to that of Texcoco, which was directed by the celebrated historian Torquemada."[18] From the Venta del Carpio they went northeast nine leagues, or some twenty-two miles (a league equals about 2.5 miles), in order to visit San Juan Teotihuacan and explore the ancient temples of the Toltecs. Traveling toward Otumba another ten miles (four leagues), they stopped at the Hacienda de Zoapuyucan, "on whose northern boundary one finds the Cerros de las Navajas, so named for the abundant galenaceous

16. Commonly known as *árbol del Perú, pimiento de California*.

17. Pineda to Valdés, Mexico, 24 August 1791, MS 563, AMN.

18. "Derrotero" (in the handwriting of Julian Villar with notes added by Antonio Pineda), MS 562, AMN. The Franciscan Fr. Juan de Torquemada (1557?–1624) super-viñatero de México de los de maior crédito, y conocimientos en la materia."

stone." Two leagues to the north from Zoapuyucan they saw the Hacienda de Ometusco, and in it the famous arches of Zempoala, which were 43 yards high and 13½ yards in diameter, "a work which even now should be admired by the most knowledgeable architects." Here Pineda added a note that in Zoapuyucan, Ometusco, and nearby towns, they used great amounts of *pulque* because nowhere else could people obtain "a more complete instruction regarding the method of planting the magueys, pruning them, extracting the aguamiel, and converting this into pulque." [19]

From here they traveled six leagues by way of Zempoala to the royal mines of Pachuca and then three leagues to the mines of Real del Monte where they examined the great channel completed by the Conde de Regla, a famous mine entrepreneur who had been active in the area since 1732.[20] The channel was dug to effect a general drainage, "although in this day it is no longer useful, the floor of the mines being deeper than the bottom of the channel." At the Hacienda de Regla they saw what Pineda believed to be the "most stupendous building in the world for taking out silver, because in it one could find a particular kind of basalt forming symmetrical columns." Near Atotonilco el Chico was a stone quarry of the kind that covered the cross of the cathedral; the beautiful stone merited examination since it was neither jasperite nor marble. Passing through Atotonilco el Grande, they visited the hot springs seen by members of the Royal Scientific Expedition a few years before.

Pineda included Actopán as their next stop to find out about the preparation of the *lechuguilla,* a species of agave from which the natives made cord. Pineda noted in his diary how the thick leaves of the *lechuguilla* were cut against the grain through the epidermis and the pulpy part until the fibers were uncovered. These were taken out, pulled through the fingers, and then braided together. The fibers could not be used to weave any kind of material because they were too thick, but by twisting them together, an extremely serviceable *reata,* or lariat, could be made.[21]

19. Ibid.

20. Pedro Romero de Terreros, Conde de Regla (1710–81), was born in Huelva, Spain, and emigrated to Mexico with few means. He became one of the richest mine owners and was known for his philanthropic works, especially in founding the Monte de Piedad in 1775.

21. The preparation of the *lechuguilla,* a species of *maguey,* was described by Pineda on the trip from Ixmilquilpan to Zimapán; this document is preserved in the papers of An-

The expeditionaries left Actopán to see the lead mines at Real del Cardonal and then went east to view a spectacular gorge cut by the Río Desagüe.[22] On the road to Ixmiquilpan, Pineda noted that the earth was "generally covered by a calcareous crust" and that the rocky terrain was abundant in mesquite and various kinds of cactus similar to those found near the capital. Neé recognized as many as nine different species including the *opuntia* or *nopal* (the common prickly pear),[23] a new species called *nopalillo*,[24] the *maguey* or *Agave americana,* the *lechuguilla,* the *Yucca filamentosa* and others characteristic of that region.[25]

From Ixmiquilpan, Malaspina's scientists traveled one day to the mines of Zimapán to see how low-grade metals were utilized, and then to Tecozautla where they examined some nearby thermal baths. Their subsequent arrival at Querétaro completed the first leg of the journey. After spending some time resting and investigating in the vicinity of Querétaro, Pineda, Neé, and the companions set out in a southerly direction toward the tableland region of the Pueblo de Acámbaro instead of going directly to Guanajuato. On 10 October they examined the green waters of Acámbaro's lagoon to see if in fact the color resulted from a heavy concentration of sulfuric acid as previously thought. Pineda analyzed the water while Neé surveyed the common plants.[26]

Pineda left Acámbaro ahead of the others for Salvatierra and eventually made Salamanca, over 30 miles (12 leagues) beyond. He became lost among myriad planted fields and forests, finally coming upon an Indian pueblo called El Guaje. The weary traveler tried to hire a guide, but had no luck even after offering double pay. Pineda commented that the local Indians were disagreeable in comparison to those of South America who had been more helpful and had willingly accompanied him on his explorations.

I finally left for Salamanca, which I thought was five leagues to the northwest. I walked three hours, the major part in the obscurity of the dark-

tonio Pineda in the Museo de Ciencias Naturales, Madrid. See Standley, *Trees and Shrubs of Mexico,* p. 107ff, for a description of the many species and uses of the agave.

22. "Derrotero," MS 562, AMN.

23. *Opuntia* was and still is a popular food. Stems are peeled, cubed, and cooked. The fruit, called *las tunas,* is eaten fresh or dried.

24. Probably *Nopalzochya phyllanthoides,* a cactus plant resembling *nopal.* See Santamaría, *Diccionario de Méjicanismos,* p. 762.

25. "Viaje desde México a Guanajuato con rodeo por Zempoala, Pachuca y Real del Monte," MS 563, AMN.

26. "Descripciones de plantas por Luis Neé," 2ª división, legajo no. 1, ARJB.

ness, without a guide and with no more help than the path, which without extraordinary concentration was easy to lose. I encountered an Indian on the same
road whose malice was so extravagant that even though he knew I was following him, he hid among the bushes, thereby leaving me in danger of entering
into the woods.[27]

From Salamanca, Pineda continued on to the silver-mining center of
Guanajuato and was there reunited with Neé and the others. One of
Pineda's principal objects was to inspect subterranean constructions, so
he questioned various mine owners and officials, especially those of La
Valenciana, about the mine's workings. He visited most of the mines
personally—comparing them with those he had seen in Chile, Peru, and
other parts of New Spain and finding that the cramped spaces, oppres-
sive atmospheres, and unpleasant conditions were the same everywhere.[28]

The Malaspina scientists spent a week in Guanajuato examining the
same countryside visited by Sessé and his group. The mountains to the
north were generally rocky with light rainfall so the principal plants up
to 8,000 feet were the mesquite, huisache (a kind of acacia), agaves,
cacti, and other species of the dry tableland. On the higher slopes small
oaks and manzanita could be found while alder, madrone, thornapple,
and wild cherry appeared above 9,000 feet. They returned by way of
scenic San Miguel el Grande, southward through the hills and green
valleys in which were situated the pueblos of Chichimequillas and
Coyotillo. On 9 November, in San Juan del Río, Pineda observed
various species of *motacilla,* a small bird similar to the lark of Spain, and
a *fringilla,* very much like the European sparrow. Continuing toward
the capital, the expedition passed by way of Arroyo Zarco, Tepexí del
Río, Guatitlán, and Tlalnepantla, arriving in Mexico City on 14 November 1791.[29]

Gutiérrez sketched all the important places visited during the trip and
drew bridges, irrigation wheels, mining machinery, the arches of Zempoala, the church of Actopán, the smelting ovens of Zimapán, and several natives of the area. His drawings appear to have been done in the
field and are all in black and white.[30]

27. "Viaje desde México a Guanajuato," MS 563, AMN.
28. "Apuntes de Guanajuato," MS 562, AMN.
29. "Viaje desde México a Guanajuato," MS 563, AMN.
30. "Descripción de los borradores echos en la expedicion del Sor. Dn. Antonio Pineda
por José Gutiérrez," MS 563, AMN. The view of Guanajuato, view of San Miguel el
Grande, and the Arches of Zempoala are conserved in the Museo Naval. The others have
not yet come to light.

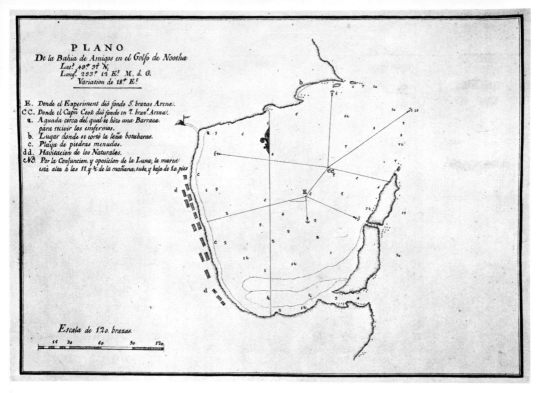

Plan of Friendly Cove, Nootka Sound, Malaspina Expedition. Museo Naval, Madrid

Tablet found on the east end of the Strait of Juan de Fuca. Drawing by José Cardero,
with inscription, "Tabla de 2 ½ varas de largo, encontrada en el Canal de su nombre."
Museo de América, Madrid

Sketch of fields and settlement at Nootka [*artist unknown*], *Malaspina Expedition. Museo de América, Madrid*

Indian festival at Nootka. Wash drawing of the dancers probably by Fernando Brambila, ca. 1791, Malaspina Expedition. Museum of New Mexico

Maquinna, Chief of Nootka. Charcoal sketch by Tomás de Suría, Malaspina Expedition. Museo de América, Madrid

Portrait of a woman of Nootka, by Tomás de Suría, Malaspina Expedition. Museo de América, Madrid

Woman of Nootka, probably by Tomás de Suría, Malaspina Expedition.
Museo Naval, Madrid

Portrait of Chief Tetaku, with inscription, "Gefe de la entrada de Juan de Fuca, Tetaku," by José Cardero on the voyage of the Sutil *and* Mexicana, *1792.* Museo de América, Madrid

Portrait of one of Tetaku's wives, by José Cardero, 1792. Museo de América, Madrid

View of the Salamanca Channel, with inscription, "Vista del Remate del Canal de Salamanca y sospechoso seguimiento de los Yndios," drawn by José Cardero on the voyage of the Sutil and Mexicana, 1792. Museo de América, Madrid

View of the Vernacci Channel inside the entrance to the Strait of Juan de Fuca, with inscription, "Vista del Canal de Bernaci y una gran Cascada," drawn by José Cardero on the voyage of the Sutil *and* Mexicana, *1792.* Museo de América, Madrid

Upon their return to the capital, Pineda and Neé set about organizing their papers and affairs immediately since they would soon be rejoining the rest of the Malaspina expedition in Acapulco. The corvettes had recently returned from their northern explorations. The clearing up of money matters was given careful attention. Pineda reimbursed Neé for one hundred pesos supplied on the trip from Acapulco to the capital and credited him with twenty-three pesos that he had advanced to Gutiérrez and Lindo. The expenses on Neé's part for the trip to Guanajuato amounted to seventy-three pesos, of which he had received seventy, so that with this he and Pineda were even except for "one and a little bit" that they would adjust in Acapulco.[31]

While Pineda was traveling throughout the kingdom of New Spain, his brother stayed in the capital collecting and assembling the numerous reports desired by Malaspina. In addition to those pertaining to methods of government, laws, customs, institutions, agriculture, Indians, and other subjects, Pineda included histories of Francisco Vásquez de Coronado and Juan de Oñate in New Mexico; the diary of the 1776 expedition of Franciscan Fathers Domínguez and Escalante; reports of the journeys of Sebastián Vizcaíno, Gaspar de Portolá, and Juan Bautista de Anza to California; extracts from journals of maritime voyages beginning with Juan Pérez in 1774 up to the latest of Manuel Quimper and Salvador Fidalgo in 1790; the plan of José de Gálvez for the creation of *intendencias* in New Spain; and various itineraries of trips throughout Spanish territories from Yucatan to the Philippine Islands. The number of separate items listed amounted to thirty-seven and, according to Arcadio Pineda, there was still a multitude of extracts and notes that were not in order or coordinated, among them being notes concerning

. . . many of the Provincias Internas and their inhabitants; accounts of this city [Mexico], of its public establishments, tribunals, residents, etc.; the history of the lagoons and their drainage, with all the works completed at various times and their costs; the privileges and donations conceded to the house of Hernan Cortés with the Marquesado del Valle de Oaxaca, the legal action which originated therefrom, and their actual state.

Mexico—26 October 1791[32]

Taking advantage of every opportunity to make a thorough investigation of New Spain, Antonio Pineda planned their return trip to Acapulco by way of Puebla de Los Angeles. The Pineda brothers and

31. Papers of Antonio Pineda, no. 168, AMCN.
32. "Nota de los papeles colectados para la expedición," MS 563, AMN.

Neé were accompanied on the first part of the journey to Amecameca by their friend Dr. Alzate, who supplied them with local information. On the road from Amecameca to Puebla, Pineda was amazed by the number of pines, oaks, madrones, and other trees that provided an abundance of shade, and the many beautiful plants in flower, which he supposed had also been observed by Martín Sessé during his explorations.[33]

On 28 November the explorers departed from Puebla in a south-southwesterly direction toward the pueblo of Guacachula. Neé observed various *loranthias* or members of the mistletoe family, the lobelias (probably *L. laxiflora*) and the *palo bobo,* or *Convolvulos arborecens,* which he had previously described.[34] Passing through the pueblos of San Juan Calmecatitlan, Mistepeque, Acatlán, Chilapa, and Petaquillas, they arrived in Acapulco early in December 1791, to rejoin the others aboard the *Descubierta* and *Atrevida.*

Malaspina was on hand to greet the returning members, but Bustamante, Haënke, and one of the officers had gone to the capital to recuperate shortly after the expedition's arrival from the northern coasts.[35] Pineda and Neé used the time remaining in port to organize, describe, and package the various materials collected during their investigations. Pineda informed Malaspina that Guío had remained in Mexico because of sickness and should probably be returned to Spain. As a result Malaspina recommended to the Minister of Marine that Guío, because of his steadfast dedication to duty "until the considerable deterioration of his health" deserved to remain employed with the expedition, especially since he could still be useful at home in mounting all the stuffed birds and animals that would be remitted from Mexico or the Philippine Islands.[36]

Another member of the expedition remaining in Mexico because of ill health was Villar, who had served not only as secretary to Antonio Pineda, but also at times as an artist. Before leaving Acapulco, Pineda prepared a statement that Villar had "fulfilled with good conduct, honor and application the work which corresponded to the copying of descriptions of birds, quadrupeds and other things pertaining to said branch in which he was employed with rather a small salary, having left

33. "Regreso de México a Acapulco rodeando por puebla," MS 562, MS 563, AMN.
34. "Descripciones de plantas por Luis Neé," 2ª división, legajo no. 2, ARJB.
35. Revillagigedo to Malaspina, Mexico, 22 November 1791, MS 279, AMN.
36. Malaspina to Valdés, Acapulco, 13 December 1791, MS 583, AMN.

from Madrid three years ago." Pineda further explained that Villar had withdrawn from the expedition only because of his poor health at sea, and that this commendation of his performance was to be used for his convenience.[37]

Both Guío and Suría, the artist who had accompanied the expedition to the north, remained in Mexico City for eight months completing the drawings they had begun during their separate journeys throughout the kingdom of New Spain. They worked in association with the two artists from the Mexican Academy of San Carlos.[38] To fill the vacancy left by the departure of José del Pozo in Peru, Malaspina had asked for replacements who could join the corvettes in Acapulco after the northern expedition. On 27 May 1791, Valdés informed Malaspina that two painters, Juan Ravenet and Fernando Brambila, were hired in Italy and had already departed from La Coruña for New Spain.[39]

On their way from Veracruz to the capital, the Italian artists made a number of drawings—Brambila concentrating on landscapes, Ravenet sketching scenes of pueblos and their inhabitants. After completing several paintings of Mexico City, Brambila and Ravenet joined Malaspina in Acapulco and remained with the expedition until its return to Spain in 1794.[40]

Shortly before departing for the Philippines, Antonio Pineda wrote a letter to his friend Gómez Ortega at the Botanical Garden in Madrid, commending the excellent assistance he had received from Cervantes in Mexico. "He earns the applause of many of this capital as much for his science and profession as for his treatment and conduct." Pineda explained that he had also corresponded with Sessé "whose brilliant talents merit the greatest recommendation truly as much as the pupils of the Botanical Garden who are distributed throughout this great continent of America." Pineda believed that when all the newly discovered plants had been presented, they would augment the inventory of the vegetable kingdom by at least one-third, "if one counts those which are

37. Statement of Don Antonio de Pineda y Ramírez, Mexico, 23 December 1791, legajo no. 5, capeta no. 1, AMCN.

38. [Viceroy] to Ciriaco González de Carbajal, [Mexico], 29 May 1792, Historia 277, AGN. Guío returned to Spain aboard the merchant ship *Concepción* for 264 pesos (Cutter, *Malaspina in California,* p. 22), while Suría remained in Mexico carrying out various artistic enterprises. He first returned to his job at the mint, was then employed at the Academy, and later yet served as secretary to various government concessions.

39. MS 279, AMN.

40. The majority of drawings by these two artists are conserved in the Museo Naval, Madrid.

scarcely known or those which the great Linnaeus has described badly."
He believed that more than seven thousand distinct plants had been
collected, over five hundred species of animals described, and at least
four hundred fossils examined.

> Their meteorological observations on the density of the air have been repeated
> in all countries, and with their calculations about the temperature, I have been
> able, by consulting the same natural phenomena inside the depths of the mines,
> in the gorges, on precipices, snow-covered peaks, and volcanoes, to learn many
> lessons that one does not learn in the best lecture-rooms nor in the most select
> books. They have collected seeds everywhere and have accumulated for our re-
> turn a respectable collection of all the objects of their respective branches.[41]

Pineda concluded by recommending, "with the greatest praises, the
merit of the young Tadeo Haënke and the indefatigable Luis Neé."
Because they were about to set sail for the Marianas Islands and would
be saying goodbye to America, Pineda hoped that Gómez Ortega and
his fellow botanist Antonio Cavanilles would know that he was at their
disposition and "would recognize him equally as a pupil and as a
friend."[42]

Malaspina was especially grateful for the help offered by Ciriaco
González Carvajal, a judge of the Royal Audiencia of Mexico, who had
contributed to the maximum progress and benefit of the expedition.
Malaspina reported that González Carvajal had surpassed their greatest
expectations by supplying them with all necessary written accounts, assisting the officers who were ill, providing them with persons informed
in natural history, and gathering together, under the direction of the
viceroy, the large number of boxes left by Pineda in Mexico City.
Malaspina said that this commendation of the judge was the only tribute the individuals of the expedition could offer such a worthy minister.[43]

The most important item prepared by Malaspina during this time
was the "account of what is included in the current remission to Madrid
from the corvettes *Descubierta* and *Atrevida.*" This list constituted a
summary of the work of the expedition during the previous year:[44]

41. Pineda to Gómez Ortega, Acapulco, 19 December 1791, 5ª división, legajo no. 5,
ARJB.

42. Ibid.

43. Malaspina to Valdés, Acapulco, 20 December 1791, MS 583, AMN.

44. "Noticia de la que comprende la actual remesa a Madrid de las Corvetas *Des-
cubridora* [sic] y *Atrevida,*" Acapulco, 20 December 1791, MS 583, AMN.

With the First Post:

In a tin box

Three spheric charts showing the coasts from Acapulco as far as the entrance of Bucareli; the chart that was sent from San Blas should contain the small piece from Port Bucareli to Cabo Engaño

Nine plans of the Ports of Mulgrave, Desengaño, Nutka, Cayocuat, Monterey and San Blas

A notebook of sketches of coastal views of the last campaign

Two drawings of perspective by the Sres. Ravenet and Brambila of the Port of Desengaño

In a package or bound in a book

Route from Coquimbo to Lima

Explanation of the charts constructed from Lima to Realejo

Diary of the stay in Acapulco the previous April

Diary of the latest navigations from Acapulco to the Northwest Coast of America until the return to said port

Astronomical diary of the same trip including the experiments of gravity on the simple constant pendulum

Meteorological diary of the same trip

Extract of the magnetic variations

Physical descriptions of the coasts examined to the north of Cabo Blanco at 43° north latitude

Political examination of the same

Discussion of the most convenient port for the stationing of Naval Forces on the Pacific Ocean

Copy of a letter to the Board of Trade of Mexico offering them an essay on the commerce of beaver furs

Continuation of the Botanical Treatise of Tadeo Haënke

In a small box No. 1, marked D.A.

Drawings of Don Tomas Suría and Josef Cardero of the most important objects of the past campaign

Those which are done in pencil have been put under glass so they would not be erased. Some, which Suría is finishing, are missing. Botanical plates of insects by José Guío. Paintings of perspectives by the two artists who accompanied Don Antonio Pineda on his excursions throughout the Kingdom of Mexico

In another Post for the necessary organization and reunion of all:

Marked General D.A., 13 Boxes (No. 1 to 13)

Contain herbaria, minerals, crystals, ores, spars, insects, and some birds belonging to the collection of natural history of the Sres. Pineda and Neé

No. 14 . . . Continuation of the Herbarium of Don Tadeo Haënke

No. 15 . . . Collection of utensils of all kinds from Port Mulgrave; a large canoe of Tinaja will be remitted from Manila

No. 16 . . . The same collection from Nutka and beaver skins from different parallels

No. 17 . . . The same collection from Monterey and stuffed birds

No. 18 . . . Small bundle with bows and arrows from the ports visited
No. 19 . . . Papers and books of Antonio Pineda
No. 20 . . . Plans and papers
   NOTE: If boxes No. 15 and 16 are opened, one should take precautions against the disagreeable odor of the seal and whale fat, which could not be eliminated entirely. The explanation of the articles included in these same boxes and in No. 17 are in Box No. 18.

Malaspina sent a copy of the list to Revillagigedo requesting him to do everything possible to assure the safe arrival of the boxes in Madrid. The boxes numbered one to thirteen were in the charge of González Carvajal, while Suría, Guío, and the two painters from the academy were finishing the relevant drawings. The boxes numbered fourteen to twenty were to be carried later to the capital from Acapulco by royal officers; and the tin box and package was to be sent by the daily post.[45] Another copy of the list was forwarded to Valdés. Malaspina hoped that when the boxes arrived, the Minister of Marine would "look at them as a new offering of our gratefulness to the generosity of the Sovereign, and as a small part of the fruits of the Expedition in this year."[46]

On 21 December 1791, the Descubierta and Atrevida set sail from Acapulco to carry out new explorations of the Pacific Islands. They bade farewell to Alcalá Galiano and Cayetano Valdés, who were preparing for their return to the Pacific Northwest in the Sutil and Mexicana.[47] Suría, Guío, and Cardero also remained in Mexico on various assignments. Malaspina and Bustamante directed their courses first to Guam and then to the Philippines, where they arrived on 26 March 1792. Neé left almost immediately on a botanical excursion to the province of Albay. In the meantime Haënke embarked in one of the corvettes to the province of Ilocos, where he collected several unusual plants, returning by land through Pangasinan to the capital.

   Pineda stayed in Manila and was joined by Juan de Cuellar from the Royal Botanical Garden of Madrid. Cuellar had been sent to supervise the transplanting of about four hundred thousand cinnamon trees and to prepare some for shipment to Spain. The two scientists traveled together through the area south of Laguna de Bay to the Hacienda of

   45. Malaspina to Revillagigedo, Acapulco, 20 December 1791, MS 583, AMN.
   46. Malaspina to Valdés, Acapulco, 20 December 1791, MS 583, AMN.
   47. See José Espinosa y Tello, ed., Relacion del viaje hecho por las goletas Sutil y Mexicana. The Sutil was commanded by Alcalá Galiano and the Mexicana by Valdés.

Calavan where the cinnamon trees were located. They took time for a detour to observe the iron mine of Santa Inés to the northeast of the lake, but Cuellar had to return to the Hacienda to complete the plantings.[48]

Pineda continued on to the province of Ilocos, when in early July, he suddenly became extremely ill and died on the sixth of sunstroke or heat prostration for, ostensibly, "having covered too much territory in too short a time."[49] Friends and fellow investigators were shocked and deeply saddened by his death. Malaspina composed a eulogy in the letter reporting Pineda's death to the governor and captain general of the Philippines, pointing out that his companion "had sacrificed himself" to promote the cause of science as much as any military man who had died in battle.[50] Brambila designed a monument to commemorate Pineda's service to his profession, king, and country. Arcadio Pineda took over his brother's duties and attempted to fulfill the obligations of the commission.

After leaving the Philippines, the expedition touched at New Zealand, New South Wales, and the Fiji Islands. On 30 May 1793, while the *Descubierta* and *Atrevida* were anchored at today's Port Refuge, near the village of Longamapu, Vavua (Tonga), Malaspina and several of the officers buried a bottle with a document claiming possession of the island in the name of Carlos IV.[51] The ceremony concluded a ten-day visit among the Tongan people and the Spaniards set sail the same evening.

Recrossing the Pacific, Malaspina and Bustamante again visited Lima, Peru, where Haënke decided to leave the expedition and continue his botanical studies by making another overland trek to Buenos Aires. Instead he investigated in the areas of Peru and Bolivia for the next seven years. He was ordered to return to Spain in 1810, but news of Malaspina's ill fortune convinced him to remain on his estate in the mountains of Yuracaré, north of Cochabamba. Haënke spent his time botanizing, operating a small mine, practicing medicine, dabbling in

48. Juan de Cuellar to Antonio Porlier, Manila, 24 October 1792, legajo 723, Manila, AGI.

49. Ibid.

50. Malaspina to the governor of the Philippines, Manila, 15 July 1792, MS 583, AMN. The entire letter appears in Wilson, "Don Antonio Pineda y su viaje mundial," pp. 62–63.

51. See Patricia Matheson, "Royal Treasure Hunt," pp. 5–6.

music, and raising mulberry trees for a potential silk operation. He died of accidental poisoning in 1817.[52]

The corvettes continued southward to Concepción and Talcahuano in Chile where Luis Neé also departed for an excursion to Buenos Aires by way of Argentina's Mendoza province. Neé successfully completed his trek, having gathered over five hundred plants on the Pampas, and finally reached Montevideo, where he rejoined the expedition. The corvettes had rounded Cape Horn on Christmas Day of 1793, sailed among icebergs to the Falkland Islands, and cruised uneventfully to Montevideo in February 1794.

The expedition soon set its course for Cádiz, culminating sixty-two months of constant travel on 21 September 1794. After a short stay in the southern port, the members transported their materials to Madrid for cataloguing and editing. Their reports were so extensive, and their illustrations so profuse, that a cost estimate for at least a seven-volume work accompanied by seventy maps and seventy plates ran to the enormous sum of two million reales. Despite financial hardships, Carlos IV's government approved Malaspina's project.

Neé began immediately to put his observations in order at the Royal Botanical Garden in Madrid. He prepared the following list of the number of plants collected in the places visited:

	Number
On the Pampas of Buenos Aires	507
Ports Deseado and Egmont	235
Chiloe and Chile	1,167
Peru	1,609
Panama	449
New Spain	2,940
Philippines	2,400
Botany Bay	1,155
Friendly Islands	160
	[10,622]

He listed various types of grasses, mosses, algae, and fungi separately, which brought the overall total to 15,990 dried specimens.[53] Continu-

52. "Sobre los botánicos y pintores que tuvieron destino en la expedición de D. Alexandro Malaspina," Aranjuez, 6 May 1797, MS 1407, AMN; See Goodman, *Explorers of South America,* p. 237.

53. "Plantas colectadas en la expedición alrededor del mundo," MS 1407, AMN.

ing in association with Gómez Ortega, the French-born botanist wrote several papers based upon the results of his investigations.[54] He was on hand in 1799 to give Alexander von Humboldt advice about New World plants when the latter visited Madrid prior to his American journey. Neé's drawings and pressed plants are still preserved in the Botanical Garden.

For a time, all members of Malaspina's expedition were praised in Madrid for their success. Suddenly, however, Malaspina's fame took an about-face because of an inopportune involvement with Queen María Luisa of Parma. In his preliminary report about the Americas, Malaspina suggested some sweeping changes in Spain's policies with regard to future colonial development. Since María Luisa was temporarily unhappy with her alleged lover and court favorite Manuel Godoy, she wanted to weaken his influence with her husband Carlos IV. She encouraged Malaspina to write a letter outlining his ideas for reform and criticizing Godoy's incompetence. María Luisa apparently hid the incriminating letter until the proper moment and, when it suited her purposes, let the contents be known. Malaspina was arrested on 24 November 1795, tried, and convicted of treason. He was stripped of his rank and sentenced to ten years' imprisonment in Castle San Anton, La Coruña.[55] His personal papers and the documents of the expedition were confiscated and all plans for publication were dissolved.

Malaspina was held in confinement for eight years and, through Napoleon's intercession, was finally released upon the condition that he never again return to Spain. His fellow commander, Bustamante, fared better in the royal service,[56] but could not arrange for the publication of the expedition's papers and drawings. Although Malaspina was eventually allowed to return to the peninsula, he could not complete his project. Publication of even a small portion of the material had to wait

54. "Descripción de varias especies nuevas de Encina (*Quercus* de Linneo)," pp. 260–78; and "De la *Pistia stratiotes*," pp. 76–82, were among those written by Luis Neé.

55. Warren L. Cook, *Flood Tide of Empire*, pp. 318–20. Alexander von Humboldt summed up the unhappy ending of Malaspina's expedition: ". . . this able navigator is more famous for his misfortunes than for his discoveries. The works of Malaspina lay buried in the archives, not because the government feared revelation of secrets that it thought useful not to reveal, but because the name of that intrepid navigator had to remain in eternal oblivion."

56. José Bustamante later became governor of Uruguay, captain general of Guatemala and director general of the Armada (see Cutter, *Malaspina in California*, p. 8).

nearly one hundred years when Lieutenant Pedro Novo y Colson compiled his large one-volume edition on Malaspina's epic voyage.[57]

Whether or not the economic and political reforms envisioned by Malaspina, including a plan for greater autonomy for the Americas, could have curtailed the growing movement toward independence can now only be a subject for speculation. Malaspina, his spirit broken, died in Milan in 1809.

57. *Viaje político-científico alrededor del mundo por las corbetas* Descubierta y Atrevida (Madrid, 1885).

8

Expeditions to
Nootka Sound, 1792

FOLLOWING THE departure of Malaspina's scientists from Mexico City, the Royal Scientific Expedition received a new commission. When Sessé arrived at El Rosario, Sinaloa, early in 1792, an official communication dated 21 December 1791 awaited him. The viceroy ordered Moziño, Maldonado, and the "best of the artists" to join Bodega y Quadra's expedition, soon to survey the northernmost limits of Spanish territories.[1] There were several reasons behind Revillagigedo's action. First, after hearing Malaspina's recommendations about the area and learning of the agreements reached in London and Madrid for a solution of the Nootka controversy, he decided to send Bodega y Quadra to meet with English Commissioner George Vancouver in an attempt to carry out the terms of the Nootka Convention of 1790.[2] Second, this solved the problem of keeping Moziño and Maldonado in the employ of the expedition in the face of cutbacks insisted upon by Carlos IV.[3] Sessé, therefore, sent a letter to Aguascalientes,

1. "La expedición de limites al norte de California." Bodega y Quadra's official journal bears the title "Viaje a la Costa N. O. de la América Septentrional por Don Juan Francisco de la Bodega Y Quadra, del Orden de Santiago, Capitán de Navío de la Real Armada, y Comandante del Departamento de San Blas en las Fragatas de su mando *Sta. Gertrudis, Aránzazu, Princesa* y Goleta *Activa* en el año de 1792," MS 145, Archivo del Ministerio de Asuntos Exteriores, Madrid (AMAE). Bodega's journal is hereinafter referred to as Bodega y Quadra, "Viaje de 1792."

2. Royal orders for implementing the terms of the Nootka agreement reached Revillagigedo in the spring of 1791. In accordance with the crown's suggestion, he selected Bodega y Quadra as commissioner and informed him in a letter of 29 October 1791 (Archivo Histórico Nacional, Madrid [AHN], estado 4287; and Historia 67 AGN).

3. Sessé to Revillagigedo, Mexico, 9 May 1793, AGN, Historia 527. The viceroy had early been cognizant of Moziño's ability and approved his employment, with that of José

where Moziño and Echeverría were making botanical collections, and ordered them to start immediately for San Blas. They would be joined there by Maldonado.

Juan Francisco de la Bodega y Quadra was the logical person to carry out the terms of the Nootka Convention. A seasoned navigator and veteran of previous expeditions to the Pacific Northwest, he enjoyed Revillagigedo's utmost confidence and was often singled out for his skillful rendering of charts and plans. A native of Lima, Peru, he entered the navy at nineteen, was trained at Cádiz, and received his commission on 12 October 1767.[4] An intelligent and personable young man, his advancement in the royal service was rapid. As a lieutenant, he commanded the thirty-six-foot schooner *Sonora* as a consort to the expedition of Bruno de Hezeta from San Blas to the Northwest Coast in 1775.[5]

On the third major Spanish expedition to the northern area in 1779, Bodega y Quadra, commanding the frigate *Favorita* in the company of Lt. Ignacio de Arteaga and the *Princesa,* reached Alaska and the Bering Sea in 61° north latitude.[6] Praised for his resourcefulness as an explorer and naval officer, he was awarded the Cross of the Order of Santiago during service in Spain. In 1789 he was promoted to captain and received his appointment as commandant of the department of San Blas

Maldonado, as an official member of the expedition. A shortage of funds made it difficult to keep the new men on the payroll, especially when the viceroy's petition for additional support was denied by Carlos IV (Orden del Rey Carlos IV [1792], 4ª división, legajo no. 15, ARJB.)

4. Bodega y Quadra's parents were Tomás de la Bodega y de las Llanas of Vizcaya, Spain, and Francisca de Mollinedo y Losada, a native of Lima whose parents were from Bilbao. The name Quadra came from a paternal grandmother, Isabel de la Quadra, and was added by Juan Francisco to honor this branch of the family. Although the British and others, including at times Bodega y Quadra himself, used only the Quadra portion of his name, it is not technically correct that it should stand alone. See Donald C. Cutter, "California, Training Ground for Spanish Naval Heroes," p. 115. See also "Oficiales asuntos particulares," MN, MS 1163.

5. "Navegación hecha por Don Juan Francisco de la Bodega y Quadra, teniente de fragata de la real armada y comandante de la goleta *Sonora,* a los descubrimientos de los Mares y Costa Septentrional de California," MN, MS 622; "Segunda exploración de la Costa Septentrional de la California en 1775 con la fragata *Santiago* y goleta *Sonora,* mandado por el teniente de navío D. Bruno de Heceta y de Fragata D. Juan de la [Bodega y] Quadra desde el puerto de San Blas hasta los 58 grados de latitud," MN, MS 331.

6. "Tercera exploración de la Costa Septentrional de Californias con las dos fragatas *Princesa* y *Faborita,* mandadas por el teniente de navío D. Ignacio Arteaga, y por el de la misma clase D. Juan de la [Bodega y] Quadra en el año de 79 desde el Puerto de San Blas hasta los 61 grados de latitud," MN, MS 331.

in time to accompany Revillagigedo to Mexico. He served at San Blas until his death in the spring of 1794.[7]

Bodega y Quadra's "expedition of the Limits to the North of California" in 1792 was intended to resolve all difficulties with England over territorial rights in the Pacific Northwest. According to the terms of the Nootka Convention, both Spanish and British ships could have free entry into any port north of the Spanish settlements, and British subjects could not form any establishments on coasts of the Americas occupied by Spain. The Spaniards were to return to the British any property Martínez had seized in 1789. When this had been done, Spain was free to maintain a post at Nootka, but Revillagigedo favored abandoning the area to the English and building a new Spanish settlement on the south side of the Strait of Juan de Fuca. The viceroy also recommended that the strait be made the northern boundary of exclusive Spanish ownership instead of the forty-eighth parallel mentioned in the royal orders. Another boundary running due north from the strait to latitude 60° north would assure the inclusion of any territories in the province of New Mexico.[8]

When Moziño, Maldonado, and Echeverría arrived in San Blas, they were welcomed by Bodega y Quadra and assigned to their respective quarters. The two vessels of the expedition, the *Activa* and *Santa Gertrudis,* cleared the Mexican port on 3 March 1792, and reached Nootka Sound without incident on 29 April. They were welcomed at Friendly Cove by both Chief Maquinna of the Nootka Indians and Presidio Commandant Pedro Alberni. Since the departure of the Malaspina expedition the previous summer, the Indians had continued their amiable relationship with the Spanish officers and soldiers, and were willing to cooperate with Moziño and Maldonado in gathering scientific information.[9] Alberni offered to give Bodega y Quadra a tour of the facilities and the two officers discussed pending political problems. Vancouver was scheduled to arrive sometime within the next few weeks.

Since the members of the expedition were going to be at the northern post for several months, Moziño decided to study the language of the

7. The career of Bodega y Quadra is treated in Michael Thurman, *The Naval Department of San Blas* and in Marcial Gutiérrez Camarena, *San Blas y las Californias.* Bodega y Quadra's health deteriorated after his return from Nootka. Despite a period of rest, he suffered a seizure and died in Mexico City on 26 March 1794.

8. Henry R. Wagner, *Spanish Explorations in the Strait of Juan de Fuca,* pp. 60–62. See also Warren L. Cook, *Flood Tide of Empire,* pp. 247–303.

9. Iris Higbie Wilson, ed. and trans., *Noticias de Nutka,* pp. 80, 83.

Nootka Indians in order to find out all he could about their history, religion, system of government, and customs.[10] Although, as he later wrote, he "learned their language sufficiently to converse with them," and compiled a brief dictionary of common words, it is likely that he relied upon the Indians' (and especially Chief Maquinna's) moderate knowledge of Spanish to compile his report. Whatever the case, Moziño's journal of more than two hundred handwritten pages is a comprehensive ethnographic and historical study of the Northwest Coast.[11] The natives also cooperated with the scientists in collecting botanical and zoological specimens. Moziño and Maldonado identified and classified more than two hundred species of plants, animals, and birds according to the Linnean system, while Echeverría made sketches to accompany the scientific descriptions.[12]

Moziño divided his report about the Nootkas into twelve separate articles. In the first he discussed the discovery of natural resources of the Island of Nootka, its relationship to the larger area of Vancouver Island, and certain physical characteristics of the Indians. He also wrote about their clothing, adornments, and weapons. Moziño thought that the climate was healthful and incomparably better than on the northeastern

10. Ibid., p. 9. The designation "Nootkan," originally applied to the Moachat by Captain Cook, is a linguistic one referring to a branch of the Wakashan stock. Within the Nootkan language there are three dialectic divisions: Nootka proper, spoken from Cape Cook to the east shore of Barkley Sound; Nitinat, used further south at Pacheena and Nitinat Lake; and Makah, used at Cape Flattery. See Edward Sapir, "Some Aspects of Nootka Language and Culture," pp. 15–28.

11. Its full title, "Nootka, an Account of its Discovery, Location and Natural Products; about the Customs of its Inhabitants, Government, Rites, Chronology, Language, Music, Poetry, Fishing, Hunting and Fur Trade: with an Account of the Voyages made by Europeans, particularly Spaniards, and of the Agreement made between them and the English," indicates the extensive nature of Moziño's work. A copy was published in several parts in vols. 7 and 8 (1803 and 1804) of the *Gazeta de Guatemala*. Alberto M. Carreño edited and published another edition, from the library of the Sociedad Mexicana de Geografía y Estadística, in 1913. Other copies may be found in the Beinecke Collection of the Yale University Library; in the Biblioteca del Palacio Nacional (Madrid); in two separate volumes in the archives of the Museo Naval, Ministerio de Marina (Madrid); and in the Agrand Collection of the Bibliotheque Nationale (Paris). The first English translation is that of Iris H. Wilson published by the University of Washington Press, 1970, complete with drawings.

12. "Breve diccionario de los términos que se pudieron aprender del idioma de los naturales de Nutka," and "Catálogo de los animales y plantas que han reconocido y determinado según el sistema de Linneo los Facultativos de mi Expedición Don José Moziño y Don José Maldonado," MS 145, AMAE. See Wilson *Noticias de Nutka*, Appendixes A and B; and "Planos geográficos y dibujos para ilustrar el diario de D. Juan Francisco de la Bodega y Quadra," AMAE, MS 146.

coast of America. The natives inhabited only the beach areas because of the deep gorges and thick underbrush of the interior regions. The mountains, he commented, were "reserved for the bears, lynxes, racoons, weasels, squirrels, deer, and so forth. I realized that birds were scarce because of the small number that I was able to arouse. I was barely able to see a woodpecker, a hooked-bill sparrow, two humming-birds, and two larks. . . . There are white-headed falcon, yellow-speckled falcon, sparrow hawks, crows, herons, geese, seagulls, and so forth." In his "Catálogo de los animales y plantas," he classifies forty different birds according to the Linnean system.

Moziño and Bodega y Quadra agreed with Malaspina's assessment of the abundant vegetable garden of Alberni and speculated about the advisability of clearing more land for cultivation. Moziño thought the problems of taking out the roots and burning the seeds of wild plants might be too difficult, while Bodega y Quadra optimistically thought that to the west "was an extension of nearly one mile which could be converted into wheat fields capable of providing bread for a thousand people." It was a place that could be used for the planting of corn and even if these both failed there would be "substantial recourse in the bulbous root of the Kamchatka Lily which grows wild throughout the entire island . . . and would serve as savory bread." [13] They both felt that goats and pigs would do better than cattle or sheep.

Describing the native peoples of the area, Moziño indicated that the Indians were of below average height and that no one was fat. Their heads, he saw, were elongated because from birth babies were held with strong bindings in an oblong box that served as a portable cradle. This caused the forehead to be raised up, the nose flattened at the bridge, and the cheek-bones to be "set wide apart, which makes the majority of them wide-faced." Their teeth were strong and even, their hair long, straight and thick, and their earlobes pierced for copper adornments. They rubbed their bodies with grease and red ochre, which obscured their natural skin tones, and tinted their faces various colors. They dressed in capes woven from beaten cedar fibers and some kind of wool. Chief Maquinna was wearing "an excellent cape made of many skins of the finest sable, jointed together with such skill that much care was necessary to distinguish the seams on the reverse side." [14]

13. Wilson, *Noticias de Nutka*, p. 8.
14. Ibid., p. 14.

The Nootka Indians wore a distinctive woven hat which Cook described as "a truncated cone, or like a flowerpot, made of fine matting, having the top frequently ornamented with a round or pointed knob." [15] According to Moziño, only the chiefs' hat contained the additional knob and was made with designs representing fishing or whaling equipment. The commoners' hat was of a coarser material and had no designs, while both hats contained chin straps of some kind of cord to hold them on against the wind. The Nootkas' only weapons were lances and bows and arrows. The bows were "small and not very flexible, and their arrows very poorly prepared." They had learned to handle all European arms of flints, sabers, swords, and muskets. [16]

Moziño's second article covered Nootkan houses, furniture, utensils, food, and drink. Echeverría made several drawings of the plank houses showing the interior design and an example of a sculptured human face called a *tlama,* which Moziño called "a simple decoration" rather than an object of superstitious worship. They had a number of special boxes inlaid with the teeth of animals in which they kept their capes, masks, and other treasures. From the ceiling beams they dried strings of sardines and other fish; they also left lying about the remains of fish and shellfish that they had cleaned. This caused an unbearable odor for anyone "who had not grown up with it."

Prior to the arrival of Europeans, the natives of Nootka had no fermented beverages and drank only water. Within a short time, however, they adjusted their tastes to include wine, brandy, and beer. They would accept whatever was given to them, although they had not yet thought of obtaining liquor by trade. They had acquired a taste for coffee, tea, chocolate, and sugar, but did not like milk, butter, cheese, olive oil, vinegar, or spices. They had become accustomed to soup, as long as it did not contain noodles, and cooked vegetables with the exception of cabbage. They ate roast mutton, beef, and deer, but beans headed their list of favorites. They were thought by the Europeans to have practiced cannibalism in the past, but "the abhorrence which they immediately perceived on our part, and the threats of punishment which they were promised for such execrable cruelty, have made them remove this viand from their tables." [17]

15. Synge, ed., *Captain Cook's Voyages round the World,* p. 433. See also Charles C. Willoughby, "Hats from the Nootka Sound Region."

16. Wilson, *Noticias de Nutka,* p. 16.

17. Ibid., pp. 18, 22.

The third article in Moziño's study analyzed the Nootkan system of government as headed by the *tais,* or chief, and discussed their religious beliefs, methods of worship, superstitions, and funeral rites. The chief served as both political and religious leader and members of his family served as princes or part of a noble hierarchy. All the rest of the people were called *meschimes,* or commoners.[18] The chief was always accompanied by two or three princes; he did no work, but was expected to make certain sacrifices as part of religious ceremonies. The Indians recognized the existence of a benevolent God Creator (Qua-utz) as well as "another malign deity, author of wars, of infirmities, and of deaths," whom they called Iz-mi-tz.

Their story of creation was to Moziño "rather amusing."

They say that God created a woman who was left perfectly alone in the obscure forests of Yuquatl,[19] in which lived deer without antlers, dogs without tails, and ducks without wings; that, isolated there, she cried day and night in her loneliness without finding the least means of remedying her sad situation until Qua-utz, sympathizing with her tears, allowed her to see on the ocean a very resplendent canoe of copper in which, with paddles of the same metal, many handsome young men came paddling. Astonished by this spectacle, the island girl remained stunned at the foot of the tree, until one of the paddlers advised her that it was the All-Powerful who had had the goodness to visit that beach and supply her with the company she longed for.

At these words the melancholy solitary girl redoubled her weeping; her nose began to run, and she sneezed its loathsome discharge onto the nearby sand. Qua-utz then ordered her to pick up what she had sneezed out, and to her astonishment she found palpitating the tiny body of a man which had just been formed.[20] She gathered it up, by order of the Deity, in a shell appropriate to its size, and was admonished to continue keeping it in other larger shells as it grew in size.

After this, the Creator got into the boat again, after having allowed even the

18. The Nootkas placed considerable emphasis upon hereditary class distinctions. The chiefs constituted a nobility set apart, purely by accident of birth, from the commoners. The principal chiefs of the district were those who owned the most property, the lower chiefs owned less, and the commoners owned nothing at all. The roles of each class were clearly defined, not only on formal occasions, but in everyday activities. Among the aristocracy (brothers or relatives of the chief), rank was based on primogeniture, and the descendants of younger sons formed a kind of middleclass. Chiefs were expected to marry women whose fathers were of the same social status. Rank and privileges are discussed by Drucker, *Northern and Central Nootkan Tribes,* pp. 243–45.

19. *Yuquatl (Yuqwot)* was the Nootkan name for the site where the Spanish were located on the island of Nootka.

20. Drucker (*Northern and Central Nootkan Tribes,* pp. 144 and 452) refers to Snot-Boy (*antokt*) as the Transformer-Culture Hero in the myths of the northern and central Nootkan groups above Barkley Sound.

animals to share in his liberality, because at the same moment the deer saw antlers grow over his forehead, the dog began to wag a tail . . . from one side to the other, and the birds were able to lift themselves by the wind and try out for the first time the gift of wings which they had just received.

The man grew little by little, passing successively from one cradle to another until he began to walk. Having left his childhood, the first proof he gave of his early manhood was to impregnate his mistress, whose first-born created the family tree of the *taises* while the other siblings formed that of the common people.[21]

The difference between commoners and princes could be seen in their funeral rites. The bodies of chiefs or princes were wrapped in sea otter furs, placed in wooden chests and suspended from pine tree branches in the mountains. Every day four or six servants would go to sing funeral hymns around the tree. The commoners were buried in the ground in order to be nearer the location of *pin-pu-la* (Hell) where there did not seem to be any suffering except that of being separated "from their old masters."

The fourth article concerned the "dignity of the *tais* and his marriage; fertility of the women; ceremonies with which they celebrate child-births; and accounts of other strange customs." The office of *tais* passed from father to son and since Maquinna's father had died in 1778 in a war against the Tlaumases, he had succeeded to the honored post. The two other *taises* in the area were Tlu-pana-nutl, who had first visited Malaspina in the summer of 1791, and Quio-comasia. Both were subject to Maquinna as head chief of the Moachat confederacy. Polygamy was practiced among the nobles and their daughters were in great demand as wives. These girls cost "many sheets of copper, otter skins, shells, cloth of cedar bark, canoes, fish, and so forth, so that the person who has four or six daughters of normal appearance can count them as so many jewels. . . ." The commoners many times could not afford to marry or at best had "to content themselves with just one wife."

Moziño, Bodega y Quadra, and others attended the elaborate puberty rites of Maquinna's daughter Izto-coti-clemot. Echeverría sketched the ceremony and the Spanish sailors participated in one of the games. The Indians appreciated the visitors' interest and were impressed by a dance that Moziño and the chaplain performed. The only sad result of the festive occasion was that Maquinna's daughter, who had visited them

21. Wilson, *Noticias de Nutka,* pp. 26–27.

every day and was always smiling and happy, could no longer share their company. Even all the pleadings of Alberni "who enjoyed the friendship of Maquinna to the greatest degree that confidence can achieve" could not persuade him to let her have dinner with them even once again. Maquinna responded only that "his daughter was now a woman and could not leave the house."[22]

In the fifth article, Moziño wrote about religious fasting and prayer, methods of fishing, the movement of villages according to the seasons, the administration of justice, and some native crafts. Maquinna's scattered villages began at Woody Point (Cape Cook) and were separated by two or three miles. As winter approached, villagers would all move on to Tahsis at the foot of the mountains and remain there during December and January. They transported most of their furniture by means of two or three canoes joined together by the planks that formed the walls of their houses. In constructing canoes, which were usually of a single piece and extremely maneuverable, the carpenters used only fire, shells, and flints as tools. The paddles served both to propel the canoe and to repel enemies trying to board.[23]

The sixth article concerned whaling, sea otter hunting, other hunting methods, and some occupations of the women; the seventh was devoted to the Nootkan language and its comparison to the Náhuatl language of Mexico.[24] Moziño spent considerable time trying to understand verb conjugation, patterns of sound, and the Nootkan system of counting. "All the numbers from one to ten have a particular name. Twenty is expressed among them by two times ten, thirty by three, and so on successively." In order to express a very large number they would repeat the word *ayo* (ten) five, six, or seven times. Moziño also tried to understand their music and describe some of their songs. He was convinced that they understood forms of poetry and thought their dances were very interesting. Decency, however, compelled him "to omit the detailed description of the obscene dances of the *meschimes* because the movements with which they carry them out are extremely scandalous. . . ."

The final five articles of Moziño's study reviewed the chronology of the native inhabitants and the history of all European contact with Nootka Sound from the time of the arrival of Juan Pérez in 1774.

22. Ibid., pp. 29, 32, 36.
23. Ibid., pp. 41–45.
24. Ibid., pp. 46–50, 53, 54.

Moziño attempted to record the events that had taken place and understand the activities of the English from the point of view of the Spanish and Indians. After reflecting upon the situation carefully, he became firmly convinced that Spain's retention of a fort there offered no possible advantage to the crown for either military or commercial purposes. Moziño warned: "Anyone can see that six or eight thousand men would scarcely be enough to guard the area, and that, even if we took exclusive possession of the fur trade, it probably would not defray the enormous expense which our defense would require."[25]

On the other hand, Moziño was favorably impressed with California. "There our conquest has taken roots, our religion has been propagated, and our hopes are greatest for obtaining obvious advantages to benefit all the monarchy." He also recommended that individual Spaniards be encouraged to enter the fur trade because of the availability of Indian trade goods within the empire. Moziño predicted that

One active trader can make at least two trips every three years and realize a minimum of 300 percent on each one of them despite the reduction which the initial price of sea otters has suffered and the frequent restrictions of the emperor of China. . . . As the Spanish traders along the coast increase in number, necessity itself will make the English and other foreigners retire. In this way, by reaping benefits instead of incurring expenses, we will succeed in securing our possessions and bringing about happiness and prosperity.[26]

While Moziño was busy observing native customs and compiling his *Noticias* during the summer of 1792, his friend Maldonado accompanied the expedition of Lt. Jacinto Caamaño in the frigate *Aránzazu,* destined to explore the Northwest Coast in the neighborhood of fifty-three degrees.[27] The vessel, although not large, drew fourteen and one-half feet of water and could not enter the smaller inlets. Nevertheless, all of the better vessels were in service, so Caamaño and his first pilot Juan Pantoja y Arriaga had to be content with the slow-sailing ship and the use of longboats. They departed from Nootka on 13 June and reached Bucareli Inlet on the twenty-fourth. Caamaño described the port as being seven miles wide, very deep, and free of shoals. They found

25. Ibid., p. 93.
26. Ibid., p. 97.
27. Caamaño's journal is contained in "Extracto del diario de las navegaciones, exploraciones y descubrimientos hechos en la America Septentrional por D. Jacinto Caamaño," MS 10, AMAE. See also "The Journal of Don Jacinto Caamaño," edited by Henry R. Wagner and W. A. Newcombe and translated by Captain Harold Grenfell, pp. 189–222, 265–301.

some good anchorages affording complete shelter from the winds and made preparations to stay for about two weeks to survey all the channels in the area not previously examined in 1779.

Caamaño was "desirous of acquiring information in regard to the customs and manner of living" of the Haida Indians, natives of this area. He noted that their language was totally different from that spoken at Nootka, some of which he had learned during his service there in 1791. He found the people eager to trade and learned that they wanted only cloth or "small shells, provided these were green. They never asked for either iron or copper, articles that they seemed to hold in small account, and with which they appeared to be well supplied."

Caamaño thought the Indians were physically well proportioned, "of light colour, large-framed, with cheerful faces and good features." Their hair was straight and of medium length. They all carried a sheath knife with a sharp blade some twelve inches long tied around their necks and a smaller blunt dagger, "which is used to give the first blows, and for wounding the face. Few of them, indeed, are without ugly scars of wounds made by these or other weapons, on different parts of the body. The hilt, also of iron, is leather covered, and is fitted with a thong some seventeen inches long, for securing it to the hand." [28]

The knives were so well made that Caamaño at first thought they could not be of native manufacture, but later learned that they were made quite easily from iron obtained from fur traders and forged by beating with stones in the water.

The Haida women were about the same color and "as equally large framed" as the men. They looked healthy, with pleasing and well-proportioned features. "The mouth, alone, disfigures them, since the lower lip is pierced at birth with a wire that is left in place . . . until, finally, an oval piece is inserted." The labret never failed to shock the Spanish observers.

Through their habit of enlarging this wooden toggle, the distention of the hole in the case of some older women becomes so marked that the lower lip almost touches the nose when turned up, while it entirely covers the chin when turned down. . . . The girls, until married, wear very small earrings, and also hang little half-moons of copper or mother-of-pearl from the gristle of the nose, which is generally bored through for this purpose.[29]

28. "Journal of Don Jacinto Caamaño," p. 203.
29. See chapter 5, note 19.

Caamaño was unable to find out about their marriage customs so did not know whether or not they practiced polygamy. He noticed, however, that the numbers arriving in canoes were equally divided among men and women with no particular pattern. There seemed to be no villages nearby nor could he distinguish anyone among them who seemed to be the chief. They wore a kind of defensive armor that protected them against native weapons or, he thought, even a musket shot at moderate range. They also covered themselves with a long shirt of thick deer skin.

Caamaño commented that the women were better than the men at bargaining and were "active, vigorous, and show great vivacity." They handled their paddles by themselves and managed "any canoe extremely well. . . . They go modestly dressed; as, over the tunic made of fine deer skin or of some goods they have acquired that reaches from neck to ankle, they wear a cape made from a skin of sea-otter, bear, or other animal."[30]

After several trips to the north, Caamaño left the Bucareli area and discovered a small port at 54°20' north latitude, which he named Baylío Bazán.[31] By 20 July they crossed Dixon Entrance and anchored in a port which they called Florida Blanca, located in 54°20'. Several days later they recrossed Dixon Entrance and anchored two leagues from Cabo Muñoz in the bay that Caamaño named Córdova. After examining a number of ports and bays in the area of present-day Melville and Graham Islands, they found themselves at the end of July in the archipelago of the 11,000 Virgins in today's Brown Passage. On 1 August, Caamaño took possession, with appropriate ceremonies, of a port he named San Roque, alias Mal Fondo. Second Pilot Juan Martínez y Zayas and several others explored and mapped the area for five days and informed the commander that the northwest branch (Douglas Channel) was the principal passage. Caamaño named the channel northwest of their anchorage Maldonado, for the botanist of the expedition.[32]

Caamaño again spent much of his time recording native customs of the region. He developed a warm friendship with Chief Jammasit who saved the Spaniards from a serious attack by unfriendly Indians. When the *Aránzazu* departed, they all exchanged presents, sang songs of peace, and toasted each other with wine.

30. "Journal of Don Jacinto Caamaño," pp. 205–6.
31. Named for Minister of Marine Antonio Valdés Fernández y Bazán.
32. Henry R. Wagner, *Cartography of the Northwest Coast,* pp. 234–35.

While Caamaño concerned himself with native customs and the charting of coastlines, Maldonado studied the abundant marine life, which included various kinds of salmon, huge halibut, and several shellfish. He also prepared as complete a list as possible of the fauna and flora, noting especially the many berries of the region.[33] After spending nearly a month in the area, Caamaño returned south. On the morning of the first of September he discovered and named the Islas de San Joaquin (Scott Islands), but continued southward without anchoring until rejoining the others at Nootka Sound on 7 September. They remained there until the second of October when the *Aránzazu* sailed for Monterey.[34]

Because of several delays, the second expedition planned as a part of the campaign of 1792, that of Dionisio Alcalá Galiano and Cayetano Valdés in command of the *Sutil* and *Mexicana,* did not depart from Acapulco until late March 1792. Instead of preceding Bodega y Quadra to Nootka, they did not arrive in Friendly Cove until the end of May. Mourelle's original project to look for a new port was set aside and the former Malaspina officers were sent to examine the Strait of Juan de Fuca in a manner similar to their previous assignment.[35] Artist Cardero was to sketch the geographic features and Indians encountered in the area. He also kept the official journal of the expedition.[36]

The *Sutil* and *Mexicana* left Nootka on 5 June 1792, and reached Nuñez Gaona (Neah Bay) the following day. They found the *Princesa Real* anchored in the cove and Salvador Fidalgo scouting the shore. Fidalgo had set up some provisional buildings, befriended the Indians, and was proceeding with plans for a permanent Spanish establishment.[37] Several days later Alcalá Galiano and Valdés entered the straits

33. MS 10, AMAE. See Wagner, "The Journal of Don Jacinto Caamaño," pp. 208–10, for a translation with notes by W. A. Newcombe.

34. Wagner, *Cartography of the Northwest Coast,* p. 236.

35. Wagner, *Spanish Explorations in the Strait of Juan de Fuca,* p. 46. The 1930 English translation by Cecil Jane (Argonaut Press, London) has been reissued as José Espinosa y Tello, ed., *A Spanish Voyage to Vancouver and the North-West Coast of America,* with a brief preface by N. M. Penzer. It is hereinafter referred to as Espinosa y Tello, *Spanish Voyage.*

36. Cutter, "Early Spanish Artists on the Northwest Coast," p. 153. The official journal is entitled "Relación del viaje hecho por las goletas *Sutil* y *Mexicana* en el ano de 1792 para reconocer el estrecho de Fuca," MS 468, Museo Naval, Madrid.

37. See José Espinosa y Tello, *Relación del viaje hecho por las goletas* Sutil y Mexicana *en el año 1792,* a new edition of which was published by Ediciones José Porrúa Turanzas at Madrid in 1958. This final act of expansion was short-lived since the port was abandoned in September 1792, with Fidalgo's return to Nootka. In a letter from Alcalá Galiano and Valdés to Revillagigedo, Monterey, 22 October 1792 (Historia 67, AGN), they reiterated that Nuñez Gaona had absolutely no advantages as a Spanish port.

of Juan de Fuca and Rosario, noting the small islands and inlets. After leaving Bellingham Bay, they encountered the English vessels *Discovery* and *Chatham* under the command of George Vancouver, the commissioner sent to carry out the terms of the Nootka Convention.[38] Alcalá Galiano informed Vancouver that the Spanish commandant, Bodega y Quadra, was awaiting the Englishman's arrival at Nootka Sound.

Alcalá Galiano and Vancouver cordially exchanged results of their respective explorations in the strait and agreed to continue together. The *Discovery* and *Chatham* left their anchorage at Birch Bay and joined the Spanish vessels for a short time, but relations became strained when the British questioned the Spanish survey.

An example of their joint operations in the channel is detailed in the journal of the expedition at the end of June, when Valdés returned with the longboat after having examined a channel that he named "La Tabla." Because he saw a kind of "wooden plank on which various hieroglyphics were represented" on the east side of a nearby hill, he paused long enough for a sketch to be made of it. Valdés at first thought the channel to be of considerable importance and was disappointed when he unexpectedly reached its end. He looked at the adjacent channels, which contained many lowlying islets, and noticed some abandoned Indian villages. Upon returning from his survey of the Tabla inlet, Valdés met Peter Puget, second lieutenant of the *Discovery*, who was going to examine the same channel. He told Puget that it was closed, "but the English officer went on to examine it for himself." In view of this duplication of effort, the Spaniards pointed out to Vancouver "that the way to advance the surveys was to treat one another with perfect confidence," and they themselves were certainly being candid. Vancouver nonetheless replied that even though he had the greatest confidence in the Spaniards' work, he would not be free from responsibility unless he saw it all himself since he was expressly directed in his instructions "to survey all the inlets on the coast from lat. 45° up to Cook's river."[39]

After parting company with Alcalá Galiano and Valdés, Vancouver asked some Indians to take a message of his position overland to Bodega y Quadra. He made his way up Johnstone Strait and finally emerged into the open waters of Queen Charlotte Sound. After a brief

38. See Edmond S. Meany, *Vancouver's Discovery of Puget Sound* and Bern Anderson, *The Life and Voyages of Captain George Vancouver,* pp. 90–97.
39. Wagner, *Spanish Explorations in the Strait of Juan de Fuca,* p. 269.

exploration northward, the ships headed for Nootka; first the *Chatham* and then the *Discovery* anchored in Friendly Cove on 28 August. The *Sutil* and *Mexicana,* sailing close to the Vancouver Island shore through Goletas channel, entered the Pacific several days after the British and reached Nootka Sound on 30 August.[40]

Vancouver's arrival at Nootka in 1792 brought the problems between Spain and England again into focus. The convention signed between the two countries on 28 October 1790 had resulted from difficult negotiations. The British public wanted revenge for the alleged insult to their sovereignty caused by Martínez' seizing of British vessels and officers. Merchants demanded the undisputed right to send British traders to the area. Spain, on the other hand, claimed possession of the Pacific Northwest under the papal bull of Alexander VI in 1493, and pointed to their occupation of Nootka. The Spaniards wanted to retain the Northwest Coast mainly because they feared other European settlements would endanger their establishments farther south. Great Britain's strength, however, gave her the upper hand and Spain was eventually forced to abandon her claim of exclusive sovereignty.[41]

Bodega y Quadra's attempt to settle the controversy with England was a failure. Vancouver maintained that his instructions were to receive all of Nootka, whereas the Spanish commissioner asserted that the return of the land where British trader John Meares had built his hut in 1788 was the most that the terms of the Nootka Convention required. Despite a most cordial relationship based upon mutual admiration and respect, Bodega y Quadra and Vancouver reached a stalemate and could agree only to refer the matter back to Madrid and London.[42] In the meantime, Archibald Menzies, the Scottish botanist accompanying the British expedition, admired the results of Moziño's work, and the men exchanged notes on various plants.[43] Vancouver remained at Friendly Cove to complete his surveys even after the departure of Bodega y

40. *Relatión de las goletas* Sutil *y* Mexicana. MS 468.
41. See Warren L. Cook, *Flood Tide of Empire,* chapter 9.
42. Bodega y Quadra, "Viaje de 1792"; Anderson, *Life and Voyages of George Vancouver,* pp. 100–19.
43. Menzies commented in his journal that Moziño, Maldonado, and Echeverría "were part of a Society of Naturalists who were employed of late years in examining Mexico and New Spain for the purpose of collecting materials for a Flora Mexicana which they said would soon be published, and with the assistance of so good an artist it must be a valuable acquisition" (*Menzies' Journal of Vancouver's Voyage April to October, 1792,* edited by C. F. Newcombe).

Quadra. He set sail in mid-October with plans to visit some coastal areas to the south and rejoin his Spanish companions in Monterey.

Bodega y Quadra had sailed for California on 21 September 1792, with plans to stop at Nuñez Gaona with orders for Fidalgo's return to Nootka as commandant. Just as he was putting to sea he encountered Robert Gray in the *Columbia* accompanied by the sloop *Adventure*. Gray, knowing that the Spaniards were perennially in need of ships, offered to sell the sloop to Bodega y Quadra. The latter agreed to a price of seventy-five prime sea otter pelts if the ship was delivered to him at Nuñez Gaona. The *Activa* and *Columbia* arrived simultaneously in the Spanish port on 25 September and joined the *Hope,* commanded by Joseph Ingraham, and the *Princesa.* After Bodega y Quadra solved some anchoring problems with Gray's help, a joint dinner was held on board the *Activa.* The arrangements for the sale were completed and the *Adventure* was rechristened the *Orcasitas* as a proposed gift for the viceroy.[44]

Bodega y Quadra remained in the port for a few days because he wanted to investigate the death of Antonio Serantes, first lieutenant of the *Princesa,* who allegedly had been killed by Indians a short while before. He gave some gifts to Chief Tatlacu, who in turn persuaded his brother Tutusi to invite some other chiefs to a conference. The chiefs agreed that some neighboring villagers had killed Serantes to rob him. Bodega y Quadra was not convinced by their disavowal of any involvement, but decided to be friendly, nevertheless, and give them Fidalgo's wooden barracks since the Spaniards were abandoning the settlement. On 28 September, Gray invited the officers of the *Activa, Princesa, Hope,* and *Adventure* to a farewell dinner. They all departed the following morning and the newly named *Orcasitas,* commanded by Lopez de Haro, followed Bodega y Quadra to the California coast.[45]

When the *Activa* reached Monterey on 10 October 1792, Bodega y Quadra found Alonso de Torres at anchor with the *Santa Gertrudis,* and learned that Juan Carrasco in command of the *Santa Saturnina* was waiting for him in San Francisco with a message from the viceroy.[46] The *Sutil* and *Mexicana* were also in port and Alcalá Galiano and Valdés

44. Cook, *Flood Tide of Empire,* p. 384. Revillagigedo's given name was Juan Vicente de Güemes, Pacheco de Padilla, Horcasitas y Aguayo.
45. Bodega y Quadra, "Viaje de 1792"; Cook, *Flood Tide of Empire,* pp. 385–86.
46. Bodega y Quadra, "Viaje de 1792."

were recording further observations about the natives of the area whom they had visited the previous year with Malaspina.

Cardero wrote that even though they had attempted to learn about the religion of the Indians, they had succeeded only in "learning that the Runsienes [Rumsens] believe that the sun has the same nature as their own, so that it can assume human form in order to kill them, and that the Eslenes [Esselens] believe that after death they are all transformed into *tecolotes,* owls—birds which they hold in marked veneration." With regard to marriage and family customs, they found that

Among the Runsienes and Eslenes, no man is allowed to have more than one wife. The Runsienes do not punish their wives for unfaithfulness, but inflict blows, wounds or cuts on the body of the adulterer, these sometimes costing him his life. Among the Eslenes divorce was common, but it was their custom to make them go, or rather to hand them over, to their new lovers; these were obliged to compensate the former husbands for the expense to which they would be put in securing a new wife.[47]

The Spaniards noted that the custom of purchasing wives was common to both tribes, but that the Rumsens took the contract much more seriously because relatives of both parties took part. Members of the husband's family all contributed a share of the payment, which in turn was divided among the bride's relatives at the time she was given over. The women of both groups, who were "fertile and robust," showed great tenderness in caring for their children and would undergo any danger to protect them. It was "not uncommon to see them give birth to a child in a field and return to work as soon as the newly born baby was out of their care."

The *Sutil* and *Mexicana* were being prepared for departure from Monterey when the *Aránzazu* arrived from Nootka on 22 October. Caamaño brought the news that Fidalgo was in command at the northern post. Since Bodega y Quadra already had a full complement of men at the California capital, Alcalá Galiano and Valdés set sail for the south three days later and cruised easily through the Santa Barbara channel. They entered the port of San Diego in the company of the *Concepción*, commanded by Francisco de Eliza, and checked their positions of latitude and longitude. Leaving the *Concepción* at anchor, which coincidentally had the naturalist Longinos aboard, the schooners continued on

47. Espinosa y Tello, *Spanish Voyage,* p. 133.

southward, rounding Cabo San Lucas in mid-November and dropping anchor in the Port of San Blas on 23 November 1792. Cardero wrote:

Our crews arrived in perfect health and full of delight at the happy ending of an expedition which was very laborious and full of risk, taking into consideration the kind of vessel employed upon it. The purpose for which these ships had been fitted out having been accomplished, we handed them over to the officer commanding the department, and ourselves prepared to return to Spain by way of Mexico and Vera Cruz.[48]

Moziño, Maldonado, and Echeverría spent more than three months with Bodega y Quadra in Monterey working on materials gathered in the Pacific Northwest. They also examined the natural resources of the local area while Echeverría sketched an excellent likeness of the *Tetrao californica,* or California valley quail, and several other birds. They again accompanied Menzies, who had arrived with Vancouver on 25 November, on some botanical excursions. During the English visit, Bodega y Quadra compared some longitudes calculated by Malaspina with those of Vancouver.[49]

By early January, all reports were completed and preparations were made for their departure. Bodega y Quadra, on the *Activa,* with Lt. Robert Broughton on board, sailed on 14 January with the *Discovery.* Vancouver parted company with the Spaniards on the twentieth, heading for the Hawaiian Islands; while Bodega y Quadra sailed for San Blas, arriving in the Mexican port at the beginning of February 1793. Moziño and Maldonado, escorting Broughton, proceeded directly to the capital. The Englishman continued on to Veracruz to seek passage across the Atlantic and deliver Vancouver's reports to London.

Moziño worked on his *Noticias de Nutka* which he completed and delivered to Revillagigedo before 20 April 1793, when he left on an expedition to southern Mexico.[50] Echeverría placed the original sketches that he had made on the trip north in the hands of fellow artists at the Academy of San Carlos for multiple reproduction,[51] and joined Moziño

48. Ibid., p. 138.

49. Wagner, in his *Cartography of the Northwest Coast,* p. 243, writes that Malaspina's calculations were 15½ minutes too far west, and that Vancouver's were 19½ minutes too far east.

50. Sessé to Revillagigedo, Mexico, 9 May 1793, Historia 527 AGN.

51. "Planos geográficos y dibujos para ilustrar el diario de D. Juan Francisco de la Bodega y Quadra," AMAE, MS 146. The two sets of drawings were completed by the following artists: Tomás Suría, José Cardero, Gabriel Gil, Julian Marchena, José Gutiérrez, J. Vicente de la Cerda, José María Montes de Oca, Francisco Lindo, José María Guerro, José María Vásquez, M. García, José Castañeda Mendoza, Nicolás Moncayo,

in the south to investigate the erupting volcano of San Andrés de Tuxtla.[52]

Noticias de Nutka was so well received by Moziño's contemporaries that Alcalá Galiano thought it "preferable to study the accounts given by the distinguished Naturalist rather than rely upon one's own impressions." He believed that Moziño's insight, perseverance, knowledge of the Nootkan language, intimate friendship with the most "knowledgeable persons of the settlement, and his long residence with them are the reasons why our impartiality demands that we give preference to his investigations over our own."[53] The German naturalist Baron Alexander von Humboldt was so impressed with the *Noticias* that on his visit to Mexico in 1803 he made copious notes from a copy of Moziño's manuscript at the Royal Botanical Garden.[54] "Despite the exact accounts which we owe to the English and French navigators," wrote Humboldt, "it would be very interesting to publish in French the observations which Moziño has made about the customs of the natives of Nootka. . . ."

If Spain's plans for a universal history of North America had materialized as originally planned under Carlos III,[55] Moziño's account would have acquainted Europeans with much of the history of the Pacific Northwest and provided natural scientists with an abundance of untapped source material. But that was not to be. On the other hand, the account of the *Sutil* and *Mexicana* fortunately reached the right persons and was published in Madrid as early as 1802. Martín Fernández de

---

José Mariano de Aguila, Miguel Albián, and Manuel López. Both Tomás Suría and José Cardero had been with Malaspina at Nootka in 1791 and Cardero returned there with the Alcalá Galiano-Valdés expedition in 1792. Several of the remaining artists, especially Vicente de la Cerda and Francisco Lindo, worked with the Royal Scientific Expedition in New Spain.

52. Moziño to Revillagigedo, San Andrés de Tuxtla, 27 November 1793, AGN, Historia 558. Echeverría apparently had trouble completing work already begun and caused Sessé, at the time of the artist's departure for Cuba in 1798, to complain: "[Echeverría] shut his ears to my comments and his eyes to the state of his sketches" (Sessé to Branciforte, Mexico, 18 November 1798, AGN, Historia 465).

53. "Relación del viaje hecho por las goletas *Sutil* y *Mexicana* en el año de 1792," MS 468, Museo Naval.

54. Humbolt, *Ensayo político*, pp. 81, 212, noted that the "distinguished doctor, José Moziño," and "Señor Echeverría, painter of plants and animals and whose works can compete with the most perfect which Europe has produced of this class [of artist], were both born in New Spain and both occupy a very distinguished place among learned persons and artists without having left their native country."

55. Donald C. Cutter, "Spanish Scientific Exploration along the Pacific Coast," in *The American West—An Appraisal*, edited by Robert G. Ferris, p. 155.

Navarrete, one of the founders of the Museo Naval in Madrid, partially subsidized the project and wrote the introduction. Many of the original maps of the expedition were reproduced in this edition.[56]

56. José Espinosa y Tello, ed., *Relación del viaje hecho por las goletas* Sutil *y* Mexicana.

9

Longinos' Journey to the Californias, 1792

BECAUSE OF personality conflicts with members of the Royal Scientific Expedition and problems concerning areas of specialization, José Longinos Martínez did not participate in the third excursion to the Guanajuato and Guadalajara regions. Among the many contentions between Longinos and Sessé was the issue of the small museum that the naturalist had started in Mexico City "to celebrate the happy ascent of His Majesty [Carlos IV] to the Throne." The *Gaceta de México* reported that Longinos, to "show his affection, fidelity and love" for the king and his subjects, had, at his own expense, gathered together a collection of all kinds of natural products. He had carefully numbered and labeled each one, giving its class, order, genus, species, and variety. He also indicated the province and place where it originated, its name and use among the natives, and its possible application in case it had no current use. To teach the public some "fundamental principles," Longinos had constructed three families corresponding to the three kingdoms of nature in Linnaeus' *Systema naturae*.[1] Malaspina's scientists were favorably impressed during their visit to the museum in 1791.

In a letter to Revillagigedo, Longinos complained that Sessé had always opposed the museum and did his best to prevent collections from being placed in it—even imperfect articles rejected by the expedition. Longinos further lamented that items sent to Sessé's house were ruined by neglect or by mishandling: "The same Director, who had

1. *Gaceta de México* 4 (27 April 1790):68–69.

never held a stuffed animal in his hand, nor had any notion of this science when I arrived in New Spain, changed himself into a Master of Natural History and attempted to correct half of these animals."[2] Longinos explained that "objects of natural history need such delicate handling that an inexperienced person can destroy their value even by taking them in his hand . . . and no Professor of honor could continue under such a system." He therefore petitioned Revillagigedo that he be authorized to conduct his research independently, keeping his collections in his house, boxing them for shipment to Spain, and merely notifying the director of his progress. He asked that he be allowed to plan a separate excursion.[3]

The previous arrangement that had allowed Moziño to travel with the expedition in 1790 provided that Sensevé, also a problem to Sessé, should remain in the capital preparing specimens. In this timid pharmacist, Longinos found an ally to share his dissatisfaction with the expedition and its director. Longinos and Sensevé, therefore, planned a separate journey to make observations more nearly corresponding to their professional competency. They were able to secure the necessary passports from Revillagigedo, allowing them to collect their salary along the way.[4] They left the capital on 20 January 1791, and started out in the direction of Querétaro.[5]

Before Longinos and Sensevé departed, Sessé, who had been traveling on the third excursion since the previous May, felt it necessary to clarify the position that, in his opinion, the naturalist held with the expedition. He wrote Revillagigedo a lengthy letter in reply to the viceroy's order that Longinos be allowed to travel separately; it left no doubt about Sessé's feelings. He did not want to prevent his associate from going off alone, but wanted assurance that Longinos would not take the books and instruments belonging to the expedition and would not send work back to Spain independently. He also pointed out that the primary object of the expedition as proposed by the king had been

2. Longinos to Revillagigedo, Mexico, 25 May 1790, Historia 464, AGN.

3. In Historia 527, AGN, there is an entire *expediente* entitled "Disputas entre el director del Jardín Botánico, Don Martín Sessé, y el naturalista, Don José Longinos Martínez," Mexico, 9 January 1791.

4. In accordance with the Royal Order of 1787, they collected salary payments at Querétaro on 29 January, Villa de León on 13 February, Guadalajara on 8 March, Real Presidio de Loreto on 30 March, Tepic on 10 April, 2 May, 10 June, and 10 July (Historia 462, AGN).

5. Longinos to Porlier, San Blas, 7 July 1791, Flora Española—1791, AMCN.

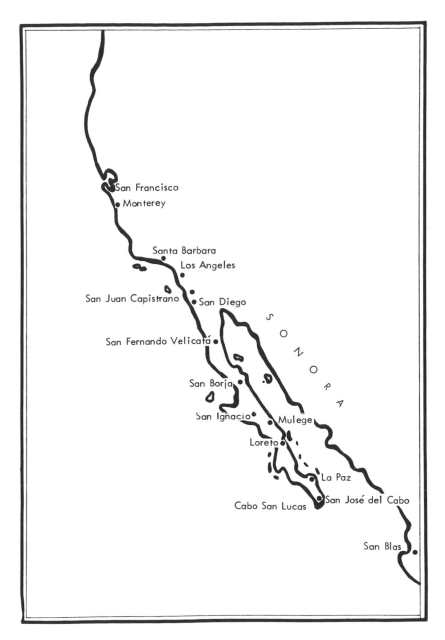

Sketch of José Longinos Martínez' route, 1792

to clarify and perfect Hernández's botanical treatise, which was to be published at royal expense. Since Hernández wrote in Latin, "of which idiom Longinos had not even the remotest idea," it was difficult for him to help. Sessé complained that in four years Longinos had not written up his first observation and now wanted to be authorized to continue spending the king's money in the interest of his own ideas. He thought Longinos was incapable of writing coherently even in Spanish and lacked a knowledge "of the Master Authors whose roads it is necessary to follow in order to travel with certainty." Instead of asking for special favors, Longinos should, like Sessé, "abandon all for his obligations, live in the mountains, suffer discomforts and dangers" and finally "occupy himself solely in the work of the institute, putting aside the gain offered by his profession, which has been the principal motive of his movements even though they have been disguised with apparent shades of better service."[6]

Sessé was convinced that Longinos could not work harmoniously within the expedition, but still thought he should be associated with one of the two "Latin Botanists" (Castillo or Moziño) so that he could produce something useful. With this help Longinos would be able to understand and illustrate what Hernández had investigated. In order to prevent further delay in the edition of this work, Sessé wanted Longinos to remit his observations and drawings monthly so they could be corrected and annotated. Sessé could not imagine what instruments Longinos had asked for since the expedition had two microscopes, the better of which was already in Longinos' hands; some thermometers that had, because of their poor condition, disintegrated on the road from Spain or on the first excursion; two barometers of which one met the same fate in Longinos' hands in the past year; two pairs of forceps for mounting butterflies, which were in the capital; a needle, chisel, and blow-torch (also in Longinos' possession); two or three tin boxes for insects; some little hoes; and some jars of tins for plants. Neither could Sessé understand why Longinos would ask for the drawings of the few animals (for the major part communal) that he had preserved from the first excursion and the short time he had spent on the second, since these had already been sent to the court. The only duplicates were those in Mexico locked up with Sessé's papers and impossible to obtain.[7]

6. Sessé to Revillagigedo, Zospotam, 13 February 1791, MS 562, AMN.
7. Ibid.

By the time Sessé's letter reached Revillagigedo, Longinos and Sensevé were well on their way. The journal of their trip, which was apparently dictated to a public scribe after their return, is described by Longinos as being "the distances from one town to the next and a brief description of the most essential characteristics of that country."[8] For example, in his journey from Mexico to San Blas Longinos observed:

Mexico City to Cuautitlán: six leagues of very level road; the countryside clear, without trees or shrubs; a great deal of land planted in maize, wheat and an abundance of maguey. Midway is a large town called Tlalnepantla. . . .

San Juan del Río to Querétaro: eleven leagues; several haciendas producing grain and horses; plains also stretching to the horizon, without trees, shrubs, plants, or water. Only near the city does one come upon a small grove of mesquite, a species of mimosa. The city of Querétaro is one of the best with respect to workshops, buildings, churches, commerce, and situation. It manufactures many textiles: blankets, baize, sackcloth, and the like. It is well provided with excellent water which is brought in over a very high aqueduct of beautiful construction. In the vicinity is a very pleasant valley in fruit and greenstuff.

On his trip to San Blas, Longinos traveled by way of Querétaro, passing through the towns of Celaya, Salamanca, Guanajuato, Zapotlanejo, Guadalajara, and Tepic. Upon arriving in San Blas, he and Sensevé spent some time in exploring the surrounding country. Longinos obtained from the Department of San Blas a list, which he copied, of the trees native to the tropical lands of the area.[9] Since Longinos' list is longer than the original, it is possible that the naturalist expanded it by giving descriptions of and uses for many of the woods previously unclassified.[10]

Longinos and Sensevé arrived on the coast sometime in May 1791, continuing their explorations for approximately two months in the vicinity of Tepic and the port of San Blas. From this port, on 7 July 1791, Longinos modestly reported that his trip had been "so successful that in three months, with only one pupil who accompanied me, I have gathered together better and more products than in the past three years." He planned to send some birds to Spain that were most difficult

8. Lesley Byrd Simpson, ed. and trans., *Journal of José Longinos Martínez*, p. 1. The original manuscript is located in the Huntington Library, San Marino, California, where Simpson's first translation was published in 1938.

9. "Relación de las maderas que se remiten del corte de San Blas, sus largos y diámetros en Píes de Burgos, San Blas," 20 April 1791, MS 127, AMN.

10. "Trees of the Hot Country of the Department of San Blas," translated and quoted in Simpson, *Journal of José Longinos Martínez*, pp. 83–89.

to conserve because decomposition in the tropics took place so fast. Besides two boxes of additional items accompanying the birds, Longinos was sending separately to the viceroy for transshipment, "a little box with one dozen birds that because of their particular and exquisite differences of color, their excellent preparation," and "their unique character" should be presented directly to Queen María Luisa for her special pleasure. He planned to leave for Loreto within a week and spend some time in Baja California examining the mines and southern coasts as far as he would be permitted by the Indians. Afterwards he planned to cross the Gulf of California, recross the provinces of Sonora and Sinaloa and investigate all of the royal mining districts before returning to the capital.[11]

Longinos requested that one of the artists of the expedition be ordered to accompany him, as well as some servants. He also asked for the books that had previously been denied to him, saying that any naturalist who travels around the world carries books valuing more than six thousand pesos, whereas the books he had in his possession were not worth twenty. There is no evidence that Longinos was granted any of his requests.

Longinos and Sensevé embarked for Loreto, Baja California, sometime in July 1791. They continued their explorations on the peninsula, first visiting Cabo San Lucas, where the journal of this portion of the journey begins.[12] Longinos commented that as one views the peninsula "from the sea, the land gives the impression of indescribable ruggedness, and thus it is in fact, for the roads from one mission to the next are over high hills and deep gorges, and stream beds sown with boulders and stones." He confidently asserted that "The name of California, or Lime Kiln, accords with the abundance of limestone found in most of the Peninsula, as well as with the great heat of the Gulf coast during the summer months. . . ."[13]

The travelers visited the mountainous region west of Mission San-

11. Longinos to Porlier, San Blas, 7 July 1791, Flora Española—1791, AMCN.
12. Simpson, *Journal of José Longinos Martínez*, p. 19. A copy of Longinos' itinerary is also found in the archives of the Real Jardín Botánico in Madrid, 4ª división, legajo 19, as "Nombre de misiones, poblaciones, rancherías de gentiles, ranchos y parajes con agua y sin ella que se encuentran en el camino recorrido y expediciones de travesía que ha hecho en la Antigua y Nueva California el naturalista D. José Longinos con las leguas de distancia que hay de una parte a otra."
13. Simpson, *Journal of José Longinos Martínez*, p. 19. This is from *cal* meaning lime and *forno* for oven or kiln. Actually limestone is not abundant in Baja California.

tiago where they encountered some interesting mineral and thermal waters. Longinos wrote:

At the Real de San Antonio there is a spring within the town plan that produces a stream the size of an orange, at a temperature of 35° Reaumur, charged with calcareous selenite. The water is used at the camp for drinking and all other necessities, and the inhabitants are strong and in good health. Two leagues west of Mission Santiago is another spring flowing from fissures in the cliffs at the base of some fairly high mountains. It yields a stream of three or four oranges, very hot, and contains a trace of liver of sulphur. The natives bathe in it, with good results in the treatment of rheums and certain other congestions from which they suffer.[14]

After visiting several mining areas including a "place called Saltillo, which is about forty leagues in a straight line from Cabo San Lucas, one can hardly go a quarter of a league without finding placer gold by fishing the sand and earth." The southern peninsula had not lost its mysterious charm since "within a radius of fifteen to twenty leagues, the same thing happens with respect to ore deposits, for the hills are criss-crossed with veins of silver, gold, lead, antimony, magnetic iron, etc."[15]

When Longinos and Sensevé again reached Loreto on their trip northward, sometime in March 1792, they parted company. Sensevé made plans to return directly to Mexico and while awaiting passage to San Blas, wrote a lengthy petition to Revillagigedo telling of his hardships and asking for the extra salary due him while on field duty.[16] Longinos reported to the viceroy that he had discharged Sensevé because "even as a student he is almost worthless." Undoubtedly Sensevé had some complaints about his "teacher," and the next word about the young pharmacist is that he arrived in Mexico City in March 1793.[17]

Longinos left Loreto almost immediately and was at Mission San Francisco Borja by the middle of April. There the naturalist wrote to Porlier that he was sending two more boxes of specimens. He wanted

14. *Selentia calcarea,* according to Adolph Pabst, "doubtless means gypsum or selenite. . . . Selenite is a very old term, and *calcarea* may be a generic term improperly used by Longinos." Simpson, *Journal of José Longinos Martínez,* p. 22, note 4.

15. Ibid., p. 28. There were some substantial silver deposits but gold deposits, especially placer gold, were uncommon.

16. Sensevé to Revillagigedo, Loreto, 2 May 1792, Historia 462, AGN. His petition was denied because of the Royal Order of 22 March 1791, which had required him to rejoin the main body of the expedition.

17. Simpson, *Journal of José Longinos Martínez,* p. xi; Rickett, "Royal Botanical Expedition," p. 48.

to know what had happened to the shipment of birds from San Blas the previous June and complained that he had received no word regarding the dozen special birds for Queen María Luisa. Longinos pointed out that despite the slight appreciation thus far shown for his "singular and distinguished efforts," he had undertaken "this long and painful journey" among Indians and over almost impassable roads to study the peninsula. He had left Cabo San Lucas three months before and intended to arrive in Monterey in September, and would "afterwards make a complete report of the products of the two Californias and of their benefits to the state and commerce." [18]

While at San Francisco Borja, Longinos spent time investigating a peculiar insect. "It walks like a beetle and is a species of cantharis, superior, because of its rapid action, to that used by apothecaries." Its effect was unfailing and acted in less than four hours. Longinos had previously experimented with this insect in the barracks of Tepic where some soldiers were dying of pneumonia. "When I applied this efficacious vesicatory to the affected parts the symptoms yielded at once and the cure was perfect." [19]

Continuing his journey northward, Longinos observed the customs, arms, and clothing of the Indians and became particularly interested in a ball game called *pelota*.

They play it very dextrously with the shoulder, arm, hand, and foot, although the most usual way is with the hand alone. *Pelota* and the manner of playing it are the same as with us. The thing is to knock the ball over a board dividing the two sides, the side upon which the ball dies losing the point. Women as well as men play it, and they [all] do so with such enthusiasm that on the feast days when it is permitted they become very fatigued and out of breath with the continuous exercise. This game is such a vice with them that on such feast days, from the time they hear Mass at seven or eight in the morning until they go to prayers at six in the evening, they are to be found playing in the sunniest spots, even in the hottest season, rarely changing players. [20]

At Mission San Fernando Velicatá, Longinos, at the request of Dominican Father Jorge Coello, acted as godfather at the baptism of two Christian Indians born at the mission. [21] Since the two ceremonies took

18. Longinos to Porlier, San Borja, 15 April 1792, legajo no. 1546, in Archivo General de Indias, Sevilla, hereinafter referred to as AGI.

19. Simpson, *Journal of José Longinos Martínez*, p. 26. Cantharis is also called Spanish fly.

20. Ibid., p. 31.

21. "Libro de Bautismos," 1 July 1792 Mission San Fernando Velicatá, St. Albert's College, Oakland, California.

place a week apart, Longinos apparently stayed in the area at least from the twenty-third of June to the first of July 1792. He then followed the trail through the area "known by the name of Fronteras among the missions that lie between," which was more densely populated than the areas previously seen. He was amazed that the "Indians of Missions San Miguel, Santo Tomás, San Vicente, El Rosario, and San Fernando, speak some fourteen different languages in that short distance" so one needed three or four "captured interpreters."[22]

As a result of his observations in the Baja California peninsula, and probably because of information supplied to him by the several missionaries along the way, Longinos was able to compile a list of medicinal plants with their various uses:

. . . the *gobernadora*,[23] which the Indians use to induce abortions (and there is no doubt that this plant has the power, at least, as I have observed, to facilitate delayed menstruation and the expulsion of the afterbirth), and the plant called *hierba del venado,* a species of *Tagetes,* which is used as a strong stomach stimulant.

What they call "scorpion root" is the *Plumbago Rosco.* Ground into a paste and applied to the sting of a scorpion or other poisonous insect, it produces excellent results, owing to its sharp and caustic property, for it forms a crust and fixes the virus.

The inhabitants of [Old] California utilize the root of the *Regalis* as a remedy for chest ailments. . . .

The root of the *tabardillo (Mimosa Californica)* abounds in the Southern District . . . [and] has been employed in several fever epidemics, the pernicious effects of which have been halted with its decoction.

Indian root (*Aristolochia Pentandria*) is used as a vulnerary, applied in powder form to wounds, and to ulcers in all stages. Plants of the same genus, according to an aphorism of Linnaeus, have the same virtues, and hence one may include all varieties of *Aristolochiae,* both long and round, which are well known.

The root of the *mesquitillo* is used as a powerful astringent in lavages for diarrheas; it is also chewed for strengthening the teeth. This root could be very useful in the dyeing and tanning of hides, if it were propagated in Europe. It abounds in the Peninsula, and with it most of the hides are dyed a beautiful scarlet.

The root of the *peyote* (the native name for the *Adiantus Trifolius,* S.N.) occurs in the highest mountains of [Old] California. There is hardly anyone who does not have this root in his possession, such is their faith in it for the

22. Simpson, *Journal of José Longinos Martínez,* p. 34.
23. *Larrea tridentata,* or creosote bush, one of the most abundant desert shrubs. See Coyle and Roberts, *A Field Guide to the Common and Interesting Plants of Baja California,* p. 104, and chapter 2, note 54.

treatment of wounds and ulcers, and, because of their experience with it, in powder form, as a miraculous specific for any contusion.

The root of the *manzo*[24] is applied in powder form for stubborn ulcers and the stings of poisonous insects. It has a rather pleasant aromatic odor and is very bitter.

The root of the *jarramatraca* (*Cactus Tuberosus*, S.N.) is much esteemed among the Yaqui and the inhabitants of Sonora, and they order it from great distances because of its marvelous effects in the treatment of headaches, as I have heard from trustworthy persons. It is applied to the temples in powder form, mixed with a little milk.

"Indian root" (also so called in the Northern District of [Old] California) is the *Aristolochia Maurorum*. It is applied like the preceding and has the same effects.

What they call *"raíz barbuda"* [bearded root] is the *Perdicium Californianum*. It is a fasciculated root thickly covered with short hairs at the joints. The hair or wool is used for toothaches, and the rest is applied in powder form to wounds as a mundificant and incarnative.

The *Mencelia Aspera* also abounds. Its purgative root is used by the Mexican Indians as an anti-venereal. It is a kind of *Lobelia*, very like the *Syphillitica*, the use of which against this virus [syphilis] is recommended by authorities. I have made it known here [in Mexico] for the treatment of this disease.[25]

According to Longinos, he left Mission Santo Domingo on 17 July 1792, "with an escort of five soldiers, three servants from the Mission, and twelve Indians." He observed the scattered roses of Castile, poppies, juniper, alder, willow, and sage along the way. They followed one creek up into the mountains and returned to continue northward along the coast. Crossing into Alta California near San Diego, Longinos was impressed by the activity at the local Franciscan mission. Even though they lacked water previously, "since the Catalans came, they have had water and such an abundance of everything that they are no longer able to dispose of their grain, livestock, fruit, etc."[26]

After a visit to Mission San Juan Capistrano, Longinos continued on to San Gabriel where he spent several days investigating the area. About the place later called Rancho La Brea, he reported in his journal:

I have also observed a different kind of spring, rare in Nature, of petroleum, pitch and other volcanic substances. At the parallel of San Juan Capistrano one finds several pitch springs on the eastern slope of the mountains. In the vicinity

24. According to Simpson the *manzo* is unidentified but may be the *maguey manso*.

25. Simpson, *Journal of José Longinos Martínez*, pp. 24–25.

26. Ibid., p. 44. The "Catalanes" referred to by Longinos were Fathers Hilario Torrent, who served at San Diego from 1786 to 1798, and Juan Mariner, who served from 1785 to 1800. See Maynard Geiger, O.F.M., *Franciscan Missionaries in Hispanic California.*

of San Gabriel are other pitch springs, and near the Pueblo of Los Angeles more than twenty springs of liquid petroleum, pitch, etc. To the west of said town, in the middle of a great plain of more than fifteen leagues in circumference, there is a large lake of pitch, with many pools in which bubbles or blisters are constantly forming and exploding. They are shaped like conical bells and make a little report when they burst at the apex.

Longinos commented that if one stood upon the more solid masses of pitch, one seemed "to be rising insensibly from the ground." In hot weather, the Indians reported, animals sank in it because their feet became stuck "and the lake swallowed them." After many years their petrified bones would come up to the surface. Longinos gathered up several specimens to take back to Mexico.

Further to the north, Longinos visited several permanent villages of Chumash Indians. He thought their houses were "very well constructed, round like an oven, spacious and fairly comfortable." They slept on mats with dividers between them. They built smaller houses nearby to store seeds, dried fish, sardines, and other foods for the winter. Outside the village was a cemetery for their dead and graves were marked with a painted board representing the dead person's occupation. He recorded that

Each of the villages has one or more sweat houses (*temescales*), depending upon the number of inhabitants. Men and women both enter them twice a day [and emerge] streaming with sweat, after which they plunge into pools or streams of cold water which they always have at hand. This rite, which truly seems repugnant to our way of life, they perform daily, even in the severest cold, which on some days is considerable. I attribute to this bad practice of theirs, which they follow from birth, their want of hardiness, unlike the nations that do not do such violence to Nature. But these people are so addicted to it that the missionary fathers, even in the missions, allow them to have their sweat houses and ponds of cold water for the daily ablutions that they all perform because of their cleanliness and their fondness for soaping themselves at all hours.

In his journal Longinos observed that the women dressed gracefully, usually wearing two very soft pieces of buckskin, one in front and the other in back, as a kind of skirt. The edges were cut into fringes and decorated with "strings of beads, snail shells, and others of various colors" giving an attractive effect. Around their shoulders they wore an oblong *tápalo* (literally, "cover it") of fox, otter, squirrel, or rabbit fur that was tied at opposite corners. They put their head and one arm through the upper opening and arranged it "gracefully so as to cover their flesh." They adorned "their heads tastefully with necklaces and earrings."

Their hair is worn in bangs, cut short and combed forward, which gives it the appearance of a brush. They trim it daily by singeing it hair by hair with a piece of pine bark, so that no hair protrudes. If by chance their forehead or hair line is ill-shaped, they correct it with black pitch, as true as if done with compass and ruler. They wear side locks (*balcarrotas*), but the rest of their back hair is worn loose, slicked down on top as much as possible. Their headdress or coiffure gives the woman a neat and graceful appearance and makes them less horribly ugly than the rest of the gentile women, giving them some attraction for the Spaniards.

It is apparent that Longinos felt comfortable with the Chumash and liked what he saw. He thought their basketwork represented the "utmost delicacy" and described their pots and pans as being of a kind of mica stone [soapstone] that was "so resistant to heat that it never wears out or becomes unserviceable." These pots were handed down "from father to son to grandson." He was obviously favorably impressed with their canoes, which

. . . are of a singular construction and extremely light, made of a number of pieces, fashioned without nails or glue, or any tools other than flints, but with such precision and neatness that they look like the work of our best master carpenter, with all his tools and rules. Their bows and arrows are different from those of the other nations, excelling them in workmanship, beauty, and effectiveness. They also make war clubs, somewhat curved, and sticks which they use with great skill for hunting rabbits and other small game. Their fishhooks are of shell or bone, which they sometimes prefer to our iron ones. They fish also with tridents (*fisgas*) and harpoons of shell or flint. They hunt sea otters in the same manner as the Indians of Old California.[27]

Longinos thought that the Chinese or "some person of great skill" had landed on the Santa Barbara coast because of the skill of the Chumash in the construction of houses, canoes, and weapons. He believed them to be superior to any of the other Indians of either Alta or Baja California who lived in "no fixed domiciles," cremated their dead, went about naked, and were too lazy to store up food. He thought the Indians of the San Diego area were "warlike and proud" and "to be feared because of their treachery," while those of San Juan Capistrano were "affable" and learned Castilian readily. The Indians of San Gabriel

27. Simpson, *Journal of José Longinos Martínez,* p. 54. See also Robert F. Heizer, "The California Indians," pp. 1–28.

had the "custom of carrying small stones" for which they paid a high price to the Indians of Catalina Island, not because they contained any metal "but because of the current belief that he who has one with him thereby acquires valor and bravery."

In regard to the natural products of both Lower and Upper California, Longinos prepared a list of those capable of being exploited commercially. Under the heading "Animal Kingdom" he placed nacre, seal fur, otter fur, whale oil, seal oil, whalebone, codfish, sardines, tallow, hides, salt meat, wool, bear skins, and bear's grease (for medicine) as being common to Upper California. Under the remaining two kingdoms for the same province he listed:

Vegetable Kingdom

Lac, hemp, flax (and other fibers, such as *Malvas Asclepias,* etc., for naval rigging), wine

Medicinal plants: Apothecary's sage, a root called *chuchupaste* (held to be a miraculous cure for headaches, by inhalation only), three species of *chia* seeds (used for a refreshment; they are abundant and could be better utilized in medicine)

Mineral Kingdom

Silver, hematite, alum, agates, colored silicas, white clay (for porcelain), mica (for crucibles and furnaces), natural soap (having the same properties as artificial soap)[28]

Longinos reached the port of Monterey, capital of Upper California, on approximately the first day of September 1792, just a month prior to Moziño's return from Nootka. The naturalist ended his extended trip at this point and boarded a ship bound for Mexico. After an absence of more than one year, Longinos returned to San Blas on 22 November 1792. A letter from Francisco de Eliza, commander of the Royal Frigate *Concepción* to Revillagigedo reported that he had arrived in the port of San Blas with a passenger, the naturalist Longinos Martínez, four mules "belonging to the widow of the late Governor" (Romeu), and "a married soldier on leave from the presidio of San Diego."[29] Back on the mainland, Longinos continued his solitary travel in the vicinity of San Blas. In May 1793, when Sessé wrote to the viceroy trying to incorporate Moziño into the expedition, he referred to Longinos as "being at a distance of 200 leagues" and needing two months to reach Mexico.[30]

28. Simpson, *Journal of José Longinos Martínez,* pp. 81–82.

29. Eliza to Revillagigedo, San Blas, 22 November 1792, Historia 69, AGN, as quoted in Simpson, *Journal of José Longinos Martínez,* p. xiii.

30. Sessé to Revillagigedo, Mexico, 9 May 1793, Historia 527, AGN.

In June 1793 Longinos wrote to Revillagigedo from the Hacienda of San Josef which was situated between San Blas and Acaponeta. He informed the viceroy that he had received the orders to rejoin the expedition and, because he was always obedient to the commands of the sovereign, would do so. Longinos again referred to the insults that Sessé had directed toward him from Querétaro in 1790, claiming them malicious and untrue. He also stated that he had not separated himself from the expedition because he disliked traveling; on the contrary, he had spent two years in "Antigua and Nueva California" where he had been exposed to the dangers of land and sea and the diseases of the coast. During this time he had collected more than thirty boxes of specimens. But, he argued, because he was four to five hundred leagues away from the capital, and the rains were beginning, he would not be able to join the expedition immediately.[31]

On 26 October 1793, Revillagigedo ordered Longinos to return to duty.[32] Two weeks later, while in Compostela, the naturalist offered to survey the entire west coast from Los Angeles to Lima, but the viceroy replied by ordering him to return to Mexico at once.[33] Apparently the message finally got through because Longinos was back in the capital by 20 January 1794, the date on which he asked for back salary. The request was granted under the condition that he write up and submit "all the observations you have made on your recent Expedition to the Coasts of San Blas, the Peninsula of the Californias, and all other territories through which you have passed."[34] Longinos had often been criticized for failure to record his observations or submit reports, so the lure of accumulated salary probably stimulated him to produce the long journal describing his travels in 1791 and 1792. He finally rejoined the other members of the royal expedition, but harmonious relations did not ensue.

31. Longinos to Revillagigedo, Hacienda de San Josef, 12 June 1793, Historia 463, AGN.

32. Revillagigedo to Longinos, Mexico, Historia 462, AGN.

33. Longinos to Revillagigedo, Compostela, 6 November 1793 Historia 460, AGN. Revillagigedo to Longinos, Mexico, 7 December 1793, Historia 460, AGN.

34. Revillagigedo to Longinos, Mexico, 22 January 1794, Historia 460, AGN.

10

The Botanical Garden
and Expeditions to the South

THE OPENING exercises held at the Botanical Garden of Mexico in May 1791 had left Arcadio Pineda and Luis Neé unimpressed. Pineda commented afterwards that the lecture room was inadequate and that the garden needed considerable work. To excuse the garden's substandard condition, Cervantes told the Malaspina group that for several years he had tried unsuccessfully to convince the crown that the Potrero of Atlampa was unsuitable for the garden. Although his complaints had previously fallen upon unsympathetic ears, Cervantes held new hope in the support offered by head gardener Jacinto López.[1] Through López's recommendation, several new sites were proposed, including the gardens of the half-completed palace at Chapultepec, but none seemed to meet all the requirements.[2]

Finally Revillagigedo presented a suitable plan proposing the use of a small garden attached to his official residence in the Royal Palace on the Zócalo. The gallery or arcade along one side could be used for a lecture room and the staff could live in inexpensive houses in the vicinity. Small plants could be grown in the garden for the use of students and for public enjoyment, while larger ones could be grown at Chapultepec and brought in as needed.[3] Cervantes and López both approved of the plan, and Cervantes commented that the garden of the palace would

1. Diario de Arcadio Pineda, MS 562, AMN. López, who had arrived from Spain in 1790, had formerly been employed at the Real Jardín Botánico in Madrid for fourteen years and was considered an expert in soil fertility.
2. Rickett, "Royal Botanical Expedition," p. 16.
3. Plan del Virrey, Historia 462, AGN.

hold about one thousand species, enough for class use, and that the students could easily visit the Chapultepec garden when necessary.[4]

Cervantes requested that the soil, which was "pure gravel and prejudicial to almost all plants," be excavated to a depth of one yard and be replaced with soil selected by López in Tlaspana. The order for removal was dated 28 September 1791, and the actual moving was done from the third to the eighth of October. The seven weeks that followed were used to make necessary alterations. The job of bringing in 6,000 loads of soil, 7,500 bricks, 12 cartloads of lime, 200 loads of sand, and enough tiles to recover the walls was done under the direction of the captain of engineers, Manuel Agustín Mascaro, at a cost of 1,556 pesos. They planted *cacaloxochitls* (a kind of plumeria), walnuts, avocados, chestnuts, figs, apricots, oranges, and pears.[5]

The Royal Botanical Garden of Mexico had at last found a permanent home and was destined to remain there until the institution ceased to exist some time after 1824.[6] Carlos IV somewhat illogically prohibited the use of the Chapultepec grounds for a botanical garden in April 1792, but fortunately did not specifically mention the garden of the royal palace. The abandoned Potrero of Atlampa was designated as the site of a new cigar factory.[7]

Sessé and Castillo returned to the capital in the spring of 1792 after completing their explorations of western and northern Mexico.[8] They examined the new sites and were pleased with the improvements. Because Longinos and Sensevé were still in California and Moziño was serving with Bodega y Quadra in Nootka, they would not see the new garden until the following year.[9] Sessé liked the small planted area in the royal palace and made several suggestions for enlarging it. Although this became the official Royal Botanical Garden of Mexico, in actuality it was never appreciably enlarged.[10]

4. Rickett, "Royal Botanical Expedition," p. 16.

5. Ibid., pp. 17, 18, 55, 56.

6. Mexico completed its Wars of Independence from Spain during the years 1821–22 and for a time the status of the Botanical Garden was doubtful. Vicente Cervantes died in Mexico in 1829.

7. Antonio Porlier to Revillagigedo, Aranjuez, 28 April 1792, Historia 462, AGN; Rickett, "Royal Botanical Expedition," p. 18.

8. Sessé returned to the capital too late to confer with members of the Malaspina expedition.

9. None of these members of the expedition would reach Mexico City until March or April 1793.

10. Plans for Chapultepec were abandoned although occasional plantings were made at the site.

While in the capital, Sessé spent the majority of his time preparing items for shipment to Spain. These were in part the result of his expedition to Sinaloa and northward along the west coast to the Yaqui River. Sessé was particularly proud of a new method discovered by a native Indian for preserving dissected birds. This discovery was crucial for the expedition since many birds had been destroyed enroute to Madrid. Sessé reported that Cristobal Quintana left Mexico City on 15 March with ten boxes of live plants for the Botanical Garden and two birds for the Royal Museum which had been "prepared by Mateo Sánchez, 'an Indian of singular dexterity and inestimable value for restoration and conservation, in which branch Ornithologists have worked unproductively.' "[11] The ingenuity of this man had eliminated the inconvenience of disjointing the feathers and, by removing the skin from the bird and mounting it over a wooden and waxed form that had been treated with cupric acetate and other poisons, prevented its being eaten by insects. The artificial bodies were of the same colors as the feathers so as not to leave an obvious mark should some of the feathers come out in the handling.

To begin the operation Sánchez would make a wooden shell of the same dimensions as the bird to be mounted and cover it with the wax preparation. He would then patiently replace the feathers one by one in the same order as they had occurred in nature. The wings were kept separate and attached in their entirety, being hooked together with pins. "Their joints are filled with this same wax in order to prevent the entrance of moths in this only place where the skin is preserved. The bill and the cranium are stuffed and secured by means of the same liquified wax, and the feet are accommodated with wires in the same manner employed by other Naturalist-Taxidermists."[12]

So that members of the court could realize how ingenious was Sánchez' handiwork, Sessé suggested that they compare his specimens to illustrations in Buffon's *Natural History*. Though the feathers were less flexible than in nature, they would last longer and maintain their specific characteristics, which, after all, was the principal reason why museums spent so much money in acquiring and conserving them. At first, because Sessé was out of the capital, Sánchez was somewhat careless in omitting the whiskers and other trifles that he thought made little difference in appearance but that in reality were important signs by

11. Sessé to Pedro de Acuña y Malvar, Mexico, 28 March 1793, 4ᵃ división, legajo no. 2, ARJB.
12. Ibid.

which the naturalist could distinguish the various genera within a class. When Sessé returned, he warned Sánchez that "many times the minutest detail consists of the essential part for recognition," so from then on he worked "with an exactitude capable of the admiration of the most scrupulous who would compare his pieces with the natural ones."

To prove the soundness of this new method, for one year Sessé neglected the first birds tested. Even without care they suffered no damage, while "those that José Longinos dissected were victims of moths in a few months, even though they were left with a friend in charge of their care." It was not difficult to imagine, he wrote, how long these birds might last considering that wood formed the body and the feathers were entombed in wax. Of course they could be attacked by moths in the same manner as writing quills if they remained a long time without being handled, but this could be avoided with a simple cleaning and exposure to the air every fifteen days. The worst that could happen would be a little picking at the feathers, but they would not be stripped like those that had been conserved in museums.[13]

Sánchez also had the ability to replace with the same perfection any other bird prepared previously that might be falling apart. For this reason, Sessé warned that the unfastened feathers should always be kept safe, because from an example or drawing as a model, he could make a new one. Sánchez demonstrated this with the yellow-headed parrot whose feathers were collected from the corner of the repository of Viceroy Florez, where they had been thrown by servants after the bird's unexpected death.[14] Sánchez could also imitate in wax any object of natural history, so the director decided to keep him employed in this activity when there were no more birds to prepare. Because of his usefulness, Sessé paid Sánchez one peso daily out of his own pocket for the maintenance of his family and continued to do so until he could get royal support for this talented person. Sessé actually hoped to get Sánchez transferred to Madrid where he could repair all decaying birds and mount those remitted from the field. If scientists had to send only the skins, the major expense—"that of conducting them in voluminous form exposed to the risks of the road and devouring moths"—would be saved.

Sessé explained that the drawings, herbarium, and descriptions of the last excursion did not accompany the letter because they had not been

13. Ibid.
14. Viceroy Manuel Florez was replaced by Revillagigedo in 1789.

coordinated nor had duplicates been made. Moziño and Echeverría were still on tour with Bodega y Quadra so could not help. Sessé thought it would be impossible to arrange this collection until the coming winter because of having to continue the explorations of that year.

Moziño returned from Nootka in February 1793, but did not start to work at the botanical garden until early April. He needed this time to arrange his notes and descriptions and write his *Noticias de Nutka*. Moziño continued with the expedition despite the royal order of 1791, which had discharged him. In April Sessé wrote Revillagigedo of his plans for Moziño and the others to continue exploring. One division formed by Castillo, Moziño, and Vicente de la Cerda would examine the Mixteca and the coast of Tabasco. Sessé, with Echeverría and Villar, would go to the Huasteca and the Province of Santander if the season permitted. In order to cover the extraordinary expenses of the trips, Sessé asked that two thousand of the six thousand pesos consigned by the king for this purpose be delivered to him together with two passports and the corresponding certifications from the royal treasury so that their salaries would be covered by the administration of Tabasco as had been done in Mexico.[15]

In addition to justifying the somewhat anomalous position held by Moziño, Sessé now found it necessary to plead on behalf of Villar, Antonio Pineda's former scribe who had left the Malaspina expedition. A native of Camprobín in the region of La Rioja, Spain, Villar had stayed in Mexico because of poor health. He had worked on the staff of the viceroyalty and "one year after submitting his application," left to travel with Sessé's group.[16]

Even in his unofficial capacity, Villar had not only helped members of the expedition extend their descriptions, but had also prepared many of the animals that were collected. A portion of these had already been submitted to the crown for display in the Royal Museum, and many others remained to be mounted for the same purpose. Villar had impressed Cervantes and Moziño both with his ability in managing the scalpel and with his scientific talent in all branches of zoology. For this reason he could work on any animal presented, prepare it with precision and describe it with exactitude.[17]

15. Sessé to Revillagigedo, Mexico, 9 April 1793, Historia 460, AGN.
16. José Moziño and Vicente Cervantes to El Rey, Mexico, 19 June 1795. Flora Española—1795, AMCN.
17. Ibid.

While the proposed expeditions were in the planning stage, Castillo again became seriously ill with "symptoms of scurvy" and could not travel. Longinos, of course, was many miles away and Sensevé could perform only the mechanical aspects of dissection. Sessé renewed his efforts to retain Moziño because he found himself "absolutely alone for the observations of this final year," which were to cover the fertile coasts of Tehuantepec and Tabasco and the provinces of La Mixteca, La Huasteca, and New Santander. "At the pain of omitting some of these worthwhile provinces" and "having to lose the precious season of spring and part of the summer," he could await the recovery of Castillo and the doubtful return of Longinos, but he felt that the loss of Moziño would prevent completion of work already begun and result in a costly waste of the king's generosity.[18]

Sessé reiterated Moziño's contributions on previous excursions and particularly his excellent report on the voyage to Nootka that had been sent to the viceroy on 20 April 1793. Upon completion of this lengthy treatise, Moziño had immediately set out again with artist Cerda to examine the Sierra de Papalotipac and Mixteca as far south as the border of Guatemala. For all the reasons Sessé had given and also because Moziño was his most knowledgeable and useful assistant and "his separation would be a bad example for the students of botany who would see this able professor abandoned with no reward for his ability," the director begged the viceroy to find some way to keep Moziño on the payroll.

Despite this final plea, Sessé's petition was again turned down because of the viceroy's inability to reverse the royal order. The situation, however, was altered by Castillo's death on 26 July 1793. This Aragonese scientist had suffered from one illness or another since the beginning of his duty in Mexico. Sessé had previously thought that Castillo had symptoms of scurvy, but Cervantes diagnosed his death as resulting from an obstruction of the pylorus.[19] In his will Castillo left the sum of 4,000 pesos for the printing and engraving of *Flora mexicana,* the great work accomplished by the members of the expedition.[20] Sessé requested that notice of Castillo's death be placed in the *Gaceta de México.* The members of the expedition decided to honor their comrade

18. Sessé to Revillagigedo, Mexico, 9 May 1793, Historia 527, AGN.
19. Vicente Cervantes, "Discurso pronunciado en el Real Jardín Botánico."
20. Testamento de Juan Diego del Castillo, Historia 464, AGN.

by naming the valuable *árbol de hule,* or rubber tree, after him; Cervantes chose the name *Castilla elástica.*[21]

Castillo's death meant that Moziño could now apply for the vacant position, and on 31 July 1793, he sent his application to Revillagigedo from Córdoba.[22] He was provisionally appointed to the expedition on 24 October 1793, at half the salary paid to Castillo. The viceroy requested approval from Carlos IV at the end of October 1793, and received it almost one year later on 16 September 1794.[23]

Prior to receiving his official status, Moziño had been sent by Revillagigedo in September 1793 to report on the eruption of the volcano near San Andrés de Tuxtla. This volcano, dormant for many years, had suddenly awakened and erupted violently on 2 May, 22 May, 28 June, and 26 August 1793. The eruptions caused considerable panic in the vicinity and the noise was so great that citizens of Veracruz, two hundred miles away, believed that the English were attacking. Moziño wrote a description of the volcano from the nearby town of San Andrés de Tuxtla after having made two trips to the edge of the crater. His report to Revillagigedo demonstrated both the courage and scientific curiosity of this thirty-six year old Mexican scientist.[24] His companions, Echeverría, who sketched the erupting volcano, and Villar, also visited the crater. Moziño described the Indians' reaction to the eruption of the volcano and their feelings toward him—a scientist who, according to their belief, had come to placate the spirit of the volcano.

As common people always see all the extraordinary phenomena of nature as a supernatural effect of the Divine Indignation, it is not strange that these inhabitants were caught up in a panic of terror that impelled them to abandon their homeland and even their possessions. Some of them did just that, but were for-

21. Cervantes, "Discurso," p. 2, commented: "This rare and new product of the vegetable kingdom, not so much because of its morphology as because of the copious amount of the substance that the modern Mexicans call [H]ule [latex or caoutchouc] and Europeans call *Goma* and *Resina elástica* that it secretes, gives me sufficient cause to describe it more fully. . . . The ancient Mexicans called it *Holguahuitl* (Hernández, edit. Roman. p. 50, *Matritens,* vol. 2, p. 336)." A short time later Longinos attacked Cervantes by means of the *Gaceta de Mexico* (5 November 1794) saying that the name *Castilla* was contrary to good botanical practice and that it should have been *Castella.*

22. José Moziño to Revillagigedo, Cordoba, 31 July 1793, Historia 464, AGN.

23. Order of the viceroy, 24 October 1793, Mexico, Historia 464, AGN. Revillagigedo to Carlos IV, Mexico, 30 October 1793, Flora Española—1793, AMCN. Royal Order of 16 September 1794, Historia 462, AGN.

24. Moziño to Revillagigedo, San Andrés de Tuxtla, 27 November 1793, Historia 558, AGN.

tunate in that these were afterwards returned to them by the zealous Magistrate who governs them. They were persuaded that I had come to put out the volcano, and did not cease to see me as some kind of Deity capable of dominating the fire with sovereignty or at least conquering its voracity with ingenuity.[25]

The Indians wanted to accompany Moziño on his first journey. He saw their tremendous fear, especially when they heard the horrible bellowing roar of the volcano, but he was able to comfort them. They became convinced they were immortal at his side and never deserted him. Their faith proved very helpful to Moziño because he often needed a hand when the effort of the climb took his breath away. "They, with their bodies, formed a handrail by which I was ultimately able to overcome the difficulties which otherwise would have been impossible for a man who was convalescing in Veracruz from a recent attack of fever." As they neared the blaze, Moziño watched the continuous motions the Indians made with some crucifixes that they suddenly took out of secret hiding places in their shirts. They all gave thanks to God for their safe arrival at the edge of the crater. The bottle that Moziño carried with a written account of their visit enclosed was a new kind of mystery for the Indians. Some believed it would serve as a barrier to contain the impetus of the flames during the next eruption, while others began to suspect that it was a "magic letter carrier" by which Moziño was informing the king of the unhappy state in which he had found the local pueblos.

While Moziño was in San Andrés he at last received his provisional appointment to the Royal Scientific Expedition as a result of Castillo's death. The Mexican botanist thanked the viceroy for finally being allowed to work officially for the King of Spain.[26] After completing their reconnaissance of the volcano of Tuxtla, Moziño, Echeverría, and Villar left to explore the territory near Veracruz. On 22 February 1794, Moziño sent a box containing collections of the previous year. The catalogue accompanying the box listed the contents as "30 birds, 15 bottles of *resina elástica,* various volcanic lavas, a package of dried plants and an

25. "Descripción del Volcán de Tuxtla por D. José Mariano Moziño, Botánico de la Expedición de Nueva España, Año de 1793," Historia 558, AGN. Another copy "Descripción de los reconocimientos hechos del Volcán de Tuxtla en el Reyno de Nueva España por el Naturalista Don Juan [sic] Mosiño—Año de 1793," MS 291, AMN. Also published by Alberto M. Carreño in *Noticias de Nutka,* pp. 104–17.

26. Moziño to Revillagigedo, San Andrés de Tuxtla, 16 November 1793, Historia 464, AGN.

American porcupine."[27] Sessé later added a sample of asphalt that Mo-ziño had left off the list and described it as "Malta, or Pisasfalto, a kind of mineral known as Chapopte, which is found in abundance on a mountain near Acayucán."[28]

In April, Sessé wrote to Revillagigedo that Moziño had ten boxes of plants in Veracruz containing "the most valuable of that coast such as *Caoba, Gateado, Cedro Fino, Bálsamo del Perú, Bálsamo de María, Pimienta de Tabasco,* and Cardamom or *Gengibre,* which, not having seen their flowers, he could not designate scientifically." Later in the spring and early summer of 1794, Moziño returned to San Andrés de Tuxtla and from this town informed the viceroy of another shipment of birds and animals. This time the items included "1 squirrel, 1 titmouse, 3 parrots, 1 toucan, 2 trogons [quetzals], 2 martins, 3 ducks, 3 pelicans, 3 herons, 1 jacana, 1 sparrow, 1 whippoorwill."

Sessé had remained in the capital during this time to recover from ill-nesses incurred on his previous explorations. He was also depressed when he reminded himself that the allotted six years for the Royal Scientific Expedition would expire in June 1794. Knowing the great expanse of territory still to be explored, Sessé petitioned the crown for an extension of time. A duplicate plea was sent to Pedro de Acuña in Madrid on 28 March and to Revillagigedo on 29 March 1794. He pointed out that the expedition had covered a tremendous area, but that "the repeated infirmities" suffered by all, Castillo's death, and Moziño's separation at a time when he could have accompanied Castillo to Guatemala had prevented the examination of the southern part of the continent. They had plans to cover the Guatemalan region in the spring.[29]

Sessé explained to the Spanish minister and the viceroy that certain inconveniences, in addition to the continued separations that had been necessary in order to examine the vast extension of more than 3,500 leagues, not including the voyage by sea to Nootka, had not allowed the members of the expedition sufficient time for coordinating and arranging the observations that each had made during the previous three years. The same reasons had prevented the artists from concluding the many drawings of rare and unknown objects that they had seen. Sessé was certain the materials gathered by the expedition formed a flora as

27. Moziño to Revillagigedo, Veracruz, 22 February 1794, Historia 460, AGN.
28. Sessé to Revillagigedo, Mexico, 3 April 1794, Historia 460, AGN.
29. Sessé to Acuña, Mexico, 28 March 1794, Flora Española—1794, AMCN; Sessé to Revillagigedo, Mexico, 29 March 1794, Historia 460, AGN.

rich as that of any other kingdom; and a fauna, which, although not being as abundant in animals, had provided a knowledge of many new species, particularly in the class of birds.

Sessé believed their work would be much more complete and useful if they could examine not only Guatemala but the Islands of Cuba, Santo Domingo, and Puerto Rico, which were "abundant in the more exquisite balsams and other products of great interest in Commerce and Medicine." A similar expedition at another time or under other professors lacking their knowledge and experience would demand more time and expense than they would spend in the two years Sessé thought sufficient for the explorations. He would send Longinos, Moziño, and one of the artists to Guatemala and go himself with the rest of the expedition to the islands.

The director also brought up the need for extending the facilities of the botanical garden in Mexico. During the absence of the others, Cervantes could direct the planting of the garden at Chapultepec, should the king approve it, and with the advantages and excellent conditions that this terrain offered at low cost, the plants of the various climates throughout America could be cultivated for demonstrations in botany courses. The garden at the Royal Palace, which presently contained sufficient plants for this purpose, gave the capital a most beautiful display in its center and "a spectacle that could be seen from its principal plaza if it could be enlarged."[30]

Carlos IV approved the two-year extension on 15 September 1794, although Sessé was not notified until the spring of 1795. The crown ordered that the extension be put into effect immediately and that additional proposals be carried out with the greatest economy. If possible, the expedition was to be completed in less time than the allotted two years.[31] At last receiving official authorization, Sessé began to formulate plans for the other members of the group.

Longinos, in his usual spirit of non-cooperation, informed the director that his term of service had terminated with the completion of the six years and, since he had not been consulted, he was not bound to the additional time. Sessé appealed to the new viceroy, Miguel de la Grúa Talamanca, Marqués de Branciforte (1794–98), and was eventually given a royal order obligating Longinos to remain with the expedi-

30. Ibid.

31. "Extracto de communicaciones sobre la expedición botánica de Nueva España," Flora Española—1794, AMCN.

tion.[32] While awaiting official word, Sessé proposed that Longinos accompany Moziño and Cerda on the excursion to Guatemala. Upon learning of this arrangement, Moziño, who had always complied with the wishes of the director, wrote to Viceroy Branciforte pleading that "he be released from this misfortune." He stated that even though he had never traveled with Longinos, neither he nor anyone else had ever been able to get along with him and that "even Sensevé had been obliged to leave him on their journey to California and return by himself, almost begging his way."[33] Longinos, who never referred to Moziño as anything but a student, was actually no more eager to accompany Moziño than the latter was to have him. Therefore, when Moziño left with the portion of the expedition destined for Guatemala in June 1795, Longinos remained in the capital.

A royal order of 29 June 1795 required that Longinos join Moziño and Cerda, and for this reason the naturalist finally left Mexico City in July 1795.[34] A later report, written in Guatemala in 1797, described Longinos as fulfilling his obligations in Mexico when "an order of the Court arrived stating that he should go to Guatemala to inspect its coasts with a new expedition." It said that Longinos had first examined the vicinities of the river Coatzacoalcos on the coast from the north. Afterwards he "journeyed up the river for fifteen days until he arrived at the border of this kingdom."[35] Longinos described the river as delightful and so entirely deserted that in those fifteen days he had seen no rancho nor a single person despite the river's great commercial advantage in transporting products to Veracruz. A few days after leaving the river he entered the provinces of Soconusco, continued on through San Antonio Suchitepeques and finally to Escuintla. He examined the shoreline, a continuation of the Costa del Sur and into which a number of rivers flowed, before leaving for the Guatemalan capital to arrange his works.

In a letter to Viceroy Branciforte, Longinos mentioned that he saw Moziño and "ordered" him to take the road through the mountains so

32. Sessé to Branciforte, Mexico, 15 April 1795, Historia 464, AGN.

33. Moziño to Branciforte, Mexico, 15 April 1795, Historia 464, AGN, quoted in Rickett, "Royal Botanical Expedition," p. 34.

34. Ibid. Branciforte reported to Eugenio Llaguno (Mexico, 30 June 1795, no. 152, Flora Española—1795, AMCN) that Longinos Martínez had departed with José Moziño and Vicente de la Cerda.

35. "Noticia del establecimiento del Museo de esta Capital de la Nueva Guatemala . . . ," legajo no. 704, AGI.

they could embrace more territory in their excursions.[36] This was probably in Tehuantepec, where Moziño had been collecting plants for about three months. Longinos arrived in Guatemala City in the summer of 1796 and proceeded to establish a Museum of Natural History under the sponsorship of Jacobo de Villa Urrutia, director of the Sociedad Económica de Amigos del Pais. Reports about the museum were highly complimentary to Longinos and it appeared that his efforts had finally been expended upon an appreciative audience.[37] The museum plan followed much the same pattern as the one he had established in Mexico. The principal salon contained three divisions of columns, arches, and cornices "forming a beautiful view in perspective" and the three rooms containing thirty-six open shelves appeared to be just one. The first division, designed for the animal kingdom, was "already adorned with more than 50 birds and as many fish, quadrupeds, butterflies, serpents, conches, snails, starfish, sea urchins, and polyps." The majority of the animals had been prepared and embalmed by students.

The second section, designed for the vegetable kingdom, held various gums and resins, the inner bark of some trees that resembled laces and fabrics, barks used in dyeing, and some rare woods, seeds, roots, and other extraordinary plants, with herbarium, in which the students would complete the Flora of Guatemala. The third section "designed for the Mineral Kingdom is the most populated with varieties of Jasperite, Marble, Silice, Quartzes, Spars, Micas, Talc, Asbestos (Amianth), stones of color, Opals, Agates, Minerals of Gold, Silver, Copper, Iron, Lead, semi-metals like bismuth, antimony, arsenic, etc. Various species of concrete, petrifactions, volcanic products and some idols and curiosities of the Gentiles."

In addition to these three sections there was a spacious study room adjacent to the museum containing necessary equipment for students as well as two large portraits of Queen María Luisa and Carlos IV. Outside the building was a provisional botanical garden on some irrigated land belonging to the president of the Audiencia. Numerous trees, plants, and natural flowers lined the street where parrots, parakeets, and other tropical birds were frequent visitors. The opening of the museum on 9 December 1796, complete with orchestral music, was attended by Captain General José Domas y Valle, his wife and daughter, the arch-

36. Longinos to Marqués de Branciforte, Guatemala 3 June 1796, Historia 465, AGN.
37. John Tate Lanning, *The Eighteenth Century Enlightenment,* p. 162; "Noticia del establecimiento del Museo," Guatemala, legajo no. 704, AGI.

bishop, and other dignitaries of the realm. Two young men having recently received the bachelor's degree in philosophy from the University of San Carlos obligingly submitted to the academic questioning of two scholars. Moziño, putting aside his personal feelings about Longinos, "'courteously' showed his respect for the occasion by joining in the questioning."[38]

The presence of the Spanish expedition in America had definitely stimulated the study of botany in Guatemala. Longinos remained there for several years making collections, supervising the work of the museum, and giving public lessons in botany.[39] In 1803 he made a journey to Campeche in Yucatan and died there of tuberculosis without having again visited Mexico City. A letter was later received by the viceroy from Antonio González in Guatemala inquiring what should be done with the effects of the "decreased naturalist Josef Longinos Martínez," which had been left in his care.[40] Thus, the second original member of the Royal Scientific Expedition met his death in the New World, but without the honor given by his colleagues to the pharmacist Castillo. Sessé, never relenting in his campaign against Longinos, warned the director of the Royal Museum in Madrid in 1804 that twelve boxes of birds and minerals labeled for the museum and one earthen jar with two valuable plants for the Royal Garden belonging to the deceased Longinos had been sent on the frigate *La Rufina*. Because the items had arrived in Mexico after Sessé's departure, they might not have been determined accurately, and Sessé insisted that they be checked before they were placed in the museum.[41]

It is difficult to evaluate fairly Longinos' contribution because of the constant criticism offered by Sessé. His inability to get along with his colleagues may have been a more serious defect than lack of training. In a day when scientific classification was far from exact and even more particularly uncertain in the Americas, there were errors made by all members of the expedition. Longinos' observations about California's natural resources and Indian life in many instances provide a unique and valuable firsthand account. Despite his pursuit of an independent course in Guatemala, where he was honored and appreciated, he always con-

38. Lanning, *The Eighteenth Century Enlightenment*, p. 164. See also Robert J. Shafer, *The Economic Societies*, p. 303.

39. Nicolás León, *Biblioteca botánica-mexicana*, p. 328.

40. 3 April 1803, Historia 465, AGN.

41. Sessé to Josef Antonio Cavellero, San Lorenzo, 15 October 1804, Flora Española— 1804, AMCN.

sidered himself a member of the expedition and faithfully remitted his collections to Mexico City until his death in 1803.

Moziño, as previously mentioned, had departed for Guatemala with Cerda shortly before Longinos began his journey. They were also accompanied by Villar for whom Cervantes and Moziño had petitioned some kind of salary. The only payment that Villar had so far enjoyed was a sum that Sessé had saved from the expenses of the expedition, but even this small amount dried up because they were traveling in distant areas. Villar, "after six years of useful and constant service, and after exposing himself to the most evident dangers like those . . . of the Volcano of Tuxtla during its most violent eruptions" had no salary. Despite his poverty, he wanted to go with the expedition to Guatemala so Cervantes and Moziño entreated the king to send Villar "an endowment which he could use to cover his needs and allow him to dedicate himself entirely to the valuable career appropriate to his genius." In addition to all his other qualities, Villar knew Latin and French.[42] The petition was remitted to Carlos IV by Viceroy Branciforte on 30 June 1795,[43] and was turned down with the following comment: "Since the expedition is finishing its charge, it does not appear necessary to the Board to augment it with individuals not being professors."[44]

With immediate plans to support Villar from their own salaries, the group headed southward toward Puebla de los Angeles. From this city they requested a tent to protect themselves, and especially their books and collections, from the rain. Moziño explained that the country was without habitations, but Branciforte refused the request because the government had no tents to spare.[45] During September they explored the territory around Tehuacán, but returned to Puebla at the end of the month. In November they reached Oaxaca and Moziño visited his wife. At this time he renewed a previous offer to her of half his meager salary, and promised her a written contract.

42. Cervantes and Moziño to El Rey, Mexico, 19 June 1795. Flora Española—1795, AMCN.

43. Marqués de Branciforte to Eugenio de Llaguno, Mexico, 30 June 1795, no. 148, Flora Española—1795, AMCN.

44. Comunicaciones del Virrey, no. 148, 22 November 1795, Flora Española—1795, AMCN. The royal order that reached Moziño in Guatemala on 3 October 1796 stated that the king would grant Julian Villar no salary as a member of the expedition to Guatemala "because he would be of no practical use to it." (Flora Española—1796, AMCN).

45. Moziño to Branciforte, Puebla, 29 July 1795, Historia 465, AGN. Rickett, "Royal Botanical Expedition," p. 37.

Early in 1796 Moziño and his companions left the Valley of Oaxaca and crossed the mountains southward into the tropical territory near the Gulf of Tehuantepec. The scientists remained in this fertile collecting area for several months making extensive records of their botanical observations.[46] Sessé reported later that Moziño, because of his medical training, "impeded the propagation of the contagiousness of smallpox by the force of his work and industry in the Río de Coatzacoalcos." The epidemic, which "was close to infesting New Spain, had caused one thousand deaths in Tabasco."[47] Moving on toward Guatemala, Moziño sent a box of specimens from Chiapas to Cervantes in Mexico.[48] By mid-September they were in Guatemala City, where they rejoined Longinos and remained through the winter.[49] Moziño, Cerda, and Villar continued their travels in early spring and were in San Salvador in March 1797, when some violent earthquakes occurred, burying their few possessions in the ruins.[50] On 31 May they had reached León, Nicaragua, the southernmost area of exploration. This city became their headquarters for the next seven months.[51]

Early in 1798 the men returned to San Salvador and by May were again in Guatemala City. Here Moziño analyzed the drinking water and studied in depth the "cultivation and benefits of indigo, about which he wrote an elemental treatise that earned him the sovereign approval of His Majesty."[52] Upon reaching Chiapas, Moziño was detained by the captain general of Guatemala and the bishop of Chiapas. These two officials had obtained an order from the viceroy of New Spain, José Miguel de Azanza, that would allow Moziño to remain in Chiapas to cure "a loathsome leprosy which was very general in those countries and in others of America."[53] Moziño did not reach Mexico City until

46. José Moziño "Descripciones de los géneros de plantas de Nueva España," 4ª división, legajo no. 3, ARJB.

47. Expediente general de la expedición donde constan los sueldos de los empleados en ella, Aranjuez, 1804; Flora Española—1804, AMCN.

48. Moziño to Branciforte, Ciudad Real, 6 June 1796, quoted in Rickett, "Royal Botanical Expedition," p. 37.

49. McVaugh, *Botanical Results of the Sessé and Mociño Expedition*, p. 164; Communicación del Presidente del Real Audiencia de Guatemala, 3 October 1796, Flora Española—1796, AMCN.

50. Carreño, *Noticias de Nutka*, p. lxxi.

51. Rickett, "Royal Botanical Expedition," p. 37; McVaugh, *Botanical Results of the Sessé and Mociño Expedition*, p. 168.

52. Expediente general de la expedición, Aranjuez, 1804, Flora Española—1804, AMCN.

53. Ibid.; Carreño, *Noticias de Nutka*, p. lxxi.

February 1799, although Cerda had returned the previous December. No mention was made of Villar. He may have sought other employment upon receiving the king's disapproval of his salary.

Following his return to the capital, Moziño arranged his notes and collections and worked with Sessé on the organization and classification of materials. In addition, he resumed his interest in medicine and assisted "constantly in the observation room of the General Hospital of San Andrés de Mexico" to study the effects on patients of the medicinal herbs whose virtues he had discovered.[54] Moziño found time to lecture at the Botanical Garden for Cervantes and to write a number of articles concerning the medicinal plants and drug remedies of New Spain. He corresponded with Alejandro Ramírez, editor of the *Gazeta de Guatemala* about the effectiveness of smallpox vaccination and sent him a practical set of instructions for carrying out the procedure.[55] Moziño also edited and enlarged a Spanish version of John Brown's *Elements of Medicine* that was printed in Mexico in 1803.[56]

54. Expediente general de la expedición, Aranjuez, 1804, Flora Española—1804, AMCN.

55. Lanning, *The Eighteenth Century Enlightenment,* p. 246.

56. *Elementos de medicina del Dr. Juan Brown, secretario de la sociedad de antiquarios de escocia* (Amplificados por D. Joseph Mariano Moziño, profesor médico en esta capital y botánico de las reales expediciones facultativas de Nueva España), Mexico, 1803.

11

Expeditions to the West Indies

IN MAY 1795, Viceroy Branciforte of New Spain informed the crown that the portion of the Botanical Expedition destined to examine the Island of Cuba and some of the Windward Islands had departed for Havana early in the month aboard the frigate of the Royal Armada *Santa Agueda*. Because the royal order of 15 September 1794 had prolonged the expedition for two additional years, the viceroy had provided passports for Sessé, Sensevé, and the artist Echeverría.[1]

Arriving in Havana in July 1795, Sessé and his companions immediately encountered difficulties in obtaining their salaries because the resident treasury officer had not yet received official authorization. Nevertheless, the expedition executed its commission in Cuba through the support of Sessé's many friends there, but they could not arrange for transportation to Santo Domingo and Puerto Rico without funds. For this reason Sessé asked that corresponding orders be communicated to the minister of the hacienda for all three islands so that members of the expedition could be paid and obtain the servants and equipment needed to carry out their duties.[2]

Diego de Gardoqui, Spanish minister of state, informed Secretary of Grace and Justice Eugenio Llaguno that he had received a letter from the *visitador general intendente* of the island of Cuba, Joseph Pablo Valiente, asking for authorization to pay the salaries.[3] Gardoqui, after

---

1. Branciforte to Eugenio de Llaguno, Mexico, 29 May 1795, Flora Española—1795, AMCN.
2. Sessé to Llaguno, Havana, 10 July 1795, Flora Española—1795, AMCN.
3. Gardoqui to Llaguno, San Ildefonso, 20 August 1795, Flora Española—1795, AMCN.

verifying the names of the members of the expedition,[4] wrote to the viceroy of New Spain ordering him in turn to issue instructions to the *intendente* of Havana to "pay the salaries and provide the assistance necessary for the good success of the commission."[5] Thus, by December 1795, the salary question was settled, but since Echeverría was sick with dysentery and the rainy season had begun, they could not take full advantage of their orders to explore the island.[6]

Sessé asked Llaguno for permission to examine the island of Santo Domingo (Hispaniola) as provided in the 15 September 1794 royal order, even though the island had been ceded to France as a result of the Treaty of Basel signed on 22 July. He believed that permission from the French government would be easy to obtain.[7] While awaiting a decision, the expeditionaries sailed for Puerto Rico on the frigate *Gloria* and began exploring that island in early April 1796. They worked until October and then received word that there were extreme problems in Santo Domingo because the Negroes were in revolt throughout the island. They decided to stay in Puerto Rico and work on their collections until they could get passage to Santiago de Cuba.[8]

At the beginning of October 1796, when the first notice of the uprising in Santo Domingo had arrived in Puerto Rico, Sessé decided they should reexamine the most elevated portion of the sierra of that island. When they had previously been in the foothills, they were unable to climb to the highest elevations because of bad weather and a lack of servants, not because the area was inaccessible.[9] By March they had completed their task and were finally ready to embark for some port of Cuba. Since so much time had passed, they were well beyond the time allowed by the royal order. The delay, of course, was beyond their control, and Sessé hoped that the crown would not be unhappy at "whatever small prolongation might be necessary for the completion of the investigations remaining in his charge."

While in Puerto Rico, Sessé, Sensevé, and Echeverría had collected,

4. Gardoqui to Ministerio de Hacienda, San Ildefonso, 9 September 1795, Flora Española—1795, AMCN.

5. Gardoqui to the viceroy, San Lorenzo, 15 November 1795, Flora Española—1795, AMCN.

6. Sessé to Llaguno, Havana, 15 October 1795, Flora Española—1795, AMCN.

7. Spain had ceded her portion of the island to France, but actual transfer of possession never took place because of the continuing war in Europe.

8. Sessé to Llaguno, Puerto Rico, 13 March 1797, Flora Española—1797, AMCN.

9. Ibid.

described, and drawn "with the greatest perfection possible nearly three hundred plants unknown in Europe." Among these was a species of laurel that Sessé was sending to Madrid for analysis to determine what advantages were offered by its similarity to the nutmeg—the name by which the islanders called it. Even the "most learned" believed it to be a variety of the legitimate nutmeg and it was used for the same purposes. Sessé put some little live laurel trees and other useful plants in boxes to be remitted at a more opportune occasion.[10]

Later in the same month Sessé wrote that they had secured passage to Cuba on the American ship *Bostonea* that would set sail after unloading its cargo. He planned to leave a duplicate of the manuscripts and herbarium collected on that island with the secretary of the governor of Puerto Rico in case they were exposed to the violence of some corsair not respecting the neutral flag. The director believed they could complete their work in Cuba by the end of August and would then return to Mexico. The expeditionaries were prepared to leave on 17 April 1797, but an English squadron blockading the port prevented their sailing.[11] They were finally taken on board another American ship, the *McGilvra,* whose captain, Florence Driscoll, charged them two hundred dollars for their passage.[12] They left Puerto Rico on 12 May and arrived in Havana on 10 June 1797.

Once again in Havana, Sessé found new justification for remaining longer than the time allotted by the extension. In a letter of 20 June he explained to the crown that a botanical expedition had arrived in that city under the direction of the Conde de Mopox y Jaruco,[13] and it appeared convenient for Sessé to compare his ideas "with those of the Professors who composed it, in order by this medium to make an examination of the Island with more certainty and economy for the public treasury." Sessé further reported that at their first conference held on 12 June, they had resolved to leave together to explore the western part of the island. He and the Conde de Mopox decided to wait until their re-

10. Ibid.

11. Sessé to Llaguno, Puerto Rico, 27 March 1797, and Havana, 20 June 1797, *Flora Española*—1797, AMCN.

12. Receipt given by Captain Driscoll of the American ship *McGilvra* to "Dn Martin Sessé Derector of the Expedison of the Botinest Company in the Windward Islands from the Cort of Spain" (Havana, 30 June 1797, Historia 460, AGN).

13. Born Joaquín de Santa Cruz y Cárdenas on 10 September 1769 in Havana, third possessor of the Countship of Santa Cruz de Mopox and San Juan de Jaruco, Knight of the Military Order of Calatrava, and *Gentil Hombre de Cámara de Su Majestad con Entrada,* the count died in Havana at the age of thirty-eight.

turn from the initial trek to negotiate the manner by which they would examine the rest of the island and coordinate the observations and findings acquired in Puerto Rico and in other analogous climates. In this way they would incur fewer costs in the conclusion of their important work.[14]

In the meantime Carlos IV, on 20 June 1797, ordered the viceroy of New Spain to have the members of the expedition return to Spain at once since the two years were up.[15] Another copy of the order was sent directly to Sessé in Havana to prevent further delay. In view of Sessé's request of 20 June to compare notes with the Conde de Mopox y Jaruco, Secretary Llaguno decided to await the report on the rest of the island before reissuing the order to return.[16] Unaware of this decision, Viceroy Branciforte wrote to Sessé at the end of October 1797, insisting that he arrange his works at once in preparation for an almost immediate departure for Spain.[17]

Finally on the twenty-second of December 1797, Sessé reported that he was awaiting a brigantine of war, which was scheduled to depart in the middle of January for Veracruz, and that he would join in Mexico the members of the expedition who had gone to Guatemala. Because Moziño and Cerda were not expected to arrive from Guatemala until March, the entire expedition would not be able to leave for Spain until April.[18] To complete the Cuban project, Sessé had made it possible for José Estévez, an enterprising pupil assigned to him by the Cuban royal consulate, to go with the Conde de Mopox. Estévez, a talented and hard-working young man, had accompanied Sessé to Puerto Rico in order to study botany and had "successfully fulfilled whatever charge this science demanded."[19]

Sessé also consented (although without informing the viceroy) to let his best artist go, with an increase in salary, on the count's expedition.

14. Sessé to Llaguno, Havana, 20 June 1797, Flora Española—1797, AMCN.

15. Royal order to the viceroy of New Spain, Aranjuez, 20 June 1797, Flora Española—1797, AMCN.

16. Note on the letter from Sessé to Llaguno (20 June 1797), Flora Española—1797, AMCN.

17. Branciforte to Sessé, Orizaba, 30 October 1797, Flora Española—1797, AMCN.

18. Sessé to Llaguno, Havana, 22 December 1797, Flora Española—1797, AMCN. Sensevé had sailed the previous September on the brigantine *San Carlos* and had landed in Veracruz on 25 September; he arrived in Mexico City on 5 October ("Expediente sobre abono de sueldos para las caxas generales de Dn. Jaime Sensevé," Historia 461, AGN).

19. Sessé to Llaguno, Havana, 22 December 1797, Flora Española—1797, AMCN.

He made Echeverría promise, however, that at the conclusion of the trip he would return to Spain to complete the work already begun.[20] In a later letter Sessé spoke of having been "deserted" by Echeverría,[21] although the two years were up and the artist was technically free.

It was clear to Sessé that with the help of Estévez and Echeverría, both well versed on American plants and on those already described by his expedition, Baltasar Boldó, chief botanist of the expedition of the Conde de Mopox,[22] could in a very short time describe all of Cuba's rare and unknown plants. Since the expedition had always been occupied with new works, it had so far been impossible to conclude or duplicate the indispensable drawings that Cerda was still working on in Mexico and that Echeverría would finish in Spain after his service with the Conde de Mopox. Sessé hoped that Llaguno would issue some kind of order for their completion. Sessé was also worried that unless duplicates of everything were made before shipment, they might "lose the major part of their work by some accident of the sea."[23]

In a final report of 25 January 1798, Sessé stated that, weather permitting, he would leave the following day with the post of Veracruz to recover all the works that remained in Mexico and to arrange the business of the garden so they could embark for Spain. Sessé had left in Havana some valuable trees and a duplicate of the herbarium, which the expedition had collected in Cuba and Puerto Rico, in the care of Mariano Espinosa, professor of surgery and correspondent of the Botanical Garden of Madrid. Espinosa was to send them on to Spain in the proper season. Sessé commended this "hardworking correspondent who, by the force of his zeal" had augmented considerably the plants of the garden by making excursions at his own expense, suffering setbacks in his profession and continually incurring expenses in the collection of

20. Ibid.

21. Sessé to Miguel José de Aranza, Mexico, 20 August 1798, Historia 461, AGN. In another, Sessé stated that Echeverría had put off finishing his sketches (Sessé to Branciforte, 18 November 1798, Mexico, Historia 465, AGN).

22. Boldó, a native of Zaragoza, practiced medicine in that city and in 1793 was named *médico de número* of the army and later *protomédico de Rosellén*. Despite his success in medicine, Boldó's major interest lay in science, especially botany. He became a correspondent of the Jardín Botánico in Madrid and made collections of natural history in Catalonia and the Balearic Islands before his appointment to the Cuban expedition. See Francisco Barras y de Aragón, "Noticias y documentos de la expedición del Conde de Mopox," pp. 513–48.

23. Sessé to Llaguno, Havana, 22 December 1797, Flora Española—1797, AMCN.

seeds and live plants. Espinosa had frequently sent plants to Madrid during the previous six years, but had never been compensated for this important service.

Sessé outlined a plan by which shipments to Spain could be made in the seasons when the plants could best travel and be transplanted upon arrival. This plan included the rental of a house with a piece of irrigated land in one of the suburbs of Havana for three or four hundred pesos a year. He hoped that his request would be attended to because "only by this medium could one benefit in Spain from the fine woods, balsams and other plants that make up a great part of the treasures of the Americas, and which could be transported much more easily from that Island as much for its lesser distance as for its greater proportion of embarkation."[24]

On 17 June 1798, a summary of the expedition's activities since 1785 was prepared, presumably by a viceregal committee in New Spain. It indicated that even though all had worked hard for little pay, the expedition had drawn criticism because of the "pretensions" of some of the members.[25]

> The Board is persuaded that Sessé and [Gómez] Ortega have not had, nor will have, any interest other than the public benefit and the honor of the nation, but there is no lack of persons who believe the opposite, reflecting that the majority of the individuals of this Expedition, and even those of Perú, Asia and Santa Fé [de Bogotá] are relatives and *paniaguados,* [26] and that many of them have thought of no other thing but to augment their interests and those of their friends.
>
> Of this there are repeated proofs, and among these are, first, the order by the Minister of State in the past year that José Longinos be permitted to place a Museum of Natural History in Mexico,[27] where one has been located since 1790; second, that of Don Casimiro Ortega in recommending the merits and services of the Director of the Botanical Garden of Mexico, Don Vicente Cervantes, in order that he be conceded honors of *Farmacéutico de la Cámara,* and to Don Martín Sessé those of *Médico,* which petition pends the informing of the Viceroy; and finally [the pretension] that Don Martín Sessé makes by taking a house in

24. Sessé to Llaguno, Havana, 25 January 1798, Flora Española—1798, AMCN.

25. Comunicaciones del Virrey sobre la expedición de Nueva España, Flora Española—1789–1798, AMCN.

26. *Paniaguados,* derived from the expression of giving bread and water (*pan y agua*) to unemployed persons, was generally applied to persons receiving government salaries without actually working.

27. In reality, Longinos' petition was to establish a museum of natural history in Guatemala, not in Mexico.

Havana and establishing in it another Botanical Garden in the charge of Don Mariano Espinosa.

The report continued sarcastically to suggest that the crown would not only have a botanical garden in Mexico, but one in Havana, another one in the Canary Islands and Madrid, "and soon there will be a project to establish one in Cádiz, the Port of Santa María, Sevilla, Ecija, Córdova and other towns until there is one in the Court, in order to place in them and give salaries to many useless persons." It went on to stress that many thousands of pesos had been spent on the expedition without any tangible benefit having resulted from so many years' activity. Measures had to be taken "to cut abuses and avoid expenses to the Royal Treasury so that the Public could begin to enjoy those great benefits and utilities from them that were said would follow." [28]

A note was added on 9 September stating that the king wanted strict orders communicated to the governor of Havana requiring that those in charge of the expedition come to Spain at once. On 16 September 1798, a royal order was sent to the governor with instructions that he find transportation for Sessé and the others if they had not already left and that he provide the court with more information regarding the house proposed as a botanical depository. The major criticism of the expedition seemed to stem from its long delay in returning to Spain. On the same date a royal order was issued to the viceroy of New Spain that "without excuse nor protest of any kind, the Director Martín Sessé and other subjects employed in the examination of the Coasts of Guatemala and Islands of Barlovento return to Spain on the first occasion." [29] Sessé had left Cuba in March 1798, but was still unprepared to return to Spain.

It seems incongruous that at the same time that the crown was recalling Sessé's expedition, it was sending out another under the Conde de Mopox y Jaruco, particularly when the latter expedition appeared to have as a major purpose the botanical or scientific survey of Cuba. A closer examination of the documents clarifies this matter at once—the principal object of the count's expedition was military and included establishing fortifications on the bay of Guantánamo, building roads, and

28. Communcaiones del Virrey sobre la expedición de Nueva Espana, Flora Española—1785–98, AMCN.

29. Royal order to the governor of Havana, San Ildefonso, 16 September 1798, Flora Española—1798, AMCN.

constructing a canal along the Río de Güines upon which lumber could be transported to Havana for the building of ships.[30] With the count were various other individuals commissioned to work out plans for the island's defense and to survey the possibilities for settling uninhabited areas.[31] A member of the commission summarized the purpose as follows:

The fertility of the Island of Cuba and its advantageous situation in the center of the Gulf of Mexico are two qualities capable not only of aiding and fomenting the commerce of the Peninsula, but also of conserving the vast dominions of the Spanish Monarchy in this part of America. These have each day been called more to the attention of our august Sovereign and his wise Ministry . . . and with this object was commissioned the Sr. Conde de Mopox, Brigadier of the Royal Armies and Sub-Inspector General of the Troops of said Island.[32]

In his report covering the work of his commission, the count explained that he was originally designated on 2 August 1796 to go to Cuba to carry out the above-mentioned military objectives, but that afterwards it was deemed necessary for the commission to investigate various branches of natural history. There were named, at the count's orders and direction, appropriate persons capable of fulfilling this purpose.[33] The botanist Baltasar Boldó, because of his long association with the Royal Botanical Garden of Madrid, was recommended by Director Gómez Ortega to accompany the expedition to Cuba.[34] Artist and taxidermist José Guío, who had previously accompanied the Malaspina expedition in South America and Mexico, was chosen as a man of competence and wide experience.[35] Apparently these two men were the only members of this expedition specifically destined for the study of natural history.

Even though the twenty-eight-year-old Conde de Mopox had the

30. "Memoria del Conde de Mopox to Don Pedro Cevallos, Madrid," 26 June 1802, Museo Naval MS published in P. Barreiro, "Documentos relativos a la expedición del Conde de Mopox a la Isla de Cuba," pp. 5–19, hereinafter "Memoria del Conde de Mopox."

31. Juan Tirry Lacy to Juan de Lángara, San Lorenzo, 20 October 1798, MS 560, AMN.

32. "Descripción de la Bahía de Nipe por Don Agustín de Blondo y Zavala," Havana, 18 March 1799, MS 551, AMN.

33. "Memoria del Conde de Mopox," p. 5.

34. Correspondence of the director of the Botanical Garden, 5ª división, legajo no. 22, ARJB.

35. José Guío had left the Malaspina expedition in Mexico City because of illness and later returned to Spain on board the merchant vessel *Concepción*.

total support of the king, his expedition followed a sad but familiar pattern. In this case, however, the British, with whom Spain had been at war since 1796, were to blame for several mishaps. The count lamented:

> From the moment His Majesty saw fit to commission me for the Island of Cuba, it appeared that all conspired against the progress of my charges: the difficulties began plaguing me before my embarkation at La Coruña. The three principal subordinates whom the King destined to my commission . . . did not arrive to fulfill their voyage to America. . . . The mathematical instruments which the Sr. Principe de la Paz [Manuel Godoy] had sent from London and Paris for the verifications of plans, observations, and altitudes, also never arrived at the Island of Cuba, having been seized by the English. Thus, without subordinates, without instruments, without help, and with nothing more than earnest desires and many times uncertain resources, I disposed myself to undertake the enterprises with which I had been encharged by the Ministry, and the many more which were later added with approval of the Ministry of State—which charges I have the pleasure of having carried out completely in spite of all the obstacles of different kinds which were presented to me at each step. . . .[36]

The count spent the first three months with the major part of the expedition examining the vicinities of Guantánamo Bay. After selecting appropriate sites for military establishments he left his three engineers and several others to complete the mapping of the area.[37] Accompanied by Boldó, Guío, and the secretary of the commission, Nicolas Pérez Santa María, the count set out by land for the western part of the island, reviewing various military troops along the way. The group arrived in Havana in June 1797, and there came in contact with Sessé and his expedition.

Boldó asked that Sessé's student Estévez be added to the count's retinue as a botanical assistant and that Echeverría be hired to help Guío, who had to double as a naturalist and could not devote full time to drawing all the plants Boldó had gathered. For the count it was a fortunate break to find both of these men in a position to work for him.[38] Boldó and Guío spent the summer collecting in the immediate vicinity of Havana.[39] They were accompanied and assisted by Estévez, whose

36. "Memoria del Conde de Mopox," p. 6.
37. See "La descripción de la Bahía de Guantánamo por Don José Martínez y Orossa, Don Anastasio Arango, Don Agustín Blondo y Zavala y Don Eleuterio Bottino," Havana, 30 October 1798, MS 554, AMN.
38. "Memoria del Conde de Mopox," p. 7, 9.
39. "Dibujos de Plantas de la Ysla de Cuba hechos por Don José Guío y Sánchez, Dibujante Botánico de la Real Comisión de Guantánamo, que se encargó por el Exmo.

presence had in part been arranged by Sessé. They gathered numerous species of both new and already known plants and examined various animals. The scientists attempted to describe, classify, and sketch each species they collected.[40] Echeverría, who was originally employed to assist Guío, was first sent to the Bay of Jagua to draw maps under the direction of the engineers assigned to that project.[41] He later completed eighty-six drawings of birds and fish from Cuba in general.

In 1798, the Conde de Mopox planned an excursion along the northern coast from Cape San Antonio to Mariel. It would experience all of the obstacles continually faced by the commission. Nevertheless, "for its assured success," the count had named as leader Brigadier Marqués de Casa-Calvo who had recently joined the commission for that purpose. Others in the company were Captain Jorge de la Torre, Antonio López Gómez, Boldó, Estévez, and Guío. They were to visit the western part of the island with the first three working up maps of Bahia-honda, Cabañas, and all the other nearby ports and anchorages of any consideration, while the naturalists made collections at each location. Eight days after the expedition departed with all its equipment, there was general alarm in Havana over a royal order announcing the coming siege of the plaza by the English.[42]

Because of the impending attack, the count immediately had to release Casa-Calvo and the others, who by this time were thirty leagues away and had begun their various operations. He felt it was his duty to suspend all non-defense projects and to require everyone to assist the captain general. Finally, when the danger had passed, the expedition was again prepared, but before it could depart, Casa-Calvo was transferred to New Orleans as interim governor of Louisiana. In view of this final blow, the count encharged de la Torre and López Gómez with the military objective,[43] and sent "the naturalists by themselves alone to their respective investigations."[44]

Sr. Principe de la Paz en 2 de Agosto de 1796 al Brigadier Conde de Mopox y Jaruco, Gefe y Director de ella," Havana, 1802, 6ª división, legajo no. 12, ARJB. Each of the thirty-four drawings gives the date and place where it was made.

40. "Descripciones de diferentes géneros y especies de plantas de la Ysla de Cuba que ha examinado la Comisión Real de Guantánamo," 3ª división, legajo no. 1, ARJB.

41. "Discurso sobre el proyecto de una población en la Bahía de Jagua, por Don Felix y Don Francisco Lemaur," Havana, 30 July 1798, MS 552, AMN

42. "Memoria del Conde de Mopox," p. 9–10.

43. See "Memoria sobre el reconocimiento de la parte occidental de la Ysla de Cuba; executada por D. Josef María de la Torre, Capitán en el Regimiento de Ynfantería de Cuba, y Don Antonio López Gómez," Havana, 1 April 1800, MS 557, AMN.

44. "Memoria del Conde de Mopox," p. 11.

By October 1800, the Conde de Mopox was ready to submit a preliminary report to the Spanish minister in Havana. He expressed hope that he and the members of his commission could sail with their equipment and collections on the first warship going to Spain, believing that they should take precedence over others who merely wanted passage home.[45] With regard to natural history, the count's report listed fifty-two drawings of birds, fish, and some plants made by "Atanacio Hecheverría"; eighty-five preserved birds; a collection of butterflies, another of insects; some curiosities of natural history; drawings of plants, fish, and insects made by the taxidermist and botanical artist José Guío; and four boxes of plants and seven hundred descriptions arranged and completed by Estévez after Boldo's untimely death, and by Lt. Col. Francisco Ramírez de Estenoz y Herrera. It also included an "analysis of the waters of Madruga" and an analysis and commentary on the virtues and circumstances of sugar cane, on the methods of using sugar to the greatest advantage according to chemical principles, and on the most adaptable machines for its manufacture. The count also reported the discovery of mines, with indications of coal, at Chapapote and discussed the minerals of Cuba in general.[46]

The count also listed the various plans, projects, and maps that other members of the commission had submitted, and included the following résumé:

Maps, without counting those pending in [Santiago de] Cuba, and more than
   30 which need to be recopied of the Canal of Güines, 105
Drawings of birds and fish by Atanasio Echeverría, 52
Same of plants by José Guío, 63
Same of insects by the same, 33
Birds preserved by the same, 85
Boxes of plants, 4
Descriptions of the same, 700
Collection of butterflies
Same of insects
Other curiosities of Natural History

He explained that Boldó had died as a result of his exhaustive explorations through the forests of Havana and had left much of the scientific

45. Conde de Mopox to Mariano Luis de Urquijo, Havana, 25 October 1800, Papeles del Conde de Mopox, AMN.

46. "Estado actual en que se halla la comisión encargada por S.M. al Conde de Mopox en la Ysla de Cuba, con expresión de los asuntos y sugetos que los han desempenado, vaxo las órdenes y dirección del referido Xefe," Havana, 14 October 1800, Papeles del Conde de Mopox, AMN.

work unfinished. The drawings of insects and reptiles by Guío lacked labels and descriptions, while the drawings of plants were only partially labeled.[47] At the end of the report prepared by the Conde de Mopox on 26 June 1802, when the expedition had returned to Spain, there appeared an index of twenty *expedientes* (files). Each one concerned a different aspect of the commission and their descriptions were, for the majority, of little variation from the ones given in the above-mentioned list.[48]

Under *expediente* no. 104 were noted Echeverría's eighty-six drawings of birds and fish, bound in a notebook. The whereabouts of these drawings are at present unknown although a folio of "descripciones de peces de la Isla de Cuba" corresponding to the expedition exists in the Museum of Natural Science in Madrid. The stuffed birds and the two bound notebooks of Guío's sketches of insects and plants are numbered as *expediente* no. 105. The drawings of insects are now located in the archives of the Naval Museum of Madrid and the plants in the archives of the Royal Botanical Garden also in Madrid.[49] *Expediente* no. 107 covers the four boxes of preserved plants and seven hundred descriptions of the same started by Boldó and completed by Estévez.

A number of other documents concerning the natural history portion of the expedition are located in the Archivo General de Indias in Sevilla. These clarify, at least, the destination of many of the items when they were first brought from Cuba. The Conde de Mopox, upon his return to Spain, spent some time at Aranjuez and on 26 June 1802 reported that he had the honor to present to the king's first secretary, Pedro Cevallos, four boxes of pressed Cuban plants, with their respective descriptions, for disposition as the minister of state saw fit.[50] He also had two boxes containing a collection of stuffed birds prepared "with the greatest accuracy by the taxidermist Guío" that he believed were still in good condition. The count was also sending an account of the minerals of Cuba prepared by Lieutenant Colonel Ramírez, accompanied by two small boxes of mineral samples. Much more would have been presented to the court if it had not been for "the misfortune which

47. "Dibujos de ynsectos de la Ysla de Cuba hechos por Don José Guío y Sanchez, dibujante botánico de la Real Comisión de Guantánamo," MS 712 bis, AMN.

48. "Memoria del Conde de Mopox," p. 13.

49. MS 712 bis in the Museo Naval, 6ª división, legajo no. 12 in the Real Jardín Botánico. "Descripciones de diferentes géneros y especies de plantas," 3ª división, legajo no. 1, ARJB.

50. Cevallos was a cousin-in-law of Manuel Godoy.

came to the great [mineral] collection of the eastern part." These minerals had been sent from Santiago de Cuba to Havana on the same ship that had "conducted the Commission of La Coruña to Cuba, and which was captured by the English in its journey." [51]

Two folders entitled "Comisión de Guantánamo" and "Conde de Mopox" contain various letters and notes regarding the files of the commission. There are three official orders dated at the palace on 15 July 1802, which transmit the botanical results of the expedition to Antonio José de Cavanilles, director of the Royal Botanical Garden of Madrid; the two boxes of stuffed birds to Eugenio Izquierdo, director of the Royal Museum of Natural History; and the two boxes of mineral samples to Christiano Herghen, also of the Museum. [52] There was no reply from Cavanilles; but Izquierdo did receive the two boxes of "bird skins" prepared by Guío, which were "well moth-eaten." These were distributed equally between Pascual Moineau and Francisco Xavier de Molina, both of the museum staff, "in order to exercise an honest rivalry between these subjects for the purpose of their both giving careful attention to their dissection." [53]

Dr. Herghen replied that he had received the minerals collected by Ramírez in Cuba, but did not find any account attached. This presented no problem since each box contained only one species of mineral that was almost unusable because of poor packaging. Nevertheless, he wrote, "the mineral-geographic collection of the dominions of His Majesty . . . remains enriched with two new species of which it had no account: one is a very interesting source of red copper, vitrious, etc. etc. and the other a black, earthy manganese." [54]

The natural history results of the expedition finally found their proper places in museums. When the Conde de Mopox completed his report about the work of the commission, telling of the obstacles that had been overcome, he hoped the king would recognize his meritorious conduct. [55] The young Cuban nobleman got his wish and became one of the few persons fortunate enough to be commended for his services. In a letter from Manuel Godoy, he was informed that the king would

51. Conde de Mopox to Pedro Cevallos, Aranjuez, 26 June 1802, estado, legajo no. 16, AGI. Contains marginal note: "The notice of minerals of which this letter speaks have not come with it nor have been found in the boxes which it cites."

52. Real Oficio de 15 de Julio de 1802, estado, legajo no. 16, AGI.

53. Izquierdo to Pedro Cevallos, Madrid, 16 July 1802, estado, legajo no. 16, AGI.

54. Herghen to Pedro Cevallos, Madrid, 17 July 1802, estado, legajo no. 16, AGI.

55. "Memoria del Conde de Mopox," p. 13.

reward his zealous service by promoting him to *Mariscal de Campo*. The appropriate papers were forwarded to the Ministry of War on 27 July 1802.[56]

After receiving his new title, the Conde de Mopox remained in Madrid for a few years with his family. He was again sent to Havana in 1807, but died shortly after his arrival on 7 April at the age of thirty-eight. In a further show of appreciation, the king conceded to the count's eldest son, Francisco Xavier de Santa Cruz y Montalvo, *la Grandeza de España,* and the same title to his widow María Teresa Montalvo during her lifetime.[57] As Spanish Grandees, they enjoyed status as if they were relatives of the king.

Such recognition was not to be given to the members of the Royal Scientific Expedition of New Spain, nor had it come to the members of the five-year expedition of Alejandro Malaspina. The Conde de Mopox y Jaruco undoubtedly merited the promotions he received, but the other two expeditions also consisted of men deserving of rewards for their service to the king.

56. Manuel Godoy to Conde de Mopox, Madrid, 27 July 1802; "expediente sobre concesión de Grandeza," consejos, legajo 5315, no. 2, Archivo Histórico Nacional.

57. *Gaceta de Madrid* (17 April 1812), no. 115; see Eugenio Sarrablo Aguareles, "La fundación de Jaruco en Cuba y los primeros condes de este título."

12

The Royal Scientific
Expedition's Return to Spain

AVING LEFT Echeverría with the Conde de Mopox y Jaruco in Havana, Sessé gathered his collections together and set sail for Veracruz in March 1798. Early in 1799 the entire Royal Scientific Expedition, with the exception of Longinos, was reunited in Mexico City. Moziño and Cerda had returned from their expedition to Guatemala, and Sensevé, having left Cuba ahead of Sessé, was already in the capital. Cervantes had remained continuously at the Botanical Garden during these years as professor of botany, directing the care of plants. Since the original term of the expedition had expired in 1794 and the two-year extension in 1796, the future direction of the institution was not clear. Sessé had received strict orders in 1797, while in Havana and later in Mexico, that all members of the expedition should return at once to Spain.

With no apparent excuse for delay, it is curious that the group remained in New Spain until 1802. Sessé and his associates were undoubtedly using this time to arrange and classify the results of the two recent excursions to the West Indies and Guatemala. Moziño spent much of his time assisting Dr. Luis Montaña in the Hospital of San Andrés of Mexico.[1] Finally, on 14 March 1802, Sessé wrote a long letter to the viceroy concerning the expedition's return. He explained that Cervantes preferred to continue in his present position and that, because the royal orders had specified the return of only those members who had to give an account of their discoveries, there was no reason why

1. "Expediente general de la expedición donde constan los sueldos de los empleados en ella," Aranjuez, 1804, Flora Española—1804, AMCN.

Cervantes should have to leave Mexico. He further argued that there was no one better qualified to fill the position of director of the garden, and that Cervantes would be entitled to half salary even if he retired to Spain. He offered the same reasons for the continuance of López as head gardener.[2]

Both of Sessé's proposals were approved and Cervantes and López remained in Mexico to battle earthquakes, an inadequate water supply, a continual lack of funds, loss of a portion of the garden for construction of army barracks, and numerous other problems of varying degrees of severity. López died in 1813 in an epidemic of fever and it took five years for Cervantes to get a replacement.[3]

The botanical garden survived Mexico's war for independence but was threatened with closure because there was no money for its support. A report made by English traveler William Bullock in 1823 testified to Cervantes' ingenuity in keeping the institution alive: "This beautiful establishment occupied one of the courts of the viceregal palace; and, though situated in the centre of a large and populous city, every vegetable production seems in perfect health and vigour." Bullock saw "the celebrated hand-tree," several species of extraordinary cacti, and a number of European fruits, such as apples, pears, peaches, and quinces "in company with bananas, avocatas, and the most delicious sapotas" he had ever tasted. The garden was

handsomely laid out in the Spanish fashion, with flagged walks, bordered with elegant large pots of flowers. The walks are rendered cool by the creeping plants that are trained over them. They diverge from a large stone basin in the centre, constantly supplied by a fountain with water, which, in small rivulets, spreads itself over every part of this little paradise—imparting freshness and life to thousands of elegant plants and flowers, unknown to the eye of an European. . . .[4]

Here in Mexico's climate of eternal spring, plants bloomed and sent forth their fragrance without man's assistance, quite unlike the "dwarfish sickly exotics" of English hothouses. Bullock decided to see if these sturdy plants could grow in London so he sent seeds of thirty-one plants that he obtained from Cervantes to the Botanical Garden in Sloane Street. The Englishman was sorry to learn that the Mexican gar-

2. Sessé to Iturrigaray, Mexico, 14 March 1802, Historia 465, AGN.
3. Rickett, "Royal Botanical Expedition," p. 67.
4. William Bullock, *Six Months Residence and Travels in Mexico*, pp. 183–84, 185–87. See Appendix E for the complete list of plants provided by Cervantes.

den "was about to be discontinued, the pension of the professor being stopped."[5] Cervantes continued to live nearby and supported himself by dispensing drugs to hospitals until his death on 26 July 1829. The garden remained for a number of years afterwards, but never again reached the state of productiveness and activity that it had enjoyed under the original directors.

The remainder of Sessé's letter of 14 March to the viceroy was directed toward enabling Moziño and Cerda to accompany the expedition to Spain even though they had not been included in the original orders. Sessé insisted that there were excellent reasons why these two native Mexicans should not be left behind. Moziño had served eleven years in place of Castillo, who would have returned to Spain had he lived, and during this time had made expeditions to Nootka, California, the Gulf Coast, and Guatemala. Consequently, Sessé believed, Moziño should be responsible, being certainly the most capable, for completing the descriptions begun on these excursions. Besides, entreated Sessé, he could truthfully say that there was no other person who could help him edit the many different works of the commission. And, finally, because Moziño would enjoy the same retirement in Mexico as in Spain, Sessé could find no reason why the crown would oppose the Mexican's desire to assist in the conclusion of the expedition's work.[6]

Cerda would be useful in Madrid because the majority of the plants were only partially drawn and their completion by another artist would be difficult.[7] Despite the director's urgings, however, Cerda remained in the botanical garden in Mexico. As a final hope, Sessé asked that Echeverría be ordered to join the group upon his return from Cuba.

Moziño's departure with the expedition was officially approved to the delight of all except his long neglected wife María. On 29 March 1803 she complained that since 1790 she had continued her suit for fulfillment of the decree granting her alimony; that in 1793 her husband had promised her half his pay; and that in 1795 on his way to Guatemala he had promised her a written contract. She said that "none of these promises have been kept except that I have had a third of his salary. Now I am afraid that he will go to Spain leaving me in poverty." Just before the expedition departed Sessé commented wryly that

5. Rickett, "Royal Botanical Expedition," p. 69.

6. Sessé to Iturrigaray, Mexico, 14 March 1802, Historia 465, AGN.

7. The original royal order had provided that the artists finish only one part of each drawing, e.g., one flower, one fruit, etc., and leave the rest in India ink to be colored later. Many of the drawings still remain in this unfinished form.

"Doña María Rita Rivera seems to live only in order to discredit her husband in every tribunal on earth." The matter was finally settled by an order of the treasurer general on 15 April 1803, that the king be informed of her claim on Moziño's salary in Spain, which was as yet undetermined.[8]

On 26 March 1802, Sessé wrote to José Antonio Caballero in Madrid that he and his associates were awaiting the arrival of a ship in Veracruz and planned to leave the capital in a day or two. He reported that he had with him more than 3,000 species of American plants, nearly 500 birds, more than 100 fish, some quadrupeds, amphibians, insects, and minerals resulting from their excursions. He explained that Longinos would remain in Guatemala because of illness.[9] It seems incredible that it took approximately one year from the date of Sessé's letter for a group composed of Sessé; his wife, María Guadalupe de los Morales, and children, Alexandro and Martina; his sister-in-law, María Josefa de los Morales; Moziño; Sensevé; a clerk, José Antonio Zambrano; a servant, Agustín Betancur; and a Negro slave, María Inés, to depart at last from the capital.[10]

José de Iturrigaray, viceroy since the beginning of the year, took over the job of getting the scientists back to Spain. He was relieved to report the embarkation of Sessé and his associates, an accomplishment achieved with no little difficulty. In a letter of 27 August 1803, he outlined a few of the obstacles that had been surmounted to comply "with the reiterated orders of His Majesty for the immediate return to that Peninsula of the individuals of the Botanical Garden."[11] At Sessé's request, on 2 March he had ordered that the group be transported without delay to Veracruz so that, at the expense of the royal treasury, they could embark on a merchant ship or storeship. Iturrigaray advised the three botanists that they would each be given 133 pesos, 2 reales, and 8 granos, in addition to an advance of two months' simple salary, in order to cover their expenses on the voyage. But the embarkation did not take effect as planned because the ships sailed directly to Spain, and Sessé had petitioned to go first to Havana to pick up certain works and specimens that he had left there. Therefore, Iturrigaray adjusted the matter so that Sensevé and a servant would go directly to Spain and carry the boxes from the botanical garden, but this too failed to take

8. Letters translated and quoted in Rickett, "Royal Botanical Expedition," p. 74.
9. Sessé to Caballero, Mexico, 26 March 1802, Flora Española—1802, AMCN.
10. Rickett, "Royal Botanical Expedition," p. 74.
11. Iturrigaray to Caballero, Mexico, 27 August 1803, Flora Española—1803, AMCN.

place. "The Ministers of the Royal Treasury of Veracruz attributed it to the fault of Sensevé for not wanting to embark, to Sessé for having failed to give him the money he requested for his passage, considering 400 pesos excessive, and to the commander of the store-ship for not wanting to provide maintenance for Sensevé." [12]

By this time the viceroy seemed willing to make almost any allowance in order to effect their departure. He advised the *intendent* of the port to provide an equitable sum for their passage, to iron out any difficulties with the royal officials, to interpose with the commanders of the ships who always make excessive demands, and to oblige the individuals of the expedition to be ready to depart. As a result, Iturrigaray could finally breathe a sigh of relief. "Sessé and Moziño," he wrote Cabellero, "have gone to Havana and Sensevé directly to the Peninsula in compliance with the Royal Order of the previous March 8, which repeated the demand for the return of the said Expedition."

Actually Iturrigaray's report was in error because Sensevé accompanied Sessé to Havana while Moziño sailed directly to Spain. Moziño arrived in the port of Cádiz on 31 July 1803 on the frigate *Nueva Mahonesa*. All those who had made the fifty-seven day voyage from New Spain were forced by port authorities to remain on board several more days in quarantine because some of the crew had had yellow fever, a sickness known as "Mal de Vera Cruz." [13] Moziño was finally allowed to disembark on 2 August and complained that the heat was worse than in Veracruz. He had planned to await the arrival of Sessé in Cádiz, but because of the weather decided to go on to Madrid. [14]

It was just as well that Moziño did not remain in the south since Sessé and Sensevé did not arrive in Cádiz until November 1803. Rumors of a new rupture with England had obstructed the departure of all ships from the port of Havana, where Sessé had stopped to collect the duplicates of the materials from the Puerto Rican expedition. [15] He had brought with him twenty-six boxes of products of natural history, unfinished, which would be deposited at the Casa de Contratación in Seville until authorized for shipment to Madrid. Sessé remained personally in charge of one other box with manuscripts and drawings that were the most interesting and valuable to the expedition, in order to

12. Ibid.
13. Moziño to Sessé, on board the *Fragata Nueva Mahonesa*, at anchor in the bay of Cádiz, 31 July 1803, 4ª división, legajo no. 22, ARJB.
14. Moziño to Sessé, Cádiz, 2 August and 5 August 1803, 4ª división, legajo no. 22, ARJB.
15. Sessé to Caballero, Cádiz, 8 November 1803, Flora Española—1803, AMCN.

present the material directly to Caballero. He was prudent to have kept this box in hand since it was not until June 1804 that the other twenty-six boxes arrived in Madrid.[16]

Apparently the manuscripts of the expedition were first given to Hipólito Ruiz and José Pavón, leaders of the botanical expedition to South America and authors of *Flora peruviana et chilensis,* for their examination. This did not seem to meet with the approval of Sessé, who petitioned the king on 10 January 1804 that "the authors of the *Flora Peruana* be ordered to deliver to him all the drawings, herbaria, and other products that they have in their power belonging to the Botanical Expedition of New Spain." Not until 7 March 1804 was a royal order issued to botanists Ruiz and Pavón requesting that they return the said items to Sessé.[17]

During these years Moziño lived with Sessé in Madrid, becoming a member and later an officer of the *Junta Suprema de Sanidad* (Public Health Commission). During the winter of 1804 he worked throughout Andalucia, and particularly in Ecija, fighting an epidemic of yellow fever. When he returned to Madrid he became associated with the Royal Academy of Medicine.[18] Sensevé, who had finally reached Madrid in June 1804, worked for a short time with his two associates, but was suddenly taken ill and died in March 1805.[19] Sessé wrote to Caballero in hopes that Sensevé's salary could be allotted to Moziño and himself to complete the task of arranging the work of the expedition.[20]

The artist Echeverría had returned to Spain following the completion of his work with the expedition of the Conde de Mopox y Jaruco.

16. Sessé to Caballero, Madrid, 13 June 1804, "por fin llego ayer Dn. Jayme Sensevé con los 26 caxones de herbario y ostros objetos de historia natural," Flora Española—1804, AMCN.

17. Petition of Martín Sessé, Madrid, 10 January 1804, Flora Española—1804, AMCN. Royal Order to Hipólito Ruiz and José Pavón, Aranjuez, 7 March 1804, Flora Española—1804, AMCN.

18. Cartas de Moziño, 4ª división, legajo no. 22, November 1804 to February 1805. Moziño worked on a treatise for curing yellow fever off and on during the next two years and gave a number of lectures at the Academy of Medicine in Madrid, of which he served as president for four terms between 1805 and 1812. His work was somewhat controversial, but finally received a favorable judgment. Arias Divito, *Las expediciones científicas del siglo XVIII,* p. 253.

19. Sessé to Caballero, Madrid, 14 March 1805, "Yesterday evening the body of Jayme Sensevé was buried . . . José Moziño and I remain alone in charge of all the work and reduced to such limited salaries that we can subsist only with the greatest economy" (Flora Española—1805, AMCN).

20. Sessé to Caballero, Madrid, 14 March 1805, Flora Española—1805, AMCN.

Through the count's influence with Manuel Godoy, in 1803 Echeverría received an appointment as second director of painting at the Royal Academy of San Carlos of Mexico, where he had originally studied seventeen years before.[21] Echeverría, because of his great merit, would receive a salary of 2,000 pesos upon the condition that before he left he conclude the work he had begun "as artist of the Botanical Expedition of New Spain, under the orders of its Director, D. Martín de Sessé, and for which the King would allow two years."[22]

Echeverría had previously asked that he be given enough money to pay for his return trip to America, and that a portion of his salary be paid to his wife in Havana. With this new appointment, Echeverría explained that if he had to remain two more years in Madrid he wanted all his salary earned from the previous March until the fourth of January 1804 paid to his wife in Cuba so she could bring his family to Spain.[23] Echeverría remained in Madrid until 1808, receiving his salary as second director of the Mexican Academy, when the French invasion forced him to flee with his family to Sevilla. He was still in southern Spain in 1821.

Of the members of the Royal Scientific Expedition, only Echeverría received a favor from the court of Spain, and this because of his later association with the Conde de Mopox. Sessé and Moziño, who had worked so many years in the service of the king, were to be crushed by the same lack of official interest that had greeted the scientist Francisco Hernández in a previous age.[24] As political considerations had interrupted Philip II's grand plans, outside forces caused Carlos IV to abandon some worthy projects. The futility of the situation is reflected in a lengthy letter written by Moziño to Pedro Cevallos reporting the death of his friend and patron, Martín Sessé:

On the 4th day of the current month [October 1808] died in this Court Don Martín de Sessé who, by Order of His Majesty, was Director of the Royal Botanical Garden of Mexico and of the Expedition which was carried out in that Kingdom, in that of Guatemala, the Windward Island, Nutka and the Californias, for the purpose of enriching the study of natural history.[25]

---

21. Oficio del Principe de la Paz a Pedro Cevallos, Madrid, 2 March 1803, estado, legajo no. 18, AGI. Rafael Ximeno, formerly in the second spot, had become director.

22. Caballero to Echeverría, Toledo, 4 January 1804, estado, legajo no. 18, AGI.

23. Echeverría to Caballero, Madrid, 11 March and 12 July 1803, 14 January 1804, estado, legajo no. 18, AGI.

24. Rickett, "Royal Botanical Expedition," p. 75.

25. Moziño to Cevallos, Madrid, 24 October 1808, Flora Española—1808, AMCN.

Moziño complained that of the four professors who were employed in the commission, he was the lone survivor, but being of more than fifty years of age he could not expect to live much longer. He did not know how he could do by himself what four persons working continuously were not able to complete. This made him fear that "the precious collection," which had been the fruit of their long and difficult voyages costing the public treasury more than two million pesos, and which could bring such honor and utility to the nation, would not only fail to rescue the work of Dr. Hernández but would itself be lost.

Moziño explained that his fear was now even greater because of the death of Sessé in whose house he had been living. Because Sessé's family planned to return to Mexico, Moziño would have to move to "some small room in which the herbaria will not fit or will be poorly defended against the mice and moths." To avoid such possible destruction, Moziño offered them to Cevallos to be presented to the government for disposition by the king. The "aging" scientist felt that the objects pertaining to zoology should be deposited in the Royal Museum of Natural History and that the botanical specimens should be placed in the custody of Ruiz and Pavón, or perhaps even better given to the professors of the Botanical Garden whose herbarium would be augmented for public display. Moziño continued:

I hope that the *Junta Supreme* will see fit to permit me to reserve for my own use an example of each dried plant, because . . . those which I keep will allow me to rectify in the solitude and quietude of my study, my own observations and those of my deceased companions. . . . In order to assure the originality which belongs to us in our discoveries, it would be convenient if my delivery be verified by detailed catalogs to remain in the *Secretaria de Gracia y Justicia*.[26]

So that the bulk of the collection could be delivered to the government in an organized manner, Moziño, then living in quarters at the Academy of Medicine, asked for Echeverría's assistance since he had "a knowledge and skill in the herbaria, animal specimens, drawings and manuscripts." According to Moziño, any other person would be less useful. The government would also save money by assigning Echeverría to the project since the artist was receiving his salary as second director of painting of the Royal Academy of Mexico.

Within a few months, with this individual helping me, the commission whose responsibility is in my charge could be concluded in a manner so that the Gov-

26. Ibid.

ernment could make of it the best use for the progress of the arts and of commerce, and not the least in order to manifest to Europe that Spain has not been careless in making investigations of its vast dominions of both Americas by persons instructed in natural history.[27]

During this particular period Spain was in political turmoil and conditions were hardly favorable for the patronage of natural history. On 18 March 1808, Carlos IV had abdicated the throne in favor of his son Fernando VII. In April 1808, the young king was invited by Napoleon to "visit" France and was then detained there as a prisoner for the next six years. In May of the same year, Fernando VII was forced by Napoleon to return the crown of Spain to Carlos IV, also in France at the time, and Spain was virtually left without a monarch. In the summer and fall of 1808, the French made numerous attacks against Spanish troops that resulted in the final triumph of Napoleon's superior forces and allowed Joseph Bonaparte to claim the throne of Spain on 4 December 1808.

For Moziño these events brought an unexpected turn for the better. The Mexican scientist was apparently able to impress the French monarch with his work, since Napoleon's brother made a considerable effort to enable the publication of *Flora de México*.[28] Under French occupation Moziño was appointed director of the Royal Museum of Natural History and made a professor of zoology. Nevertheless, his newfound good fortune did not last long and the remaining years of his life were punctuated with frustration and sadness.[29] Pablo de la Llave,[30] a native of Mexico who lived with Moziño while they both worked in the museum, and Augustin Pyramus de Candolle, a Swiss botanist who became associated with Moziño a few years before the latter's death, have chronicled the last chapter.[31]

According to Llave's account, Moziño remained at the museum when the French withdrew from Madrid in 1812, believing himself to be in no danger. The returning Spanish patriots, however, did not look

27. Ibid.

28. Raymond Weibel, "Flore du Mexique et les dames de Genève."

29. Carreño, *Noticias de Nutka*, pp. 77–81; Rickett, "Royal Botanical Expedition to New Spain," pp. 77–79; León, *Biblioteca botánica-mexicana*, pp. 334–37; Standley, *Trees and Shrubs of Mexico*, pp. 15–18.

30. Llave, "Memoria sobre el quetzaltotol, genero nuevo de Aves," pp. 43–49; and "Descripción de algunos géneros y especies nuevas de vegetales," pp. 345–58.

31. Alphonse Louis de Candolle, ed., *Memoires et souvenirs de Augustin-Pyramus de Candolle.*

with favor upon anyone holding an official post under the French and placed Moziño, along with other scientists and distinguished persons, in chains and led them to prison. Finally, at the entrance to Old Castile, a French general set the illustrious chain gang free and Moziño returned to Madrid. This time he gathered together his notes and papers and departed on foot for the French border. Moziño placed the most valuable objects of the museum and his manuscripts and drawings in an old cart that he walked beside during the day and slept in at night. Near the border a French officer seized the cart and Moziño was able to save only his papers, with which he escaped from Spain and took refuge in Montpellier.

While in Montpellier, Moziño became acquainted with the Swiss scientist Augustin Pyramus de Candolle, who was then lecturing in botany at the university in that city. De Candolle became interested in Moziño's drawings, which amounted to some fourteen hundred of plants and numerous others of animals, and offered to work with him in classifying the new species. The visiting botanist believed that Moziño's identifications were of little value,[32] but that the drawings were done with such precision that he would undertake the task of identifying the known and classifying the new species of plants. In 1816 de Candolle asked Moziño to accompany him to Geneva where they could work together on the *Flora,* but Moziño declined, saying: "No, I am too old and sick; I am too unfortunate; take them [the manuscripts and drawings] to Geneva, I give them to you, and I entrust to your care my future glory."[33]

During the following year Moziño made an attempt to secure readmittance to Spain, asking help from the Academy of Medicine. Since a number of administrative changes had taken place, Moziño finally received permission in April 1817. In view of these new circumstances he decided that *Flora Mexicana* should be returned to Spain and consequently wrote to de Candolle asking for all of his drawings with the exception of 315 duplicate originals. Not wanting to lose the drawings completely, de Candolle placed himself in charge of a remarkable un-

32. As Rickett points out, Sessé and Moziño undoubtedly made mistakes in identification since they were limited to a few standard works (mostly those of Linneaus), had no access to the herbaria upon which the works were based, and were attempting to classify a flora that was largely new to science. McVaugh, *Results of the Sessé and Mociño Expedition,* pp. 113–14, concurs.

33. De Candolle, *Memoirs et souvenirs,* p. 288.

dertaking. Since he wanted to keep at least some of the sketches of the principal plants that formed the Mexican collection, he called upon some people who had already copied some of the plants. He would have been happy to have obtained copies of a few dozen, but the artists and amateurs of Geneva were such active and friendly people that more than one hundred persons volunteered, mostly women, "and in less that eight days 860 sketches were copied entirely and 119 preserved in the form of rough drafts."[34]

This collection of drawings is especially significant since Moziño's original collection has for the most part never been found.[35] The exiled botanist had received an invitation in 1820 from Spanish Minister of Marine Juan Jabat to return to Madrid and remain in his home until other means could be found for him; but Moziño never arrived in Madrid. He did, however, reach Barcelona because a certificate of death shows that he was buried on 19 May 1820 in the parochial church of St. James of Barcelona.[36]

The major portion of the herbarium collected by Sessé and Moziño in New Spain was incorporated into the general herbarium of the Botanical Garden of Madrid in 1820.[37] This institution also houses the

34. Ibid. As a result of the drawings, de Candolle and his colleagues identified 17 new genera and 271 new species, which the Swiss botanist included in his *Systema* and *Prodomus* published during the 1830s.

35. The duplicate originals and the copies of the drawings are preserved in the Conservatoire Botanique in Geneva. Tracings of 279 sketches were made in 1874 under the editorship of Alphonse de Candolle (*Calques des dessins de la flore du Mexique, de Mociño et Sessé qui ont servi de types d'especes dans le Systema ou le Prodomus*). These were sent to the ten principal botanical museums of the world (Paris, Kew, Berlin, Vienna, Leiden, St. Petersburg, Copenhagen, Brussels, Florence, and Cambridge in North America) because botanists were having difficulty identifying the new species in de Candolle's original *Systema* and *Prodomus*. At Kew Gardens in London the tracings proved useful in identifying a collection of Mexican plants made by Parry and Palmer in Central Mexico. See W. B. Hemsley, *Short Notes*, pp. 275–76.

36. Llave, "Descripción de algunos generos y especies nuevas," p. 345, note 1. The death certificate printed in Rickett, "Royal Botanical Expedition," p. 79, reads: "I certify that in one of the books of obituaries of this parish is found an entry in Catalonian that translated into Castilian says: On 19 May 1820 in the Parish Church of St. James of Barcelona, disposition was made of the body (se hizo la disposición del cadaver) of José Moziño, doctor, widower, native of Oaxaca in America, sixty-two years of age, who died of a hemorrhage, receiving the sacraments of penitence and extreme unction." This is followed by the original Catalán version.

37. In a letter from Antonio Cavanilles to Sir James Edward Smith (first president of the Linnean Society of London), Madrid, 6 April 1804, the director of the Jardín Botánico states that the herbarium contained more than 4,000 plants; Smith papers, Archives of the Linnean Society of London.

original descriptions of the *Flora de México* and *Flora de Guatemala,* in addition to the descriptions of plants made on the expeditions to Cuba and Puerto Rico. There are eighty-four colored drawings that were identified and labeled by the botanists of the expedition and thirty-seven drawings without identification.

A portion of the herbarium was sold to an English botanist and collector, Aylmer Lambert,[38] during the early 1800s, together with a larger number of dried plants belonging to the herbarium of Ruiz and Pavón. In 1842 these were sold at a public auction and the priced catalogue of the sale in the botanical department of the British Museum shows that the collection of Sessé and Moziño brought £1 8s.[39] The purchase was made by an agent for the Baron De Lessert, the eminent botanist and banker of Paris. The herbarium of Ruiz and Pavón, which was purchased for the British Museum for £270, contained, however, a number of Mexican plants that undoubtedly came into Ruiz and Pavón's hands after Moziño fled from Spain, since Ruiz and Pavón were never in Mexico. These are today preserved both in the British Museum and the Kew Herbarium and marked "Herbarium Pavón."

Had the Royal Scientific Expedition returned at the expiration of its original term, it might have been provided with the facilities necessary to organize and print its findings. In addition to losing this possible opportunity, its long delay in leaving New Spain opened the door for serious criticism. Certain accusations were made in 1798 that Sessé and his associates, as well as other scientists, were spending public funds merely to promote their own interests.[40] The charges made, however, seemed to reflect a lack of full understanding on the part of individuals rather than an overall censure by the crown. This was illustrated by the crown's continued interest in botanical activities, especially in Cuba. The later difficulties brought about by unstable conditions in the court of Carlos IV contributed to the incomplete state of the expedition's work much more than any motives of self-interest on the part of the scientists involved.

Thus, the several tragedies that befell the returning Spanish scien-

38. See H. W. Renkema and John Ardagh, "Aylmer Bourke Lambert and his description of the genus *Pinus.*" His private collection contained 30,000 specimens.

39. *Catalogue of the Highly Valuable Botanical Museum of the late A. B. Lambert, Esq.* published by the Executor of the Estate and preserved in the British Museum. Judging from the price the collection should have contained less than one hundred specimens.

40. Communicaciones del Virrey sobre la expedición de Nueva España, Flora Española—1789–98, AMCN.

tists—Malaspina's banishment, the Conde de Mopox y Jaruco's death, Sessé's inability to get enough help, the French invasion, and Moziño's exile—resulted in the consignment of a disorganized mass of information to archives; the forced sale of documents, drawings, and herbaria to foreigners; or the disappearance of such material.[41] In addition, these unfortunate occurrences were overshadowed by an even greater force that would prevent not only the assembling and publication of the evidence gathered, but the repetition of similar efforts. The loss of Spain's colonial empire meant that Spanish scientists would never again have such free rein in exploratory enterprises. The same spirit of enlightenment that awakened Old World interest in scientific investigation subsequently promoted a wave of liberal thinking that led to ideas of revolution.[42] With the success of the American wars for independence, Spain could not be expected to maintain its interest in studying the natural resources of territories no longer belonging to the crown. The scattering of material collected during these great expeditions of the late eighteenth century simply reflected the breaking away of Spain's possessions overseas. The treasures of natural history taken from the New World benefited the mother country no more than the gold of an earlier century that had been squandered in European conflicts.

Because of their country's misfortunes, these pioneers of Spanish science failed to receive proper credit or recognition. It seems only fair that they now be rescued from obscurity. Although the botanical and zoological species that they discovered may not bear their names, at least the modern generation can appreciate the great labors of these enlightened and dedicated men.

41. Although certain documents and drawings were lost, the Sociedad Mexicana de Historia Natural did, after correspondence covering a fifteen-year period, finally secure copies of the botanical descriptions made by the Royal Scientific Expedition and publish them in two volumes. *Flora mexicana* in 1888 and *Plantae novae hispaniae* in 1889. The volumes were without illustrations and, as McVaugh points out, obsolete at the time of their printing. Coincidentally, Pedro Novo y Colson had just a few years previously (1885) edited the publication of a one volume summary of the Malaspina expedition (*Viaje político-científico*). Thus, after one hundred years, Malaspina, Sessé, and Moziño received recognition in print.

42. Arthur Whitaker in *Latin America and the Enlightenment,* p. 16, believes the final days of the Spanish empire in America to be exemplified by the case of Alexander von Humboldt. The German naturalist's favorable report showed, according to Whitaker, that "Latin America's active role as participant in the Enlightenment was at last altering its passive role as an exhibit in the case prepared by the Philosophers; but the change had been too long delayed, for by the time Humboldt's new portrait was completed, the waters of the Enlightenment had run out in the marshes of war and revolution."

Appendix A

List of Books . . . for the Use of the Botanical and Natural History Expedition [1]

	Reales [2]
Tournefont. *Institutiones Rei Herbariae.* Lugduni, 1719.	0184
Linneo. *Parte Practica de Botanica* por Dn. Antonio Palau. Madrid, 1787.	0000
Bergman. *Opuscules Chimiques* eraduits par M. de Monveau. Dijon, 1780 y 1785.	0060
Dictionnaire Botanique. Roüen, 1782.	0020
Linnaei Amenitates Academicae. Volumen octavum et nonum. Exlangae, 1785.	0042
Gilibert. *Systema Plantarum Europae.* Colonie Allogrobum, 1785.	0096
Gilibert. *Botanica Philosophica.* Colonie Allogrobum, 1786.	0060
Linnaei Philosophia et Critica Botanica. Colonie Allogrobum, 1787.	0090
Linnaei Species Plantarum. Editio tertia Vindobonae, 1764.	0074
Brisson. *Ornithologye.* Paris, 1760.	0750
Cavanilles. *Dysertatio Botanica de Sida.* Paris, 1785.	0000
Plumier. *Tractatus de Filicibus Americanis en Latin y Frances.* Paris, 1750.	0180
Perrault. *Memoires pour servir a l'Histoire Naturelle des Animaux.* Amsterdam, 1758.	0180
Gautier. *Observations sur l'Histoire Naturelle.* Paris, 1752.	0090
Malpighi. *Opera omnia seu Thesaurus Botanico-Medico-Anatomicus.* Lugduni Batavorum, 1687.	0090
Reichar. *Systema Plantarum.* Francofurti ad Moenum, 1779 y 1780.	0016
Eiusdem. *Genera Plantarum.*	0030
Gesneri. *Liber quartus, qui est de Piscium et Aquatilium Animalium Watura.* Francofurti, 1604.	
Gesneri. *Liber primus de quadrupedibus oviparis.* Francofurti, 1603.	

1. "Lista de los Libros que se envian a México en dos Caxones para el uso de la Expedición Botánica y de Historia Natural de aquel Reyno."
2. One *real* was ⅛ of a peso.

Gesneri. *Liber secundus, qui est de quadrupedibus oviparis.* Francofurti,
  1617, et *Liber quintus, qui est de Serpentium Natura.* Tiguri, 1587.

Gesneri. *Liber tertius, qui est de Avium Natura.* 1604.   0240

Baume. *Chymie raisonée.* Paris, 1775.   0084

Salerne. *Ornithologye, o Histoire des Oiseaux.* Paris, 1767.   0090

Scilla de Corporibus marinis lapidescentibus. Romae, 1747.   0040

Bonarni. *Ricreatione nella Conchiologia.* [With plates]   0090

Diccionario de los Animales. Paris, 1759.   0180

Diccionario de la Lengua Castellana.[3] Madrid, 1780.   <u>0090</u>

                                              2876

[Signed by Sr. Casimiro Gómez Ortega, 21 June 1788, in Madrid.]

3. Flora Española—Año 1788, AMCN. The dictionary was added to the list in the handwriting of Gomez Ortega.

Appendix B

Plants and Grasses in Cuernavaca [1]

Texaxapotla means *Yerba Oradadora* [2] because by smearing it on a stone of a thickness of one-half vara, [3] its odor penetrates to the reverse part with such sharpness that the other side appears as if it were the smeared one. Its leaves appear like those of flax, and its flowers are yellow; all the flowers have the flavor and odor of oranges.

Acocotli, [4] or *chichicpatli,* resembles the *Nardo Montano* [mountain spikenard] in its leaves; it has flowers in the form of stars, of a yellow color which inclines somewhat to red.

The *Huitzilxóchitl* tree, [5] or tree like the *Eneldo* [common dill], secretes gum; others call it *anetlinán*. It has leaves like sweet basil, the pale flowers are white but incline toward yellow, similar in odor and taste to the *heneldo*.

Cacalictlacopatli, which others call *tlacocacalic* and *tzotzoltic,* also *apitzalizpatli* and others *huelicpatli* or *quauhxíhuitl*. It has leaves in the figure of a heart.

Copalquáhuitl, [6] or tree which carries gum, *patláhuac;* it has very wide, jagged leaves, and in the extreme is similar to the plant which in Spain is called *Zumaque*. It secretes a white, transparent gum.

Ezquáhuitl, [7] one finds this tree toward Tepeguaculco, and it secretes a gum called *Sangre de Drago*.

Quauhxilo xóchitl is a very beautiful tree, the flowers it produces open from a very well composed little head in the form of a wig.

Yzquixóchitl is a tall tree with leaves like those of the orange tree, and the

---

1. "Plantas y hierbas que ay en Cuernavaca," 4ª división, legajo no. 14, ARJB.
2. *Hierba Horadadora* (perforating plant).
3. One vara was equal to 32.9 inches.
4. *Plantae novae hispaniae,* p. 137, lists it as *Coreopsis coronata* with the common name of *tallo hueco* (keck). The current classification is *Bidens leucantha*.
5. *Antheum graveolens* in *Plantae novae hispaniae,* p. 43.
6. *Euphorbia edulis* in *Plantae novae hispaniae,* p. 76.
7. *Croton sanguiferum,* ibid., p. 153. Commonly called *El Drago* (the Dragon).

flowers appear like the *Rosa Canina* [canine rose], comparable in taste to ours.

Chichiltic tlapalezquáhuitl is a tree that produces obtuse and long leaves which narrow toward its stem; it secretes milk, at first white and afterwards inclining toward red.

Ahuehuete [8] or *Atambor de Agua* [drum of water], also called *teponáztli,* is a tree that has red wood like the Sabina; it grows near the water and in its fruit and stature it resembles the silver fir or spruce fir.

Quamóchitl [9] is a prickly briar tree whose leaves resemble those of the pomegranate tree. It has little clusters at the ends of the small branches; it produces little vines, which are green inclining to a gold color and which contain a little black seed that can be eaten.

Tzina cancuitlaquáhuitl is a tree that produces a gum like incense, which the pharmacists call lacca; it is pegged to the branches of the tree in little layers similar to those of the wings of birds.

Chilaptali is a little bush whose leaves resemble the rose. Its flowers are of the color of grain and are formed two by two at the roots of the leaves all along the course of the stem.

Noxocopatli is a little bush, which has long jagged leaves, clusters of flowers, and the seed joined to the base of the leaves.

Tlatlancuaye or *Acapatli* is a plant that has twisting stems in the manner of vine-runners; it gives a large and plump fruit which they call long pepper, and it is used as a condiment for food, although it never ripens to the perfection needed in order to. be able to plant it.

Ezpatli or *quauheztli,* which means medicine of blood, is a little bush with thick leaves and white acorns almost in the figure of a heart, which when cut secrete blood, from which [the plant] takes its name.

Mecaxóchitl is an herb of two palms in length [ca. sixteen inches] that grows on the ground; it has large, thick leaves, almost round, which are odorous with a strong flavor; it bears a fruit similar to a long pepper. [10]

8. *Cupressus disticha* (a kind of cypress) in *Plantae novae hispaniae,* p. 152.

9. Guamúchil or *Pithecollobium dulce* in Martínez, *Catálogo de nombres vulgares,* p. 400.

10. Martínez, *Catálogo de nombres vulgares,* p. 309, lists it as a species of *Piper.*

Appendix C

List of the Woods Sent from the Parish of Chicontepec of the Bishopric of Puebla de Los Angeles to Captain Joseph de Flores. [1]

Woods of Colors

No. 1 . . . First, a dark, very compact, and heavy wood that with grease, oils and other preparations, or only from use, becomes very black and close-grained. It is a species of Ebony. Here they know it as *Palo-Negro*, and the Indians call it *Tlilticquáhuitl*. It serves for works of a hand-lathe or for inlays. It is found in some mountains of the territory of this parish, although somewhat distant from this Headquarters. Thus, this one, like almost all of the colored woods, has its color in the heart or center.

No. 2 . . . The *Moralillo* [black mulberry tree], known by the Indians as *Chichictli*, is greenish yellow; very appropriate for inlaying, interpolated with Ebony. It also serves for canes, shotgun boxes, and other similar things.

No. 3 . . . Another wood of a soft yellow color, known here as *Quiebra-hachas*,[2] because it is so hard and compact that it almost always breaks the hatchets or axes that are employed in cutting it. The Indians call it *Ocpactli*. It serves for the preceding uses and also, because of its consistency, it is used for the pillars of houses, and for the provisional machines which are called *Trapiches*[3] and which serve here for taking out the juice from the sweet cane, from which they make *Piloncillo* [loaf of sugar].

No. 4 . . . Known here by *Palo-Colorado*, the Indians call it *Tlatlal-quáhuiltl*. They use it for dyes of flesh-color, preparing the water, in which it is boiled, with alum and lemon. This mixture results in the dye color. It also serves to make curious utensils. Its infusion or dye-bath is applied with good success to

1. Lista de las maderas, cuyas muestras se dirigen del Curato de Chicontepec, del Obispado de la Puebla de los Angeles, al Señor Capitán Dn. Joseph de Flores, Castellano del Puerto de Acapulco; con expresión de sus colores y propiedades respectivas, y de los usos, a que se aplican, 4ª división, legajo no. 15, ARJB.

2. Break-hatchets, a name commonly used for very hard woods including species of *Hymenaea, Leucaena, Lysiloma* and *Poeppigia.*

3. Grinding machine or fruit press.

those who suffer from skin ulcers, especially when these come from syphilis. Just after it is cut it is almost white, but as it becomes dry it changes and reaches its color.

No. 5 . . . It is known here by *Palo-Gateado* and the Indians say *Tlalcuilol quáhuitl;* it has beautiful veins. It is used for moldings, picture frames, and for many other curious things, such as wastebaskets, and also for chairs, settees, and all kinds of seats, and also for tables and wardrobe closets.

No. 6 . . . Another species of *Gateado* of softer colors, called by the Indians *Xiquili quáhuitl.* It is applied to the same uses as is the one that follows.

No. 7 . . . Another *Gateado* of more vivid colors called by the natives *Chomict-li.* Neither this one nor the two preceding ones are found in this Curacy, but there are those which are found in Tzontecomatlán, and Yzquatlán, and others of that jurisdiction situated in the center of the Sierra.

No. 8 . . . The *Huayal,* which the Indians have named *Tziquáhuitl,* and promiscuously *Cochizquáhuitl,* is equivalent to *Palo Dormilón,* because its leaves in the summer contract as if they were ready for sleep. It is a very hard and solid wood, it serves the same purposes as No. 3. The heart is a dark maroon; it becomes very black with time, especially if it is handled continuously. It is abundant in these proximities and is very appropriate for works of hand-lathes and inlays.

No. 9 . . . The *Palo-Encerado,* which the Indians know as *Cozaquáhuitl,* serves for the same as the preceding one and is almost as hard and solid; but its heart has grains of various colors, which, with use or with the chamois, become more vivid and beautiful.

No. 10 . . . The *Orejón,* which in Mexican is *Necazquáhuitl,* is so-called because the fruit resembles an ear. Its heart, which effects the color of coffee, becomes, with use and time, darker and more beautiful. Because of its little weight, it is used for boxes of Arquebus. This quality, and that of its corpulence, makes it appropriate, like the Cedar, for small one-piece boats like canoes or dugouts.

No. 11 . . . The *Trigolillo,* which the Indians call *Hequáhuitl,* has several veins of various colors which improve with use and time.

No. 12 . . . El *Chicozapote*[4] is called *Xilo-Tzápotl* by the Indians. Its heart is light purple; it becomes darker with time. It produces a fruit of the same name, which is more delicate and flavorful than that of the following species and of a different shape. The shape of the *Xilo-Tzápotl* fruit is somewhat prolongated or eliptic as an egg; that of the *Xaltzápotl,* which follows, is of a spheroid type, like an orange.

No. 13 . . . The *Chicozapote,* named by the Indians *Xaltzápotl,* contains fruit of more diverse shapes than the preceding one and although it is also very sweet it is not quite as smooth. For this reason its Mexican name is equivalent to *Zapote arenoso.* But another quality is held in esteem in Mexico and other cities and pueblos where it is scarce: that is, in the mountains of this Huasteca the fruit are produced spontaneously with such abundance that those which

4. Sapodilla plum in *Plantae novae hispaniae,* p. 48.

fall ripened to the ground serve as food for the cattle and horses and for the wild boars and other beasts, which become fattened from May onward from the benefit of this delicate and delicious fruit. The birds partake of those that do not fall to the ground, as do the various quadrupeds, which are able to climb for them, like the badgers, squirrels, wild dogs, monkeys, and similar animals, and even the fierce carnivora like the lion and the tiger.

The heart of the *Xaltzápotl* is dark purple, and with time becomes black; thus from its wood, as from that of the *Xilo-tzápotl,* are manufactured very stiff and very beautiful canes, cues for the game of billiards, night-sticks, arrows and strong stakes, and also small ones used for nailing wood together, and all the staffs of authority used by the Indian officials of the municipality, and other things of this type.

No. 14 . . . The *Cedro colorado* or *Macho* [*Cedrela mexicana*], whose properties are as well known as the uses for which it serves, is called *Teoquáhuitl chichiltic* by the Indians.

No. 15 . . . The *Cedro blanco,* or *Hembra* [*Cupressus* sp.], differs from the preceding only in its color; it is called *Teoquáhuitl chipáhuac* by the Indians.

No. 16 . . . The *Guachalala,* named by some *Iris,* and by the natives *Chichic quáhuitl,* which is the same as *Palo amargo.* When it is well-dried, one discovers some beautiful buff-colored veins like the small sample that accompanies this.

Medicinal Woods

No. 17 . . . The *Palo azul,* whose name is given because water which has been thrown into some little cup or other cavity or receptacle of this wood, takes this color [blue]. To the water thus tinted, they attribute various qualities and virtues, especially that it is very diuretic, and in this concept those who are dropsical use it, as do those who are constipated. In some parts they call it *Taray* but it seems that the description which Dr. Laguna makes of the *Tamaris* or *Tamarisco,* which is the same as the *Taray,* does not fit it. The Indians call it *Coáctli.*

No. 18 . . . The *Palo-Mulato,* known here by the name of *Chaca,* is used specifically against the sickness called by the common name of *Vómito prieto* or *Mal de Veracruz* [yellow fever], and against the malignant fevers or Tabardillos [spotted fever]. It facilitates perspiration, and its crushed bark cures the beasts of wormy wounds, and its resin or gum mixed with wax serves for the making of candles.

No. 19 . . . The *Palo de Rosa,* called promiscuously by the natives *Coyol Xóchitl* or *Tepexilo Xóchitl;* its bark, crushed or reduced to dust, is excellent for curing surface wounds rapidly.

No. 20 . . . *La Arinilla,* named by the Indians *Tamal quáhuitl;* they attribute to its roots the virtue of curing the bites or itchings of little vipers and to its leaves that of curing the grave sickness known here and in Havana as *Mal de pazmo* [tetanus].

No. 21 . . . *El Drago* is called by the Indians *Ezquáhuitl, Palo Sangriento,* because, from an incision, it secretes a liquid, which is given the name *Sangre de Drago,* whose virtues are well known.

See in Number 4 the medicinal virtues of *Palo Colorado,* and in No. 23 those of *Palo Volador.*

For Dyes

No. 22 . . . The *Colorín* or *Hiquimite,* which the natives call *Pemoch* [coral tree], tints yellow with its bark.

No. 23 . . . *Palo Volador,* which the Indians call *Petlácotl,* tints with its bark lion-colored or tawny; it secretes by incision a gum very efficacious for the curing of wounds, and they are assured that this is the famous cure commonly called *Azeyte de Palo.*

No. 24 . . . The *Chalahuite* also tints lion-colored with its bark.

No. 25 . . . The *Incienso,* which in Mexican is called *Xochiatl,* has leaves which tint black.

The *Orejón* (No. 10) serves in order to dye *timbres* and cowhides. See also *Palo Colorado* (No. 4).

Aromatics

No. 26 . . . The *Palo de Pimienta* is called as such because it produces this aromatic fruit, which is called Pimienta. The Indians know it by *Xoco Xóchitl.*

No. 27 . . . The *Copal,* in Mexican *Copal quáhuitl,* is a species of incense whose aromatic gum serves as Incense in the Churches.

No. 28 . . . The *Candelilla,* or *Mahpil xóchitl* in Mexican, produces some very odorous vines.

El Incienso (No. 25) produces an aromatic gum or resin which is employed in ecclesiastic functions.

Specialties because of other properties

No. 29 . . . *El Chijol:* The Indians call it *Nexquáhuitl,* which is equivalent to *Palo cenizo,* with allusion to its color. It is very compact and hard, of a form which is extremely resistant to the hatchets or machetes used in cutting it, from time to time throwing off sparks from the blows of the hatchets, like the flintstone. It serves for pillars, and it is incorruptible in the fact that instead of putrefying through the side which is nailed to the ground, after many years it petrifies; not because in reality it is converted to stone, but because it is of a constitution which is more apt to admit into its pores some subtle lime, which insinuates itself in its intestines and occupies the place of the corroded vegetables . . . although it may not be a true conversion to stone, it has all its configuration and properties (and even with steel creates fire, the same as with the flintstone). There remain only certain imperceptible lines which serve merely to indicate that it was wood before. One is able to recognize it in the petrified fragment that accompanies the piece of the referred *Chijol.* Some are certain that they have seen pieces of this same vegetable species converted into iron.

No. 30 . . . The *Lixa* [sandpaper] is so called because its leaves, which are very rough, serve, like the skin of the fish of the same name, for sanding and smoothing woods, which are worked and designed. It is also called *Raspa sombreros* because hats are cleaned with other leaves used like a brush. The Indians call it *Zaza*.

Appendix D

List of the Books and Instruments Necessary for the Fulfillment of the Obligations of the Branch of Natural History . . .[1]

Caracteres generum Plantarum Forsterii . . . with 78 well-drawn plates: this work is absolutely necessary; if by rare chance it cannot be found in Paris, it should be asked for in London; similarly with whatever other work published about natural history by *Forster, Banks* and *Solander,* or another naturalist, which is not listed here, which treats the latest voyages.

La Flora Ceilánica de Linneo

La Flora Lappónica by the same author

Genera Plantarum by the same, of the latest edition which seems to be that of Reichard, Chez Mequignon . . . . there can also be found in the same house and of the same editor the following works of Linneus: *Sistema Natural, Species Plantarum* and *Sistema Plantarum.*

Rumphius, *Herbarium Arborense* in the same house as above

Nicolai Joseph Jacquin, *Stirpium Americanarum*

Historia Vindebonne (in Vienna) . . . the latest

Plumier, *Genera Plantarum Americanarum*

    Idem., *Species Plantarum American.*

    Idem., *Filices Americani* [*Tractatus de Filicibus Americanus*]

Forskael, *Descriptiones animalum, avium* . . . price 9 pounds. Idem., *Icones rerum naturalium* . . . price 16 pounds

Dillenius, *Historia Muscorum*

Petrum Johanem, *Descriptiones Plantarum* . . .

Gronovius, *Flora orientali*

Idem., *Flora virginica*

Adamson, *Familles des Plantes* . . .15 pounds

Carolus Thunberg, *Genera Plantarum*

1. Antonio Pineda, "Lista de libros e instrumentos que considero precisos para desempeño del ramo de historia natural en la expedición que se prepara alrededor del mundo," Malaspina Papers, YALE.

Books of Zoology

Andreas Spazman Holmia, *Museum Calsornianum* . . . (Stockholm) If this
work, which was begun in 1786, has not been continued, omit it.
Buffon, *Su Historia de Quadrupedos y de Aves*
Pallas, *Specimen Zoologicum*
Brison, *Su Sistema de Quadrupedos*
Pennant, . . . *Zoology*
La Ornithologia de Edwards
Artedii, *Ictiologia* . . . one of the best in Stockholm
Willoughby, *Su Ictiologia,* or *Tratado de Pezes*
O. M. Agustin Brouset, *Ictiologia* . . .
Gouan, *Species piscium*
Commerson, *Su Ictiologia*
Caroli Lib. Bar. de Geer, *Genera et species*
Ander Johanes Vetzius in Strasburg, *Insectorum* . . .
The works of Brunich and Scopoli, which treat insects
Johanes Christ., *Polyc. Exl. Sistema regni animalis* . . .
Papillons, *Exotiques de l'Asie, Afrique et Amerique*
Scaffer, *Elementa Insectorum*
La Conchilogia de Martin Lister

Books of Mineralogy

Manuel du mineralogiste of Bergman, translated by Mongez . . .
Reinold Forster, *Methode aise pour esayer et classes les minereaux*
Ferber, *Voyages en Ytalie,* in English or French
Pallas, *Observations sur les Montagries et diverses changemente arriueir au Globe*
M. Lamanon, *Origine des Montagnes et Vallees* etc.

Instruments

2 hygrometers of the best construction . . .
1 thermometer . . . to measure sea temperature
1 aerometer of M. Perica
1 hydrostatic balance of the most simple construction and portable
1 thermometer of Dollard . . .
1 scaphander or swimming suit of cork
The collection of meteorological instruments of Manheim
1 pocket goniometer if it can be found in Paris
1 eudiometer
2 air-guns with their attachments in order to fuse the shot and pumps to prime
them. Those of the most safety and capacity should be procured.

Additional Items

La Mineralogía de Wallerius
M. Lunay, *Essay sur l'Histoire Naturelle des Roches*
Lehman, *Essay d'une Histoire Naturelle des couches de la terre*

Los Viages de Abate Torni en Ytalia y Dalmacia

M. Daubenton, *Tableaux Methodique des Minereaux* . . .

M. Romee, *Caractères extérieurs des Minereaux*

Las Cartas de Hamilton sobre el Vesuvio, in English or French

M. de Luc, *Recherches sur l'atmosphere*

Scaphandre ou le Bateau de l'homme

M. Bugge, Royal Astronomer of Denmark, *Observations astronomiques jusqu'à 1783 et depuis*

Summary Observations and Facts, etc., discusses Russian navigations to find the pass to the north and pretends that in the great latitudes the sea is free and without islands. L. Yelo in London

Tables de la Lune by Mr. Mayer, perfected by Mr. MacKelyne, in English or French

Appendix E

Plants Sent to England from the Botanical Garden

(All those printed in italics are new) [1]

1 Lobelia Surinamensis.
2 *Turrea tinctoria.*
3 *Hedysarum virgatum.*
4 Bignonia stans.
5 Bignonia linearis. Cavanill.
6 *Dahlia gigantea.*
7 *Malva arborea.*
8 *Ipomœa involucriflora.* An genus novum?
9 Salvia involucrata Cavanill.
10 *Fuchsia arborea.*
11 *Datura scandens.*
12 *Nocca latifolia.*
13 Psoralea glandulosa.
14 Datura arborea.
15 Hedyotis fruticosa.
16 Cactus Phyllanthus.
17 *Cactus coccineus.*
18 *Solanum scandens.*
19 *Euphorbia pulcherrima.*
20 Varietas ejusdem flore lutea.
21 Brassica crispa.
22 Ipomaea violacea.
23 Lexarcea. Genus Novum
24 Hoitzia coccinea. Cavanill.
25 *Crinum uniflorum.*
26 *Pancratium pulcherrimum.*

1. Bullock, *Six Months Residence,* pp. 186–87.

27 Variae species Novae Cactorum, inter quas valde' singularis *Cactus senescens*.
28 Crinum Zeylanicum.
29 Ferraria Pavonia, Tigridia quorundam.
30 Sicyos angulata.
31 Dahlia coccinea, variat floribus purpureis, coccineisque.

Bibliography

Manuscript Collections

Archive of the Linnean Society of London
  The Smith Papers
Archivo del Ministerio de Asuntos Exteriores, Madrid (AMAE)
  Extracto del diario de las navegaciones, exploraciones, y descubrimientos
    hechos . . . por D. Jacinto Caamaño, MS 10
  Viaje a la Costa N.O. de la America Septentrional por Don Juan Francisco de
    la Bodega y Quadra, MS 145
  Planos geográficos y dibujos para ilustrar el diario de Don Juan Francisco de
    la Bodega y Quadra, MS 146
Archivo del Museo Nacional de Ciencias Naturales, Madrid (AMCN)
  Flora Española—Años 1785 a 1808
  Flora Española—Communicaciones con el virrey de Méjico sobre el jardín,
    sobre la expedición y sobre de personal, 1785–1798
  Miscelánea, legajos nos. 3, 4, 5
  Papeles de Antonio Pineda
Archivo del Museo Naval, Madrid (AMN)
  Corbetas, vol. 3, MS 92 bis
  Corbetas, vol. 5, MS 94
  Pacífico América, vol. 2, MS 127
  Expediciones, vol. 2, MS 142
  Malaspina correspondencia, vol. 1, MS 278
  Malaspina correspondencia, vol. 1, MS 279
  Observaciones Seno Mexicano, MS 291
  Papeles varios, vol. 3, MS 316
  Reino de México, vol. 3, MS 335
  Apuntes, noticias y correspondencia pertenecientes a la espedición de Mala-
    spina, MS 427
  Navegación y viajes, vol. 3, MS 468

Proyecto de Agustín de Blondo y Zavala, MS 551
Proyecto de Félix y Francisco Lemaur, MS 552
Descripción de Guantánamo, MS 554
Reconocimiento de la parte occidental de Cuba, MS 557
Descripción de la Isla de Pinos, MS 560
Pineda, Nueva España, vol. 1, MS 562
Pineda, Nueva España, vol. 1, MS 563
Correspondencia relativa a la expedición de Malaspina, vol. A, MS 583
Dibujos de ynsectos de la Ysla de Cuba, MS 712 bis
Libro de guardias para la corbeta *Atrevida,* MS 755
Colección Guillén, MS 1407
Informes reservados, Miscelánea 6
Papeles del Conde de Mopox y Jaruco
Depósito hidrográfico de Madrid, figuras y animales, vols. 1 and 2
Bauzá Collection, photocopies
Archivo del Real Jardín Botánico, Madrid (ARJB)
2ª División: Papeles de la expedición de Malaspina, legajos nos. 1, 2
3ª División: Papeles de la expedición de Baltasar Boldó a la Isla de Cuba, legajo no. 1
4ª División: Papeles de Sessé y Moziño, legajos nos. 1, 2, 3, 5, 14, 15, 16, 19, 20, 21, 22
5ª División: Correspondencia del director, legajos nos. 5, 6, 22, 26
6ª División: Láminas de plantas de la Isla de Cuba; Luis Neé, dibujos de plantas, vols. 1, 2, and 4
Archivo Generel de Indias, Sevilla (AGI)
Estado, legajos nos. 16, 18
Guatemala, legajo no. 704
Indiferente general, legajo no. 1546
Archivo General de la Nación, México D.F. (AGN)
Historia 277, 460, 461, 462, 463, 464, 465, 466, 527, 558
Archivo Histórico Nacional (AHN)
Consejos, legajo no. 5315
Bancroft Library, University of California, Berkeley
Bibliotheque du Conservatoire Botanique, Genève
Collection De Candolle
British Museum of Natural Science, Botanical Division, London
Catalogue of the A. B. Lambert Collection
Herbarium Pavón
Yale University Library, New Haven (YALE)
Frederick W. Beinecke Collection

Selected Documents

Caamaño, Jacinto. "Extracto del diario de las navegaciones, exploraciones y descubrimientos hechos en la America Septentrional por D. Jacinto Caamaño," MS 10, AMNE.
Gómez Ortega, Casimiro. "Lista de los libros que se envian a México en dos

caxones para el uso de la expedición botánica y de historia natural de aquel reyno," Flora Española—Año 1788, AMCN.

"Juan Francisco de la Bodega y Quadra, del Orden de Santiago, Capitan de Navío de la Real Armada, y Commandante del Departamento de San Blas en las Fragatas de su mando *Sta. Gertrudis, Aranzazu, Princesa* y Goleta *Activo* en el ano de 1792," MS 145, AMAE.

"Lista de las maderas, cuyas muestras se dirigen del curato de Chicontepec, del obispado de la puebla de Los Angeles, al Señor Capitán Dn. Joseph de Flores, Castellano del Puerto de Acapulco; con expresión de sus colores y propiedades respectives, y de los usos a que se aplican," 4ª división, legajo no. 15, ARJB.

Malaspina, Alejandro. "Plan de un viaje científico y político a el rededor del mundo remitido a el Exmo. Sr. Bailío Fray Antonio Valdés de Madrid en 10 de Sept. de 1788," MS 316, AMN.

Mopox y Jaruco, Conde de. "Estado actual en que se halla la comision encargada por S.M. al Conde de Mopox en la Ysla de Cuba, con expreción de los asuntos y sugetos que los han desempeñado, vaxo las ordenes y direccion del referido Xefe, Havana, 14 October 1800," Papeles del Conde de Mopox, AMN.

Moziño, José. "Descripción del volcán de Tuxtla por D. José Mariano Moziño, botánico de la expedición de Nueva España, Año de 1793," Historia 558, AGN.

———. "Descripción de la isla de Mazarredo, junto a la Quadra o Vancouver y noticias de aquellos países" [Noticias de Nutka] Museo Naval, Madrid, MSS 143 and 468.

Pineda, Antonio. "Expedición al cerro de Guadalupe en compania de Don Josef Alzate," MS 563, AMN.

———. Lista de libros e instrumentos que considero precisos para desampeño del ramo de historia natural en la expedición que se prepara alrededor del mundo," Malaspina Papers, YALE.

———. "Viaje de Acapulco a México, 8 May 1791," MSS 562, 563, AMN.

———. "Viaje desde México, a Guanajuato con rodeo por Zempoala, Pachuca y Real de Monte," MS 563, AMN.

"Plantas y hierbas que [h]ay en Cuernavaca," 4ª división, legajo no. 14, ARJB.

"Real cédula de 20 de Marzo de 1787, por la que se establecia en su forma definitiva la expedición de Nueva España," Flora Española—Año 1787, AMCN; 4ª división, legajo no. 20, ARJB; Historia 527, AGN.

Sessé, Martín, y José Moziño. "Descripciones de los géneros de plantas de Nueva España," 4ª división, legajo no. 3, ARJB.

Sessé, Martín. Letter of Martín Sessé to Viceroy Revillagigedo, Mexico, 9 May 1793, Historia 527, AGN.

"Testimonio del expediente sobre haberse resuelto que el botánico Don Jaime Senseve quede en Mexico y que en su lugar salga con la expedición el Medico Dn. José Mosiño, nombrado para la diseccion de los animales al Cirujano Maldonado," AMCN.

Published Sources

Aguado Bleye, Pedro, and Cayetano Alcázar Molina. *Manuel de historia de España*. Vol. 3: *Casa de Borbón 1700–1808*. Madrid: Espasa-Calpe, 1964.

Alvarez López, Enrique. "Las tres primeras campañas de la expedición científica dirigida por Sessé, y sus resultados botánicos," *Anales del Instituto Botánico A. J. Cavanilles de Madrid* 1 (1952):39–141.

———. "Noticias y papeles de la expedición científica mejicana dirigida por Sessé," *Anales del Jardín Botánico de Madrid* 2 (1951): 5–79.

Anderson, Bern. *The Life and Voyages of Captain George Vancouver*. Seattle: University of Washington Press, 1960.

Anna, Timothy E. *The Fall of the Royal Government of Mexico City*. Lincoln: University of Nebraska Press, 1978.

Arias Divito, Juan Carlos. *Las expediciones científicas españolas durante el siglo XVIII*. Madrid: Ediciones Cultura Hispánica, 1968.

Barras y de Aragón, Francisco de las. "Noticia de la vida y obras de Don José Antonio Alzate y Ramírez," *Boletín de la Real Sociedad Española de Historia Natural,* sección biológica 48 (1950):339–53.

———. "Noticias y documentos de la expedición del Conde de Mopox a la Isla de Cuba," *Anuario de Estudios Americanos* 9 (1952):513–48.

Barreiro, P. "Documentos relativos a la expedición del Conde de Mopox a la Isla de Cuba, durante los años 1796 a 1802, publicados ahora por vez primera," *Revista de la Real Academia de Ciencias* 30 (1933):5–19.

Barreiro-Meiro, Roberto (ed.). [*Diario de*] *Esteban José Martínez (1742–1798)*. Madrid: Instituto Histórico del Marina, 1964.

Beaglehole, J. C. *The Life of Captain James Cook*. Stanford: Stanford University Press, 1974.

Benítez Miura, José Luis. "El Dr. Francisco Hernández, 1514–1578 (cartas inéditas)," *Anuario de Estudios Americanos* 7 (1950):367–405.

Bullock, William. *Six Months' Residence and Travels in Mexico*. London: John Murray, 1824.

Burke, Michael E. *The Royal College of San Carlos: Surgery and Spanish Medical Reform in the Late Eighteenth Century*. Durham, N.C.: Duke University Press, 1977.

Calderón Quijano, José Antonio. *Los virreyes de Nueva España en el reinado de Carlos III*. 2 vols. Sevilla: Estudios Hispano-Americanos, 1967.

———. *Los virreyes de Nueva España en el reinado de Carlos IV*. 2 vols. Sevilla: Estudios Hispano-Americanos, 1972.

Carreño, Alberto M. (ed). *Noticias de Nutka*. Mexico, D. F.: Sociedad Mexicana de Geografía y Estadística, 1913.

Cervantes, Vicente. "Discurso pronunciado en el real jardín botánico de Mexico el 2 de Junio de 1794," *Suplemento a la Gaceta de Literatura de México,* 2 July 1794.

Chappe d'Auteroche, Jean Baptiste. *Voyage en Californie pour l'observation de Venus sur le disque du soleil*. Paris: Chez Charles-Antoine Jombert, 1772.

Clark, Phil. *A Flower Lover's Guide to Mexico.* Mexico, D.F.: Minutae Mexicana, 1968.

Colmeiro, Miguel. *La botánica y los botánicos de la península Hispano-Lusitana.* Madrid: M. Rivadeneyra, 1858.

Cook, Warren L. *Flood Tide of Empire: Spain and the Pacific Northwest, 1543–1819.* New Haven: Yale University Press, 1973.

Coyle, Jeanette, and Norman C. Roberts. *A Field Guide to the Common and Interesting Plants of Baja California.* La Jolla: Natural History Publishing Company, 1975.

Cutter, Donald C. "California, Training Ground for Spanish Naval Heroes," *California Historical Society Quarterly* 40 (1961):109–22.

———. "Early Spanish Artists on the Northwest Coast," *Pacific Northwest Quarterly* 54 (1963):150–57.

———. *Malaspina in California.* San Francisco: John Howell, 1960.

———. "Malaspina at Yakutat Bay . . . encounters between the Spaniards and the Indians in 1791," *Alaska Journal* 2 (1972):42–49.

———. "The Return of Malaspina: Spain's Great Scientific Expedition to the Pacific, 1789–1794," *American West* 15 (1978):4–19.

———. "Spanish Scientific Exploration Along the Pacific Coast," in *The American West: An Appraisal,* Robert G. Ferris, ed. Santa Fe: Museum of New Mexico Press, 1963.

Cutter, Donald C., and Mercedes Palau de Iglesias. "Malaspina's Artists," *The Malaspina Expedition.* Santa Fe: Museum of New Mexico Press, 1977.

De Candolle, Aphonse Louis. *Calques des dessins de la flore du Mexique de Mociño et Sessé.* Geneva, 1874.

——— (ed). *Mémoires et souvenirs de Augustin-Pyramus de Candolle.* Geneva, 1862.

Destéfani, Laurio H., and Donald C. Cutter. *Tadeo Haënke y el final de una vieja polémica.* Buenos Aires: Secretaria de Estado de Marina, 1966.

Diccionario universal de historia y geografía. Vol. 5. Mexico D.F., 1854.

Dixon, George. *A Voyage Round the World but more particularly to the North-West Coast performed in 1785, 1786, 1787, and 1788 in the King George and the Queen Charlotte: Captains Portlock and Dixon.* London: George Goulding Publisher, 1789.

Drucker, Philip. *Northern and Central Nootkan Tribes.* Smithsonian Institution Bulletin 144. Washington, D.C.: U.S. Government Printing Office, 1951.

Engstrand, Iris Wilson. *Royal Officer in Baja California: Joaquín Velázquez de León, 1768–1770.* Los Angeles: Dawson's Book Shop, 1976.

Espinosa y Tello, José (ed.). *A Spanish Voyage to Vancouver and the Northwest Coast of America . . . in the Year 1792 by the Schooners* Sutil *and* Mexicana *to Explore the Strait of Juan de Fuca.* New York: AMS Press, 1971.

———. *Relación del viaje hecho por las goletas* Sutil *y* Mexicana *en el año 1792.* Madrid: Imprenta Real, 1802. Reprinted in Colección Chimalistac. Madrid: José Porrúa Turanzas, 1958.

Fernández, Justino. *Tomás de Suría y su viaje con Malaspina.* Mexico, D.F.: Porrúa Hermanos y Cia, 1939.

Fireman, Janet R., and Michael Weber. "In Pursuit of Knowledge: The Malaspina Expedition," *Terra* 15 (1977):18–24.

Fireman, Janet R. *The Spanish Royal Corps of Engineers in the Western Borderlands*. Glendale: Arthur H. Clark Company, 1977.

Gaceta de Madrid, no. 115, 17 April 1812.

Gaceta de México, 6 January 1789; 27 April 1790; 5 November 1794.

Galbraith, Edith C. "Malaspina's Voyage around the World," *California Historical Society Quarterly* 3 (1924):215–37.

García Ramos, José. "Elogio histórico del farmacéutico Don Vicente Cervantes," *Boletín de la Sociedad Mexicana de Geografía y Estadística,* vol. 2, no. 1, 1869.

Gastil, R. Gordon; Richard P. Phillips; and Edwin C. Allison. *Reconnaissance Geology of the State of Baja California*. Memoir 140. Boulder, Colo.: Geological Society of America, 1974.

Geiger, Maynard. O.F.M. *Franciscan Missionaries in Hispanic California, 1769–1848*. San Marino: Huntington Library, 1969.

Goldman, Edward A. *Biological Investigations in Mexico*. Smithsonian Miscellaneous Collections, vol. 115. Washington, D.C.: Smithsonian Institution, 1951.

Goodman, Edward J. *The Explorers of South America*. New York: Macmillan Company, 1972.

Guest, Francis F., O.F.M. *Fermín Francisco de Lasuén (1736–1803): A Biography*. Washington, D.C.: Academy of American Franciscan History, 1973.

Guillén y Tato, Julio F. *Indice de la colección de Fernández de Navarrete que posee el Museo Naval*. Madrid: Ministerio de Marina, 1933.

———. *Repertorio de los M.SS., cartas, planos y dibujos relativos a las Californias, existentes en este Museo [Naval]*. Madrid: Ministerio de Marina, 1932.

Gutiérrez Camarena, Marcial. *San Blas y las Californias*. Mexico, D.F.: Editorial Jus, 1956.

Heizer, Robert F. "The California Indians," *California Historical Society Quarterly* 41 (1962):1–28.

———. "The Introduction of Monterey Shells to the Indians of the Northwest Coast," *Pacific Northwest Quarterly* 31 (1940):399–402.

Hemsley, W. B. "Short Notes," *Journal of Botany* 8 (1879):275–76.

Herr, Richard. *The Eighteenth-Century Revolution in Spain*. Princeton: Princeton University Press, 1958.

Howay, Frederick W. (ed.). *The Dixon-Meares Controversy*. Toronto, Ont.: Ryerson Press, 1929.

Humboldt, Alexander von. *Ensayo político sobre el reino de la Nueva España*. Edited by Juan A. Ortega y Medina. Mexico, D.F.: Editorial Porrúa, 1966.

Jepson, Willis L. *The Silva of California*. Berkeley: University of California Press, 1910.

Juan, Jorge, and Antonio de Ulloa. *A Voyage to South America* (John Adams Translation, abridged). Introduction by Irving A. Leonard. New York: Alfred A. Knopf, 1964.

Krause, Aurel. *The Tlingit Indians*. Translated by Erna Gunther. Seattle: University of Washington Press, 1956.

Kuhnel, Josef. *Thaddaeus Haënke, Leben und Wirken eines Forschers*. Prague, 1960.

Langman, Ida Kaplan. *A Selected Guide to the Literature on the Flowering Plants of Mexico*. Philadelphia: University of Pennsylvania Press, 1964.

Lanning, John Tate. *Academic Culture in the Spanish Colonies*. New York: Oxford University Press, 1940.

————. *The Eighteenth-Century Enlightenment in the University of San Carlos de Guatemala*. Ithaca: Cornell University Press, 1956.

La Pérouse, Jean Francois Galaup, Compte de. *A Voyage around the World in the Years 1785, 1787 and 1788*. 3 vols. London: J. Johnson, 1799.

León, Nicolás. *Biblioteca botánico-mexicana*. Mexico, D.F.: 1895.

Llabrés Bernal, Juan. *Breve noticia de la labor científica del Capitán de Navío Don Felipe Bauzá y de sus papeles sobre América (1764–1834)*. Palma de Mallorca, 1934.

Llave, Pedro de la. "Descripción de algunos géneros y especies nuevas de vegetables," *Registro Trimestre* 1 (1832):43–49.

————. "Memoria sobre el quetzaltotol, género nuevo de Aves," *Registro Trimestre* 1 (1832):345–58.

Manning, William R. "The Nootka Sound Controversy," *American Historical Association Annual Report of 1904*, pp. 279–478. Washington, D.C.: U.S. Government Printing Office, 1905.

Martínez, Maximino. *Catálogo de nombres vulgares y científicos de plantas mexicanas*. Mexico, D.F.: Ediciones Botas, 1937.

————. *Las plantas medicinales de México*. México, D.F.: Ediciones Botas, 1944.

Matheson, Patricia. "Royal Treasure Hunt Gives Tongans New Awareness of Past," *Pacific Islands Monthly* 44 (1973):5–6.

McKelvey, Susan D. *Botanical Exploration of the Trans-Mississippi West, 1790–1850*. Jamaica Plain, Mass., 1955.

McVaugh, Rogers. *Botanical Results of the Sessé & Mociño Expedition (1787–1803)*. Contributions from the University of Michigan Herbarium, vol. 2, no. 3, pp. 97–195. Ann Arbor: University Herbarium, University of Michigan, 1977.

Meany, Edmond S. *Vancouver's Discovery of Puget Sound*. New York: Macmillan Company, 1907.

Menéndez y Pelayo, Marcelino. *Historia de los heterodoxos españoles*. 2d. ed., 7 vols. Madrid, 1911–32.

————. *La ciencia española*. 4th ed., 3 vols. Madrid, 1915–18.

Munford, James K. (ed.). *John Ledyard's Journal of Captain Cook's Last Voyage*. Corvallis: Oregon State University Press, 1963.

Neé, Luis. "De la *Pistia stratiotes*," *Anales de Ciencias Naturales*, 4 (1802):76–82.

————. "Descripción de varias especies nuevas de encina (*Quercus de Linneo*)," *Anales de Ciencias Naturales* 3 (1801):260–78.

Newcombe, C. F. (ed.). *Menzies' Journal of Vancouver's Voyage, April to October, 1792*. Victoria, B.C.: W. H. Cullin, 1923.

Novo y Colson, Pedro de. *Viaje político-científico alrededor del mundo por las corbetas* Descubierta y Atrevida *al mando de los Capitanes de Navío D. Alejandro Malaspina y D. José de Bustamante y Guerra, desde 1789 a 1794.* Madrid, 1885.

O'Gorman, Helen. *Mexican Flowering Trees and Plants.* Edited by Ella Wallace Turok. Mexico, D.F.: Ammex Associados, 1961.

Paláu y Verdera, Antonio. *Parte práctica de botánica del caballero Carlos Linneo.* Madrid, 1784–88.

Pesman, M. Walter. *Meet Flora Mexicana.* Flagstaff: Northland Press, 1962.

Presl, Karel B. (ed.). *Reliquiae Haenkeanae.* Prague, 1825–35.

Quesada, Vicente G. *La vida intelectual en la América española durante los siglos XVI, XVII, y XVIII.* Buenos Aires: La Cultura Argentina, 1917.

Renkema, H. W., and John Ardagh. "Aylmer Bourke Lambert and His Description of the Genus *Pinus,*" *Journal of the Linnean Society of London* 47 (1930):439–66.

Rickett, Harold W. "The Royal Botanical Expedition to New Spain, *Chronica Botanica* 11, 1 (1947):1–81.

Rubio Mañe, J. Ignacio. "Síntesis historica de la vida del Conde de Revilla Gigedo, virrey de Nueva España," *Anuario de Estudios Americanos* 6 (1949):451–96.

Sanfeliú Ortiz, Lorenzo. *62 meses a bordo. La expedición Malaspina según el diario del teniente de navío Don Antonio de Tova Arredondo, 2ª comandante de la Atrevida 1789–1794.* Madrid: Biblioteca de Camarote de la Revista General de Marina, ca. 1943.

Santamaría, Francisco J. *Diccionario de mejicanismos.* 2d ed. Mexico: Editorial Porrúa, 1974.

———. *Diccionario general de americanismos.* 3 vols. Mexico, D.F.: Editorial Pedro Robredo, 1942.

Sapir, Edward. "Some Aspects of Nootka Language and Culture," *American Anthropologist* 13 (1911):15–28.

Sarrablo Aguareles, Eugenio. "La Fundación de Jaruco en Cuba y los primeros condes de este título," *Anuario de Estudios Americanos* 8 (1951):443–501.

Schendel, Gordon. *Medicine in Mexico: From Aztec Herbs to Betatrons.* Austin: University of Texas Press, 1968.

Servín, Manuel P. "Instructions of Viceroy Bucareli to Ensign Juan Pérez," *California Historical Society Quarterly* 40 (1961):237–48.

Sessé y Lacasta, Martín de, and José Mariano Mociño. *Flora mexicana.* Mexico, D.F.: Sociedad Mexicana de Historia Natural, 1885.

———. *Plantae novae hispaniae.* Mexico, D.F.: Sociedad Mexicana de Historia Natural, 1889.

Shafer, Robert Jones. *The Economic Societies in the Spanish World (1763–1821).* New York: Syracuse University Press, 1958.

Simpson, Lesley Byrd (ed. and trans.). *Journal of José Longinos Martínez, Notes and Observations of the Naturalist of the Botanical Expedition in Old and New California and the South Coast.* San Francisco: John Howell, 1961.

Standley, Paul C. *Trees and Shrubs of Mexico.* Contributions from the U.S. National Herbarium, vol. 23. Washington, D.C.: U.S. Government Printing Office, 1920–26.

Steele, Arthur Robert. *Flowers for the King: The Expedition of Ruiz and Pavón and the Flora of Peru.* Durham: Duke University Press, 1964.

Synge, M. B. (ed.), *Captain Cook's Voyages Round the World.* London: T. Nelson and Sons, 1897.

Thurman, Michael. *The Naval Department of San Blas.* Glendale: Arthur H. Clark Company, 1967.

Torre Revello, José. *Los artistas pintores de la expedición Malaspina.* Buenos Aires, 1944.

Toussaint, Manuel. *Taxco: su historia, sus monumentos.* Mexico, D.F., 1931.

Vaughan, Thomas; E. A. P. Crownhart-Vaughan; and Mercedes Palau de Iglesias. *Voyages of Enlightenment: Malaspina on the Northwest Coast 1791/1792.* Portland: Oregon Historical Society, 1976.

Wagner, Henry Raup. *Cartography of the Northwest Coast of America to the Year 1800.* Vol. 1 Amsterdam: N. Israel, 1968.

―――. "Four Early Sketches of Monterey Scenes," *California Historical Society Quarterly* 15 (1936):213–16.

―――. "Journal of Tomás de Suría of His Voyage with Malaspina to the Northwest Coast of America in 1791," *Pacific Historical Review* 5 (1936): 234–76.

―――. *Spanish Explorations in the Strait of Juan de Fuca.* Santa Ana, Calif.: Fine Arts Press, 1933.

Wagner, Henry R., and W. A. Newcombe (eds.). "The Journal of Don Jacinto Caamaño." Translated by Capt. Harold Grenfell. *British Columbia Historical Quarterly* 2 (1938):189–222, 265–301.

Weibel, Raymond. "Flore du Mexique et les dames de Genève," *Les Musées de Genève,* June 1949.

Whitaker, Arthur P. "Changing and Unchanging Interpretations of the Enlightenment in Spanish America," *Proceedings of the American Philosophical Society* 114 (1970):256–71.

Whitaker, Arthur P. (ed.). *Latin America and the Enlightenment.* 2d ed. Ithaca: Cornell University Press, 1961. (First published in 1958.)

Willoughby, Charles C. "Hats from the Nootka Sound Region," *American Naturalist* 37 (1903):65–68.

Wilson, David Scofield. *In the Presence of Nature.* Amherst: University of Massachusetts Press, 1978.

Wilson, Iris Higbie [Engstrand]. "Antonio Pineda y su viaje mundial," *Revista de Historia Militar* (Madrid) 8 (1964):48–64.

―――. "Investigación sobre la planta maguey en Nueva España," *Revista de Indias* (Madrid) 23 (1963):501–10.

―――. (ed. and trans.). *Noticias de Nutka: An Account of Nootka Sound in 1792* by José Mariano Moziño. Seattle: University of Washington Press, 1970.

―――. "Pineda's Report on Beverages from New Spain," *Arizona and the West* 5 (1963):79–90.

―――. "Spanish Scientists in the Pacific Northwest, 1790–1792," in *Reflections of Western Historians,* John A. Carroll, ed. Tucson: University of Arizona Press, 1969.

Woolf, Harry. *The Transits of Venus: A Study of Eighteenth-Century Science.* Princeton: Princeton University Press, 1959.

Zavala, Silvio. *América en el espíritu francés del siglo XVIII.* Mexico, D.F.: Colegio Nacional, 1949.

Index
